Women Warriors:

Stories from the

Thin Blue Line

John M. Wills

TotalRecall Publications, Inc.

TotalRecall Publications, Inc..
1103 Middlecreek
Friendswood, Texas 77546
281-992-3131   281-482-5390 Fax
www.totalrecallpress.com

Copyright © 2013 by: John M. Wills
With a Foreword by Ellen Kirschman, Ph.D.
Edited by Adele Brinkley
Cover Graphic by Greg Bean
ISBN: 978-1-59095-696-0
UPC: 6-43977-46966-3

Printed in the United States of America with simultaneously printings in Australia, Canada, and United Kingdom.
FIRST EDITION
1   2   3   4   5   6   7   8   9   10

To the women in law enforcement
who have made the ultimate
sacrifice.
May they rest in peace.

To: Carrie
Never Give Up On
Your Dreams! You
are a great friend!
Thank you for always
being so supportive!

Amy Michalik
8/2012

Praise

"*Women Warriors* provides a window into the challenges of day-to-day policing—told from a woman's perspective. From a gripping account of the 9/11 aftermath when Chicago police officers descended on New York City to help search the wreckage to the humorous and sometimes tragic on-the-beat episodes, Women Warriors Stories from the
Thin Blue Lineis an intriguing and worthwhile read."
Alan Jacobson, National Bestselling Author of Inmate 1577

"Wills shines a light on the courage and tenacity of the profession's female Warriors."
Dave "Buck Savage" Smith, Internationally renowned police trainer

"A rare glimpse into the lives of women in law enforcement."
Noah Boyd, NYT best-selling author of The Bricklayer

"A powerful, deeply moving book. Filled with tales of courage, sacrifice and steely warrior determination. Powerful proof that the warrior spirit knows no gender!"
Dave Grossman, Lt. Col. USA (ret.) Author of On Combat and On Killing

"Often dismissed is the true warrior role so many women play in law enforcement. Wills brings that role into sharp focus."
Frank Borelli, Editor, Officer.com

"John's book reminds us there are women in this profession taking their turn 'Walking the Point.'"
Terry G. Hillard, Retired Superintendent Chicago Police Department

Table of Contents

Foreword

The young officer who has come to talk with me is named Lulu. She's very upset. Her field training officer had given her a low rating for failing to control a handcuffed prisoner who was cursing at her as she filled out a booking sheet. To Lulu, being called names was not worth escalating the situation nor provoking a physical confrontation. Her training officer, a male, had other ideas. He accused her of being afraid to go hands-on with the suspect and doubted she had what it took to be a cop. When he discussed her performance with the other trainers, the cursing incident overshadowed her many other acceptable ratings. Her next training officer was overprotective, fearful that she would get hurt or get someone else hurt. The one after that held her to a higher standard than he did the male rookies. Lulu hesitated to call for help in volatile circumstances, thereby creating a safety hazard for herself. She worried that calling for backup would reflect badly on her ability to take control of a situation. At the same time, she was criticized for not asking for help.

I've heard versions of this story many times in my thirty years as a police psychologist. It doesn't matter if it's municipal, state, or federal law enforcement, from patrol officer to chief, despite small increases in the number of women in law enforcement, policing is still predominantly a male profession. As such, women are stuck between a rock and a hard place that men rarely visit. It makes little difference whether they are lesbian or straight, women have to prove that they are as good as any male officer and they have to do this at every rank. Men need only be as good as each other, they don't have to redefine who they are to be successful. On the other hand powerful, competent women may get a reputation as castrating or pushy. Some may feel unfeminine, forced to act in ways that defy their true nature. They act "macho" at work and nurturing at home.

Men and women often approach their law enforcement jobs differently. Women emphasize helping over controlling. They regard physical tactics, control and command actions, and officer safety as crucial skills but prefer to talk through a situation without the need for force. Over the years, many women I have known thought their male colleagues relied too much on control and intimidation tactics, overreacted to minor challenges to their authority or actively looked for ways to provoke a fight.

Women in law enforcement, including dispatchers and correctional officers, have suffered a rash of indignities ranging from sexual harassment to rape. They've been left without backup, shut out of elite assignments, treated as second class citizens, mocked for being too emotional, and discriminated against in promotions. They've had to fight for properly fitting uniforms, smaller weapons, and bullet-proof vests designed for the female body. Those who spoke up risked ostracism and retaliation.

Many women have told me that being in law enforcement has put a damper on their social life. Some men don't want a relationship with a woman who carries a weapon and shoulders so much authority and responsibility. Some are too insecure to date a woman who spends most of her working life surrounded by men. Others are confused by women who can suppress their feelings at work and become emotional at home. They don't recognize how much gear shifting women who work in male dominated professions have to do, perhaps because they don't have to do it themselves.

Women and men in law enforcement all work long hours with mandated overtime, unpredictable schedules, and shiftwork. But working women in all occupations still spend more hours on housework and childcare than do men. And many are subjected to outdated and punitive maternity leave policies.

In my opinion, women bring unique talents to law enforcement and perform their duties with the same effectiveness as men, even when the job involves danger and aggression, which is a relatively small percentage of time. The way women are socialized prepares them verbally to defuse potentially explosive situations. Culturally conditioned to be nurturing, they are suited to deal with quality-of-life issues and relationship building which are the foundations of community policing. Women are at an advantage in undercover work because they are unexpected. They may be more resistant to stress than their male coworkers because they are more likely to seek help when they need it and less likely to become alcoholic.

So why do the women I've counseled and the women whose stories you're about to read want to work in law enforcement? For the same reason men do. They want to make a difference in the world. They want a secure, well-paying job that matters. They want variety, excitement, respect, autonomy, and opportunities for advancement. Women in law enforcement have the opportunity to exert their influence, both politically and tactically. They can modify some of the authoritarian practices that have contributed to negative public opinion and distrust of the police. They provide a needed service for victims, especially women and children.

What challenges women specifically is not so much the physical rigor of the job or the danger, but a lingering mythology about what actually constitutes law enforcement. The ideal cop is neither man nor woman, but an androgynous combination of psychologist, minister, politician, doctor, parent, stunt-car driver, athlete, warrior, and sleuth.

Ellen Kirschman, Ph.D. is the author of *I Love a Cop: What Police Families Need to Know* and *I Love a Fire Fighter: What the Family Needs to Know.*

Preface

The book you hold in your hands is unique in that it contains stories written solely by women in law enforcement regarding their experiences on the job. Some of the narratives will make you laugh, others will make you weep, and some will outrage you as you try and understand why people act as they do.

Women working the streets in law enforcement are a relatively recent phenomenon. In 1970, only 2% of all law enforcement officers were women, but by 1991, that number had risen to 9%. Numbers from the years 2007 and 2008 suggest the number of women involved in policing is almost 100,000, or just over 15%. (Bureau of Justice Statistics, 2010).

Having been involved in law enforcement since 1971, I can attest to the fact that the ranks of women in policing have increased dramatically. There are a number of reasons for this uptick, not the least of which is that law enforcement is no longer regarded as only a "man's job." We've learned over the years that women perform equally as well as men do in this vocation. Obviously, both genders bring different skills and abilities to the job, but in the final analysis, both sexes put the bad guys in jail.

Why write about women in law enforcement? Because during my career, I've trained scores of women in a variety of disciplines: defensive tactics, firearms, and fitness, to name a few. I've seen their determination and tested their mettle. I've watched as some quit, not unlike their male colleagues, and marveled as others fought through adversity and won. I've mentored some who have gone on in their careers to be highly successful. Sadly, I've seen a few make the ultimate sacrifice and lay down their lives for their fellow man. Needless to say, I am inspired by the daily battle waged by our women in blue.

We will forever be grateful to those who have unselfishly put themselves in harm's way and ultimately lost the battle. Their reward, however, is eternal life. For us who remain behind, we take comfort in seeing their names inscribed on the sacrosanct walls of the National Law Enforcement Memorial in Washington, D.C. alongside those of the men who also died in the line of duty.

The stories you are about to read are compelling and give us, the readers, an insight into the minds of these exceptional women. I refer to them as Women Warriors because, as you will see, they fight tenaciously and savagely to uphold the oath they swore: To Serve and Protect. May the patron saint of police officers, St. Michael, protect each of them as they risk their lives each day so that we may live in peace.

About The Book

Women Warriors: Stories from the Thin Blue Line features a compelling collection of stories about women in law enforcement. From a dispatcher on the radio trying to remain calm and do her job while her husband is involved in a gun battle, to a desperate search for a missing child during a frightening storm, to a courageous lone officer staring down the barrel of a gun inside a crowded department store, the tales in this book will have your pulse racing.

Police officers, federal agents, chaplains, corrections officers and dispatchers, all share their stories, each one written in their own hand. The diverse tales will make you laugh, cry and cheer as these **Women Warriors** face unknown dangers during their shifts.

From the red-hot streets of Texas, to the frozen Alaska tundra, these true stories will capture your imagination and give you a true sense of what today's women encounter as part of **The Thin Blue Line**

Acknowledgments

Greg Bean

The artwork, to the right, and on the cover of Women Warriors is a creation of Greg Bean. Greg has been a police officer with the Bellevue, Washington Police Department for twenty-three years. The last twelve years he has served as a detective and forensic sketch artist. His expertise is as a composite artist including forensic facial imaging.

Contact Greg if you would like a copy of his work at: gbean325@gmail.com

Kate Lehman and Michelle O'Hearn

My heartfelt thanks to Kate Lehman and Michelle O'Hearn for their work in reading my manuscript and spotting errors that escaped me.

Part One:

Patrol Officers

Arlene Ajello

is a native New Yorker and a retired Chicago police officer. Her father was an NYPD officer who discouraged her from joining the force, encouraging her instead to get an education. Arlene took her father's advice and has two PhDs. She became a stock broker on Wall Street and then an options trader in Chicago on the OEX.

Arlene dreamed of becoming one of "Chicago's Finest," and one day she sold her Options company and took the test to become a Chicago police officer. Her dream finally became reality, and she spent most of her career as a tactical and gang officer. She reached the pinnacle of her career near the very end when she became a member of Special Operations, the most elite unit in the Chicago Police Department.

When the events of 9/11 occurred, Arlene felt compelled as a police officer, an American patriot, and as a hometown girl from New York to lend a hand in the city's recovery. She and her team of 11 were the first officers from the CPD to arrive on September 12th. She lost many friends and family that fateful day. Arlene worked on the pile, the bucket brigades, and in many other capacities while at Ground Zero. It was a time that changed her life. Arlene spent a good part of a year going back and forth to NYC and helping in any capacity the NYPD needed.

Arlene suffered a broken back and retired from the CPD in 2009. Since then she has continued to help and heal others by volunteering at animal shelters, raising funds for 9/11 charities, and helping people cope with the tragedy of that event. She is active in the 9/11 community. Arlene is an avid equestrian and an international competitor in dressage. Although she is retired, her horses and devotion to duty keep her motivated. She has been published in Grant Wolf's book, Stories of Faith and Courage from Cops on the Street.

A Beautiful Day

by Arlene Ajello

I came home for Christmas that year as I did every year. My family had seen more of me that particular year than they had in the sixteen years since I'd left. I am a New Yorker, born and bred. However, I had buried myself in Chicago, working first as an options trader for a while, and eventually back to my first love as a Chicago police officer. Sitting at the Christmas table with my family, my brother-in-law pulled out his new gadget, an Apple iPod. He played music on the strange machine, mixing songs from Sinatra, Christmas tunes, New Age, and U2. When the band, U2, began to play "It's A Beautiful Day," a faraway look came over his face. He blurted out, "Yes, it was a beautiful day. I can't believe it happened; I can't believe I made it home alive."

The big Italian Christmas feast we had all been enjoying suddenly became silent. I wept silently as I sat at the once joyful table. My brother-in-law quickly explained his harrowing ordeal, his sixteen perilous hours trying to escape New York City when the World Trade Center was bombed. He had never before talked about it, and I wondered why he chose this moment, particularly with my sister expecting her first child. I was surprised. He told us he'd hummed this U2 song while trying to get home that fateful day. Silence.

I noticed everyone looking at me. I had been working at the bomb site for months, first on the pile and then upstairs at One

Police Plaza, in the "war room." An extended family member had been callous during the aftermath of the bombings, and I have no idea why. She nicknamed me "The Ground Zero Hero." I never said a word to her about her insensitivity and continued with my efforts at the towers through the year. I prayed that one day she might understand the magnitude of what had happened, and hoped no one she knew had been hit by the deadly terrorist attack.

I sat silently as they all stared at me as if I were an alien. I sensed they wanted to ask, "Why? Why did it happen?" I knew they were probably still in shock and denial about what happened. No one realized the full scope of what occurred on September 11, 2001. Frankly, I didn't either. I only knew I had to be there; I had to help any way I could. My team of twelve and I went in on September 12, 2001. I was frantic; I was in shock. I was worried about my family and friends. We organized a crew from the Chicago Police Department to go in. Although I am a Chicago police officer, I'm also a New Yorker. Nothing was going to prevent me from getting to the incident site. New York is my home town, it is everyone's hometown. For God's sake—it is New York City! Everyone had friends and family in the buildings: firefighters, officers, brokers, accountants . . . many I knew and know.

Initially, on that beautiful day I had no contact with my family; I just kept driving from Chicago to New York, accompanied by eleven heroes. We had one mission: to do whatever we could to help the people of New York City. An hour outside of the city, the cell towers graced me with a signal and I was able to reach my parents in Staten Island. My father, a retired veteran of the NYPD, told me to turn my car around and go home. "The air is too dangerous," he said, "and the government is lying about the air quality."

We had words. I told him, "I am here, and so is my team. Please help us. We'll need showers, and where and how can we get into Manhattan? The radio said the bridges are closed down."

He fought me, and I could hear my mother growl in the background. Nevertheless, they alerted the entire block where they lived that I was coming in with a team of rescue workers. Neighbors, some whom I've never met, welcomed us into their homes for showers, packed us lunches and dinners that fed us for days, hugged and kissed us, and extended to us their best wishes and thanks. My mother and father, true to their nature, kept their game faces on, but I could read my father's face. It was the face of a war-tested veteran who was worried about me and my team. I simply smiled, not wanting to feed into his fear. I waved. "Mom, Dad, I'll see you in a few days." Months later I still hadn't seen them.

Our arrival at the scene of the attack was surreal. My father had instructed me to go to Jersey City. The boats were loading there for those of us "stupid enough to go in." My last name carried weight within the departments running the crews. Dad had called ahead, making sure our crew was on the list. We drove in with pickups and SUVs right under the noses of the media, just us, silent and prepared.

But were we? Parking the vehicles and unpacking our gear while wearing our Chicago Police uniforms caused silence to spread among the huge crowd gathered at the waterfront. Groups of people had been staring across the river at the still smoldering towers, that is, until our vehicles rumbled up. Then their attention turned to us. We could feel their eyes upon us, and strangely, we somehow felt their pain. Their votive candles were laid out in circles on the ground, the names they represented written in chalk by loved ones. We were driven, empowered to do our job by the audacity of those who would dare to attack our nation, and strengthened by our countrymen who could only sit and stare in bewilderment at the utter destruction. We immersed ourselves in our work.

A man stood up on top of his pickup truck and started applauding, a solemn, heart wrenching clap I will never forget. He started yelling, "Thank you Chicago Police!" Other people began to clap in unison, a low, structured rhythm of applause. Tears flowed freely from my eyes, cascading down my cheeks onto my sacrosanct police star. I knew family and friends were across the river of darkness, most likely dead. One of my partners approached me, put his hand on my shoulder, and said, "Ar, it's all good. Let's get that boat your dad promised."

We were swamped by a sea of desperate family members, handing us fliers that contained identifying data of their missing loved ones, beautiful pictures, clothing descriptions, jewelry worn, names of the companies they worked for, what floor, and what building they worked in. It took everything we had to accept those fliers; we put them in our pockets as we navigated the path on our way to the boats. We promised them we would do what we could to find their loved ones and call when we knew anything. Unfortunately, those fliers are still with me; I never had the pleasure of calling with good news.

We waited and waited for those boats to come and go. Our number on the list was agonizing. I felt like an excited race horse in the gate, waiting to run the Kentucky Derby. I just wanted to get to the other side of the river. A group of iron workers spoke to some of my team and begged to get on the boat with us, asking if we would say they were cops too. My team members pointed at me, and said, "Ask her." I didn't know what to do. All I knew was they were better equipped than we were with their torches and equipment. I knew from reports of the rescue workers coming out that they were under staffed and under equipped.

Instantly, our team went from twelve to twenty-two. My last name was called for the Army Corps of Engineers boat, and they yelled out, "Do you have twelve?" My response was, "No we have twenty-two." We all loaded. In the middle of that deep black river, the iron workers knelt, grabbed our arms, pulled us down, and we all recited the Lord's Prayer. Once again, tears rolled down my cheeks. God's hand hovered over us. Even in that inky sea and with the devil's inferno burning in front of us, we all felt His presence. Silence.

The engine hummed as we crossed the river, while the waves splashed against the side of the boat. No other sounds were heard. No one spoke. Silence.

Our arrival was chaotic. Our boat docked, and we set off into a scene that could only be described in one word: mayhem. We were greeted with bright lights and a smell that anyone who was there will never forget. Uniforms were everywhere. No one knew whom to report to, who was in charge. Everyone simply converged in spots throughout the many acres and began to dig. At first, we were on The Pile like a bunch of idiots when huge horns began to sound. People yelled at us to get off the pile, the ground was shifting, and fires were burning our shoes and pants. We weren't told about the danger, nor were hundreds of others.

Chaos was the theme as the days and dark nights seemed to merge together. I lost all sense of time. Nonetheless, we quickly got into a routine, as did all the other rescue workers. Days were not important, helicopters flying overhead were barely heard, and news people sticking cameras in our faces were ignored. Nothing mattered. Everyone walked away, climbed into a tent for a few hours of shut eye, retreating into a shell, cocooned from the daily horror. We got used to finding body parts and never entire bodies. Soon everyone began to whisper in their respective circles in camp at Ground Zero that no one would be found alive. Our tears were not shed at The Pile; instead, they were reserved for when there was a free moment to use the bathroom. Odd as it may sound, I found God and copious tears in a toilet whenever I could find one.

I guess I am biased, being a native New Yorker, but the

people of the city came out in droves as I secretly hoped they would. They brought with them food, water, socks, gloves, anything they thought might make our jobs easier. Nothing went unnoticed or without a hug and a thank you. The myth of arrogant, rude New Yorkers was dispelled at Ground Zero, but I already knew that. I was proud of my fellow New Yorkers. I knew all along in my heart they would all pull together. New York will forever be my home.

One evening on The Pile, I heard my name called. I thought perhaps I was on fire again. You get used to that. The shout out actually came from the first partner I ever worked with when I was a rookie on NYPD, my first job as a police officer before hiring on with Chicago. He hopped over the rubble, and we hugged until we almost fell over, crying, laughing, and shaking our heads. He just looked at me, kissed me on the forehead, and said, "I knew you were here." Nothing else needed to be said. I worked with his crew for a long while, and also alongside the English bobbies who were simply amazing. Months later, I worked with my former partner and his team in the war room. As usual, he tried protecting me, but nothing could protect us from the toxic fumes or the absolute horror that was Ground Zero.

Years later as I look back at my team, two are dead from tragic accidents, and a few of us are sick from the toxic fumes. We sat on The Pile, opened up a few beers, and said, "If this kills us, it's worth it." I still believe that to this day. Osama Bin Laden took more than three thousand lives on that "beautiful day." He killed many souls whose hearts are still beating. We call ourselves the Walking Dead. The ones who can't forget the white dust covering our uniforms or the deadly air we breathed. We remember the families begging us every time we came outside of the roped area of Ground Zero for help or for any tidbit of news. If it didn't kill our bodies, it killed our minds and souls, but I would never turn back on that beautiful day. I would do it again ten thousand times. Who else but a Warrior would?

As I sit and watch a video of the band U2 play "A Beautiful Day," I find irony in that it's about an airline flight on a beautiful day, a day just like September 11, 2001, a day that brought so much horror and pain. However, as I travel home every year, that same memory brings many of us who were there, who survived the attacks, the widows, widowers, the children, and the mothers and fathers of those killed in the day care, all much closer. I host an annual Christmas party where it is safe to talk about 9/11 without the hush that some have begun to use. There is nothing to be quiet about. September 11, 2001 was a beautiful day, marred by savages who murdered so many in New York, Pennsylvania and Washington, D.C. May God rest their innocent souls.

Dawn Higgins

is a 28-year member of the Indianapolis Metropolitan Police Department, (formerly Indianapolis Police Department). She has a B.S. in Public Affairs from Indiana University, Bloomington and is an alumnus of the IUPD Cadet Officer Program and a graduate of the 172nd Session of the FBI National Academy.

Sergeant Higgins was a member of her department's police officer support team and hostage negotiations unit. She is presently a member of the Event Response Group, which responds to major incidents and events in the Indianapolis metro area. Sergeant Higgins spent the majority of the first half of her career in the field, and the second half working investigations, specifically investigating cases of domestic violence and stalking. She has attended numerous domestic violence training seminars and conferences and has taught and spoken publicly on the topic of domestic violence. Sergeant Higgins is presently assigned to the Special Investigations Unit and serves on several committees dedicated to reducing domestic violence and domestic violence fatalities in the Indianapolis metropolitan community.

Sergeant Higgins is the proud mother of daughter, Maria, and is the zookeeper of a menagerie of pets. She enjoys Crossfit and participating in Highland Games, music, reading, Euchre, fishing, camping and spending time with friends and family.

She would like to thank her fellow officers throughout the country, who, on a daily basis, bravely volunteer to lay their lives down for others. She would also like to thank those many amazing "women warriors" who came before her and set the foundation so she could pursue her lifelong dream of being a police officer.

It's Over Tonight

by Dawn Higgins

lthough I had been a police officer for nineteen years and had spent approximately fifteen of them on the street, my most critical situation occurred much closer to home when I was involved in a shootout with my brother-in-law.

The holidays were winding to a close in 2002. It was December 29th, Christmas was over, and the New Year loomed close. Of course, it was cold. I had been to a movie with Becky, a fellow officer and friend. We were doing some last minute shopping when I received a page. My pager was the type where a third party could type in only their number and/or a numerical code of some sort. Checking the display, I saw my sister's phone number followed by the numbers 9-1-1. Thinking my niece or nephew might be sick, I immediately made the call, only to hear the desperate voice of my sister. "He's got a gun!" She was being held at gunpoint by her husband, my brother-in-law.

I have no recall of what I said after learning of her desperate plight. I do remember immediately calling our dispatch center and providing as much information as quickly as possible for responding officers. Becky and I ran to the car, which was fortunately a marked police vehicle, and raced to my sister's house. The whole time we were en route, I continued to talk with the dispatcher and repeatedly asked her to make sure everything was being recorded.

Screeching to a stop at my sister's house, we ran to the door. We were unable to see into the downstairs area, which was where my sister and brother-in-law were located. I recall having a discussion with Becky about the children's safety and then grabbing each of them individually and handing them off to Becky. I grabbed Becky's gun while she ran to cover with my niece and nephew, secreting them behind the front wheel well of our car.

I managed to keep my phone flipped open, thus transmitting what was occurring. As I crept downstairs and entered the room, I tried to move tactically while maintaining a good eye on what was in front of me. My sister was sitting in a chair in the middle of the room, my brother-in-law off to one side. I was at the apex of the triangle.

Although I cannot remember in what order some things occurred, I recall trying to conjure up as much of my negotiator training as I could. I remember talking to him, trying to minimize what had already occurred, and pleading for him to not make things worse. At this point, I learned he had already taken a shot at my sister, the round striking the floor by her feet and not physically harming her.

"Hang up your phone!" he shouted.

Rather than doing so, I merely put my phone down and maintained the connection so the dispatch center could monitor what was occurring.

My sister was still sitting in the middle of the room between the two of us. During my exchange of words with my brother-in-law, she was able to dart to the safety of a bathroom located in the basement. Then, in a surreal scene, one that defied comprehension, it was just my brother-in-law and me facing each other with guns drawn. All negotiations had ended.

I heard other officers arriving on the scene, and both my brother-in-law and I began yelling to them.

"Stay out!" I yelled.

"No, I want you in here," shouted my brother-in-law.

My concern was obviously for the welfare of my sister, but I was also afraid that if any officers entered the room, the chances for a peaceful resolution would diminish greatly. My personal and professional knowledge of the "suicide by cop" phenomenon, wherein individuals goad the police into shooting them, was weighing heavy on my mind. I didn't want to see him lose his life.

Then, the most critical moment in this situation occurred. My brother-in-law and I began yelling at one another.

"Please, drop your weapon, everything will be okay."

"You're a negotiator, Dawn," he cried. "Negotiate!"

"This is my sister!" I screamed at him.

His reply was lost in a haze of frightening moments, but I'll never forget what happened next. He brought the weapon up to his head. "It's over tonight," he said.

The words resonated in my mind. Then he made a slight movement with his wrist, barely perceptible, but in conjunction with his statement, it seared into my mind. I was certain he was about to pull the trigger and shoot himself.

Screaming at him, I shot him once in the center mass of his body, striking him in the stomach. In response, a barrage of bullets came my way. Instantly, I felt my left hand and arm burning, and I was no longer able to hold my weapon. I fell to the ground while hearing my sister screaming for me. As quickly as it began, the shooting stopped. I later learned he had emptied his gun.

I was down but not out. I heard the officers in the foyer and recall yelling to them. "The gun's on the floor—it's empty—lying next to the shooter in the middle of the room." I tried to provide them with as much tactical information as possible.

I picked up the phone that I had previously set down. The line was still open. "Send an ambulance; there's been a shooting." There was some confusion as to which one of us was shot, and I am sure that my racing adrenaline caused me to be less clear than normal.

Once the EMTs arrived and things were secured, my brother-in-law and I were transported to the same hospital. I had been shot at nine times and hit with four rounds. One bullet went through my upper left arm, nicking a nerve, thus causing the burning in my arm and hand. That round is also what caused me to drop my gun. Two shots went through my left knee, though neither of them hit any bones. There was another round that went through my left calf, through the meaty part, and didn't hit anything vital.

My brother-in-law suffered a wound to his abdomen.

Ironically, I remember being worried about him. Although others have questioned why I did not "shoot to kill," the truth is I never wanted him to die. In fact, when I began to think clearly once again, I kept hoping maybe something good could come from this situation. I was hopeful for an epiphany on his part, and I worried about my sister, niece and nephew. What would happen now?

Ultimately, a plea agreement was reached and my brother-in-law went to prison. To my knowledge, he fully recovered from his wounds. He has since been released and has visitation rights with my niece and nephew. Needless to say, I still worry about their safety.

I have permanent nerve damage in my left arm, which affects my hand. Half of my left hand is numb but I can still function, and I'm able to continue to work as a police officer. My left knee is problematic and arthritic, which is to be expected from that type of trauma. I also fell on the ice while recovering from the gunshots and sustained a tibial plateau fracture. As one would expect, this injury exacerbated the already tenuous state of my knee. I have had no further issues with the bullet wound through my calf.

It is exceptionally difficult for me to write about something so dynamic and explosive. I am not sure I am capable of completely articulating the events of that day; nevertheless, that experience was life altering in many ways. And while I play the events over and over again in my mind, I am certain I would do things the same way. Those of us in law enforcement willingly accept danger and have no qualms about risking our lives in order to protect others, most of whom are strangers. To have been given the opportunity to protect my own family is something I consider a gift.

Kimberly B. Owens

Dallas, Texas, has been with the Dallas Police Department (DPD) for fourteen years. She is currently assigned as the night Watch Commander at the Southwest Patrol Division. As a Lieutenant, she has had assignments in the Central Business District of downtown Dallas and the Central Patrol Division. She has previously been assigned to the In-Service Training Academy, including the Firearms Training Center and the Caruth Police Institute, which provides leadership training for supervisory level officers. Kimberly's last assignment was as the Administrative Lieutenant in the Personnel and Development Division, which is responsible for all recruiting, hiring and training in the Department.

Kimberly has been tasked with planning and managing several major special events within her assigned areas. She has been responsible for Dallas Emergency Response Team Conference displays of emergency equipment, The Beat Car Show, Prairie View vs. Grambling after parties, Texas vs. Oklahoma events on Greenville Avenue, and several smaller special events. Most recently, she was the Interior Commander of the NFL Experience for Super Bowl XLV. For three years, she has planned and managed the Greenville Avenue Saint Patrick's Day party, which is a portion of one of the largest Saint Patrick's Day celebrations in the country.

Kimberly is married to Senior Corporal James Owens, who is also with the DPD, and they have one child. She holds a Bachelor of Arts in Sociology and a minor in English from Louisiana Tech University. Lieutenant Owens is from Louisiana and remains a fan of the New Orleans Saints and LSU football teams. She also enjoys reading, photography, and spending time with her family.

A Rookie's Tale

by Kimberly B. Owens

To say I was gullible early in my career would be an understatement. As I moved up through the ranks, I had to grow up and wise up. Still, those early times continue to leave me with fond memories that I share when reflecting on my career.

I was fortunate to have worked with trainers and partners whom I greatly admired and trusted, sometimes to my embarrassment. They convinced me to do some of the dumbest things, that, although somewhat perturbing at the time, still make me chuckle today. I invite you to laugh with and at me as I paint myself as the quintessential Keystone Cop.

During my first phase of field training, I had a fabulous field training officer named Steve. I think it was his goal in life to see what he could get me to do, regardless of how off the wall it seemed. Sometimes, against my better judgment, I did the things he told me to do because I rationalized that it must be my job, right?

We all know it's the rookie's job to be alert and listen to the radio at all times. Getting used to that job can be horrible, particularly with Metallica blaring on the good time radio while trying not to spill Steve's dip cup as he tells me to drive faster. We made our nightly trip to the 7 Eleven for drinks and extra napkins, for the free dip cup, and of course, I had to pee. For those who don't know, peeing in uniform is a feat in itself for a woman. There is no zip and go, but rather one must undress and hope nothing touches the nasty bathroom floor where half the drunks in town have spit, peed, vomited, and done God knows what else. And don't forget, you have to hover over the seat while trying to accomplish all this.

As I hovered and held things, the dispatcher called "371," our unit number, over the radio and gave us a call. I waited for Steve to answer; surely he knew I was performing a circus act in here. Crickets. The dispatcher calls again. Cursing, I fumble for the radio, cut off my stream (ouch), and answer. She gave us the call. I hurriedly dressed, and stomped out to the car, only to see Steve sitting there laughing so hard he almost had tears in his eyes. I got in the car, flung a few nasty words his way and backed out. While still laughing, the jerk had the nerve to say, "I couldn't even hear you pee."

Knowing Steve had an evil sense of humor, and remember, I'm gullible, I continued to trust him and do what he told me. Spring was in full swing, bugs were out and about by the thousands, including crickets. I hated having any kind of bug jump on me. Girly? Yes, but still a fact. Steve and I responded to an alarm call at an area church. He drove and I got out and checked the doors as he circled the building. We came around to the well-lit parking lot, which had attracted hundreds of bugs. The concrete was literally black from all of the bugs, almost like a blanket had covered the parking lot.

Steve drove up to the main doors and told me to put a false alarm notification on the door. I asked if he was serious—he was. I told him I was not getting out of the car. He told me that I was because policy required we leave the notification. I asked him to do it, but he quickly reminded me that I was the one in training not him. As I looked out the window I told him the bugs would jump on me so I couldn't do it. He assured me they wouldn't, that they would all run away when I stepped out. I asked if he was sure because it would freak me out if those crickets jumped on me. He replied that it would be all right and not to worry.

Stupid me, I trusted him and stepped out of the car. Yep, what felt like millions of crickets swarmed, attacked, and violently assaulted me. At least that's how I felt. I screamed and jumped around like a nut in the parking lot and tried to get back in the car. The jerk locked the door and wouldn't let me in until I put the notification on the church door. I ran through the mine field mauled by bugs to put the damn sticker on the door. I stuck it as firmly as I could, knowing it would take razors and massive elbow grease to remove. Yes it was a church, but those were their bugs, right?

I streaked back to the car and found Steve laughing like a hyena as he finally allowed me back inside. I was furious and dove into the car, cussing him and calling him every name in the book. He told me I did a good job, and I asked him why he wouldn't help me. I reminded him that he told me it wouldn't happen. He laughed and said he knew it would, but he didn't help because he wouldn't step out and let them jump on him. I asked what would have happened had I not been there to do it. The jerk told me, "Hell, I would have just driven off and not left anything." Ass!

Finally, after several months, I completed training in one piece. I was then assigned to work with a fabulous partner named Jim. He was fun, got along with everyone, and had a great sense of humor, one that was often directed at me. Jim taught me the art of talking people into jail rather than fighting with them, and how to chase stolen cars. He was one of the few people who didn't scare the living crap out of me when he drove fast and chased cars.

When we first started riding together, Jim and I were assigned to an alarm call at a junkyard. We already knew how well those calls go for me. It was pouring rain when we pulled up and saw the place was surrounded by a six foot fence. The building whose alarm was ringing was located in the middle of the yard. I asked Jim how we checked on a place with a fence we couldn't get through. He said we had to climb the fence and inspect the building to see if it was secure.

I sat there because I wasn't fool enough to get out in the monsoon. I had to figure out how this was going to happen. I'm smaller so Jim said I had to be the one to climb the fence. I let him know that climbing fences wasn't exactly my forte, but he said he would help. I asked if we could just leave and write a report stating that we couldn't access the location. "No," he said. Jim insisted we had to make sure it hadn't been burglarized.

"Fine," I replied. He told me he would help me. I asked how I would get back over when I finished checking the building, and he said he would help pull me back.

The plan was that he would pull the car against the fence; I would stand on the hood and be able to reach the fence. He pulled up and parked the front bumper against the fence. I got out in the freaking rain and climbed on the car. As I reached up to grab the fence, I slid off the hood and fell against the fence with my foot wedged in the buddy bumper. Jim jumped out, burst out laughing and said he would help get my foot loose. His brilliant idea was to get in the car and back up so my foot would come out. Rather than listen to my pleas to him not to try that, the car was thrown in reverse and my foot did come loose. Of course, as he dragged my butt with the car I couldn't hold on to the fence any longer and fell right on my rear in the mud. I got in the car and said it was his turn, I was done. With the car still rolling, Jim told me that he wasn't climbing the fence. "We can just do a report that we couldn't get inside to check," he said and drove off!

Jim and I were partners for a while. Time with him was a riot. He continued to play jokes on me, embarrass me, and make me laugh at myself and everyone else. In hindsight, my favorite Jim moment happened one night when we made a traffic stop. I drove that night and Jim did the paperwork. The driver of the car we pulled over had warrants and we arrested him without incident. Jim sat in the car with the driver and completed the book-in paperwork while I searched the vehicle. There were no problems until I searched the trunk.

The car had a sloped trunk, similar to a hatchback, except it didn't open into the backseat like a hatchback. The trunk wouldn't stay up, but there was a wooden pole the driver used to hold it open. I tried to prop the trunk open with the pole but dropped it into the trunk, which was very deep. I leaned into the trunk to retrieve the pole while I held the lid up. As I leaned further into the trunk, I lost my balance and fell inside, losing my grip on the lid. The lid came down on me, pushed me further into the trunk, closed on my ankles, and left only my feet sticking out. The trunk was so deep, I couldn't get enough leverage to push myself up or push the trunk lid up. I yelled and kicked my feet, hoping Jim would come and, yes, I will say it, rescue me.

Nothing. And after several minutes I tried figuring a way out of my seemingly hopeless situation. I decided if I could get completely inside the trunk I could stand up and push the lid open. Apparently my socks, boots, or perhaps my shoelaces were caught on the trunk latch, and I couldn't move forward. I was basically hanging upside down inside the trunk at this point. Finally, I struggled, kicked enough to move the lid, and was able to kick, push the lid, and inch backwards a little at a time. I worked my way back until I could get leverage to open the lid and get out of the guy's stinky car.

I stomped back to our car and asked Jim why he didn't see me. I found him sitting in the car, laughing, tears streaming down his face. I yelled and demanded an explanation. He quit laughing, turned to me with a straight face said, "I had a prisoner in the car and couldn't leave him," and burst out laughing again.

I yelled, "&*!@ you," and got back in the car to wait on the wrecker.

Needless to say, I've grown older, moved up in rank, and hopefully become a little wiser. Looking back though, those times were the most fun I've ever had. My war stories always seem to involve the group of guys I worked with for years on nights, which included Steve and Jim. We were a close-knit, specialized unit that focused on narcotics, high crime areas, and illegal nightclub operations. We worked hard and we had fun. I was treated like the little sister, and no matter what they did to me (these stories were just the tip of the iceberg) nobody was even allowed to look crossed-eyed at me without having to answer to one of them. Those guys taught me how to laugh at myself and have fun doing it. How much fun would life be if we couldn't do that?

Deborah "Kay" Hughbanks

was born 1963 in Grand Prairie, Texas and raised in the Dallas Metroplex. She began her career with the Dallas Police Department as a civilian dispatcher in November of 1991. Deborah entered the Dallas Police Academy in May of 1994 and graduated December of 1994. She trained at the Southwest Patrol Division and later transferred to the Southeast Patrol Division. She was promoted to senior corporal in August of 1998 and to sergeant in May 2000. She was then transferred to the Northeast Patrol Division. In April 2008, she transferred to the Property Unit as the Drug Team Sergeant. Deborah presently supervises both the Drug Team and Gun Team at the Dallas Police Property Unit.

Blue Candy

by Deborah "Kay" Hughbanks

I worked first watch, midnight to eight, most of my career in the so-called bad part of town. On this particular night, I responded to a burglary call near the end of my shift; it turned out to be a good burglary, good being a relevant term, for it meant a real crime had occurred and not a false alarm.

It had been a long night. As I headed back to the Southeast Substation, westbound on Lake June Road, a six lane residential road divided by a median, I saw a very large black male standing inside the westbound lane of traffic—my lane. I thought, "Crap, I just want to go home." The man wasn't watching traffic, and it was about fifteen minutes to eight on a weekday. I had to get him out of the road.

Slowing my squad car, I pulled up beside him. He had a blank stare. "Step out of the road, sir, so you don't get hit." The man simply nodded and stepped up on the concrete median. I continued driving, all the while knowing I needed to go back. I looked in my rear view mirror and saw him still standing on the concrete median, so I turned around and told the dispatcher to mark me out.

I stopped my car, turned on the overhead lights, and got out. This was a big man. Experience told me he was what we call "exceptional," meaning mentally ill or challenged. Standing six feet four, he must have weighed close to three hundred pounds.

Paradoxically, he looked like a lost five-year-old. He wore a long-sleeved button-down dirty shirt with a woman's three-quarter sleeve white sweater with pastel horizontal stripes over it. The sweater would have fit my five-foot-four, one hundred seventy pound stature. He had on dirty brown Dickies pants and was barefoot.

The man carried a plastic grocery sack containing clothes and a pair of shoes. "What are you doing?" I asked.

"Waiting for a ride," he answered.

Immediately I knew he needed help. "Do you take any medication?"

"Yes," he said, so I asked if he had been taking it and replied he had not.

"Is anything wrong?"

His response was to reach down, un-zip his pants, and pull out his penis.

"That's ok, you can keep that, I don't need to see it," I quickly responded. Thankfully, he put his penis back inside and zipped up his pants.

It was apparent he had mental difficulties, so I asked him if he wanted to go to the hospital and get some help.

"Yes," he replied. I told him I would give him a ride to Parkland Hospital, the county hospital for our area. Since he did not appear to be a danger, I couldn't admit him. He had to admit himself. After getting his name and birth date, I verified he didn't have any warrants for his arrest and wasn't a known felon. Next, I told him I would have to pat him down. No one gets in my squad car without having been searched for weapons.

He was very agreeable and didn't hesitate to do whatever I asked. So I patted him down and placed him in the back of my car because my duty bag was in the front passenger seat. Getting back in the car, I adjusted my rear view mirror so I could see the man's eyes. The mirror allowed me to talk to him and observe him during the trip.

I marked out at the hospital with the man in the back seat and off we went. While we were en route, I asked him some questions, trying to keep him talking, albeit just small talk, but as I watched him in the rear view mirror, I sensed he was seeing something I couldn't see. I called his name, asking him what he was seeing.

He said, "Candy." I thought, that's good, at least it wasn't demons. I sped up a little. The man started rocking while saying, "Candy canes, chocolate kisses, lollypops," naming all kinds of candy. I sped up a little more. Then he paused and looked into the rear view mirror, into my eyes and said, "And blue candy," as if that was the good stuff, and he smiled.

We were almost there, and I got him off the candy topic. We pulled into the parking lot of the hospital, and I walked him in through the emergency room door so he could admit himself. It was very crowded and loud. After I got him registered, I recognized he was becoming anxious. I had doubts whether this trip to the ER would work or not, so I walked him back out to the parking lot. I told him he really needed help and that I could help him, but I would have to handcuff him to take him where I could help.

He looked at me and replied, "Yes. I want help." He placed his bag on the back of my squad car and put his hands behind his back; he looked so worn out. I walked him in through the police entrance so I could admit him for help. As he sat down, it seemed all the air went out of him. He was clearly exhausted.

While I started on the paper work, a nurse and doctor came in. The doctor was very arrogant. He spoke rudely and acted put out. Meanwhile, the man I had brought in began to rock back and forth, and as the doctor asked questions, the man became more and more agitated. He looked at me and said "I've already answered these questions." I told the doctor he was upsetting the man, but the doctor replied that he had to ask the questions.

At this point, two large male nurses entered the room, causing the man to begin to talk about candy again. He rocked faster. I put down my pen and said to the doctor, "You're pissing him off." The two male nurses took a step back. The doctor continued. The man continued listing candies and rocking faster. Once again, I warned the doctor about the impending problem, but the doctor continued with his litany of questions.

Suddenly, a nurse in a blue uniform entered the room. The man looked at her, stopped listing candies, and then looked at me as if he had finally found it and said, "And blue candy." As he finished the statement, and while still handcuffed, he rushed the female nurse in the blue uniform like a football player going for a tackle. The two male nurses and I dove for the man and took him to the ground. I wrapped myself around both of his legs, while each male nurse got an arm. The four of us just lay on the floor holding him down. The man barely touched the nurse because we caught him in time. Nevertheless, she screamed and ran from the room.

The doctor stood there, his mouth agape, as if to say, "What the hell?" The two male nurses and I were laughing at the situation because we saw it coming, and, of course, we were laughing at the look on the doctor's face. Recovering, the doctor ordered the nurse to bring him a shot of Adivan and Haldol. She ran out of the room, happy to get away from her near-attacker.

While we waited for her to return with the injections, we continued to utilize our body weight to hold the behemoth down. It seemed like forever until the nurse came back. She gave the man the cocktail injection, and once it kicked in, he relaxed so much we had to drag him to a room. The first thing I told the doctor after I got up off the floor was, "I told you, you were pissing him off."

After that incident, I never transported any "blue candy" people without cuffing them first. While the incident was somewhat funny, I also realized it could have turned out much worse.

Kaneisha Collins

is a 38-year old single mother of one who joined the Dallas Police Department (DPD) on a whim. Little did she expect it to turn into a career she would love. She was told her background as a CPS case worker and Supervisory Probation officer would serve her well as a police officer. Ten years later, she still enjoys every minute of her job. She also has developed a new found respect for trainers and sergeants.

Kaneisha was promoted to Senior Corporal in 2007, marking the beginning of her career as a trainer. She was given the huge task of helping to mold the minds of the future officers, a task which is scary in more ways than one. Over the past several years, training has resulted in many ups and downs, but overall has taught her more about her own capabilities. She admits to being tough on recruits at times, but recalls that she was told, "What doesn't kill you can only make you stronger." She prides herself on her work, and even when not training, is open to lending a hand to younger officers in need of help. Kaneisha believes that life is too short, so she makes sure she smiles and laughs each day.

She has gained a popular reputation for her training style and ability to help several recruits realize what their true life goals are. Kaneisha is a movie addict and loves taking yearly vacations. Her leisure time is spent shopping, relaxing, vacationing, and watching her large collection of DVD's. She also loves spending time with family, friends, and the special man in her life. She looks forward to advancing her career, but until then, she is content to sit back, enjoy, and see what other funny and crazy adventures come her way.

5

Halloween Came Early

by Kaneisha Collins

Routine patrol took on a whole new perspective on a June night in 2010. My rookie and I were driving around checking the businesses along the South Buckner corridor around 2:00 A.M. when we observed a vehicle commit a traffic violation. I instructed the training officer to conduct a traffic stop so we could speak to the driver about the violation he just committed. The squad car's overhead lights were turned on, and the driver pulled over in a parking lot in the rear of a check cashing business at the next corner. The trainee marked out, and we immediately approached the vehicle to speak with the driver. As we spoke with the driver, I observed a young male walking through the parking lot. He continued to walk so I thought nothing more about him or where he was going.

Once we collected the driver's information, we returned to the squad car to check the driver and write the necessary citations. After a few minutes a co-worker stopped by our location just to check on us and make sure everything was okay. I walked up to his car and began to chat with him as my trainee continued to write the citations. As I stood on the passenger side talking with him through the window, I noticed that the same young man that walked by our traffic stop was now sitting on the curb as if he was waiting to talk to someone. My co-worker asked "Do you know why he's here or what he wants?"

"No, I saw him walk by earlier, but didn't know he had returned."

We were intrigued about why he was just sitting there, but we also questioned his actions for safety reasons since he was to my back when we were conducting our traffic stop. I stood up, peered over the car at the man, and asked "Hey, guy, what are you doing? Why are you sitting there?"

Neither one of us expected the answer we got. The guy stood up, slowly approached the car, and stated, "What if I told you I wanted to show you something? What if I told you I had a piece of real human skin that I wanted to show you?"

As he walked toward the squad car, we noticed that he had something black in his hand, something that looked more like a dead bird shriveled up. We weren't sure what to make of this development so we both stayed at the car with shocked looks on our faces. Then without blinking an eye he told us, "I have a foot too, do you want to see it?" He proceeded back to where his backpack was laying by the curb and pulled out another dried, shriveled up object that neither of us was sure what to make of.

My mouth dropped and I had to ask, "Are you shitting me?"

My co-worker decided to get a closer look, so he exited the car and walked over to where the object was lying on the ground. He turned to me and said, "It looks like it could be a real foot!"

At that point, I was truly creeped out to the extreme. Just as I was trying to get up the nerve to walk over to the object and take a closer look, a sergeant and a female officer pulled up. "Good, you found him," they said, sounding relieved. "We've been looking for him."

What? I was trying to conduct a traffic stop. It was at that moment I realized this same young man had already spoken to this female officer regarding his strange situation approximately an hour before making contact with me. She had not believed his story. She found the story odd, but just thought the man was a little "off" and offered him some food, but after thinking about it a while later, she decided to discuss the man with her sergeant and see what he thought about the situation.

The sergeant walked over to the object and with a surprised expression stated, "I think this is a human foot because I think I can see toenails." What the hell! A human foot laying on the ground in front of me . . . OMG! Curiosity finally got the best of me so I had to walk over to see what it was that was lying on the ground. My curiosity should have stayed put because now I was sure that there was indeed a dead human foot on the ground in front of me. Well now we had to figure out where it came from and why this guy had it. So of course I asked, "Why do you have a foot in your bag? And why are you carrying it around in your bag?" The guy admitted that he was a lover of 'dead' things and has always wanted to have a human head. Now I had to know, "So where did you get the foot from?" His next statement, "Oh, I got it from the cemetery down the street. I thought I was gonna die because I was digging for six hours straight and I didn't have any water." Digging at midnight? "And whose grave were you digging up?" His reply, "Oh, I don't know, some Jew girl." Hmmm.....now we all had to know why and from where. He quickly told us that he would show us where he got the foot from because he was so very proud of himself. So since I was the trainer with the trainee, guess who had to take the suspect into custody along with the foot...ME and the rookie of course.

We loaded him up in the squad car after a search and the rookie put on gloves so he could also take the evidence into custody. I was so freaked out that I wouldn't allow him to put it in the trunk of our car anywhere near my bag, so our co-worker put it in his trunk. The medical examiner was called and down the street we went to check the place from where this human foot was removed. We drove approximately three blocks, turned left, and found an open gate to the rear of a dark cemetery. We parked the squad cars and entered through the gate with nothing more than flashlights to light the way. As the five officers, one sergeant, and one suspect walked down the drive, we all were shocked that at around 1 A.M. on a Friday morning we were walking thru a graveyard. Continuing down the path, we came upon a large three-foot by six-foot hole in the ground with several pieces of wood lying on the ground around the hole. The hole was found in between four headstones so trying to figure out which one it belonged to was a chore. By this time all I could do was beg God for forgiveness for being in a graveyard in the middle of the night and disturbing the sacred resting place of these deceased Jewish people. So now we had to figure out why he dug up this person's foot. He told us that he was trying to find the head, but got to the feet instead so he took the foot.

After almost nine years on the department, no one could have ever told me that I would be standing in a cemetery in the middle of the night, or better yet that there was actually an offense related to stealing from a dead person/grave. The evidence team was called, a possible name for the victim was found, the foot was on its way to the medical examiner's office, a homicide detective was contacted, and now it was time to figure out how to write up a report that described this very bizarre arrest. I called the jail in hopes of getting some kind of guidance, but due to the nature of this beast, I was on my own. This eighteen year old kid, who stated he loved dead things, was on his way to the county jail for a felony arrest for stealing from a corpse/grave. Who would have ever thought in a million years something like this could happen, but I made the arrest and the story continues to this day. All of my friends regularly ask me to tell the story again. I oblige simply because to this date no one's stories can top the man who stole the foot.

Brittni King

is from Red Oak, Texas and works at Red Oak Police Department as a reserve officer. Before joining the department, she worked as a reserve Deputy Sheriff at the Ellis County Sheriff's Office. She has three years of experience as a police officer. When not performing the duties of an officer, she can be found working full time at a local elementary school. Brittni is the second of five girls and is the first in her family to venture into a law enforcement career. She enjoys being able to serve her community as a police officer when not working her full time occupation.

He's Got a Gun!

by Brittni King

In the police academy, some cadets arrive having already been employed in an area of law enforcement, while others have never been exposed to police work, yet they know they have a passion to become a police officer. I was one who lived a pretty sheltered life, having never been exposed to much of anything, causing some to question if I would make it in this challenging profession.

I remember my academy instructors showing us some very graphic pictures of scenes they had worked. They were trying to prepare us for what we would likely see for ourselves one day. I've often heard of officers who would make off-color or inappropriate remarks when confronted with gruesome or tragic situations, and I never really understood why they acted in such a manner. I never realized how many different emotions sweep over a cop each day until I became one myself. Sometimes snide remarks are just a mechanism that helps us cope. It has often been described as "gallows humor." It's not meant to be disrespectful—it just keeps us from being swept up in the abject horror of some incidents, one of which I'll describe below.

It was approximately 10:30 on a Saturday night. I had just finished filling out the paperwork for a prisoner I had booked into the jail. My partner and I were joking around as he was getting his boots shined. It was a calm night; we both felt relaxed. Little did we know that in the next few minutes, our calm night would morph into a terrible storm. As we finished up at the jail, the dispatcher called our radio numbers. I recall hearing her voice and knowing the call we were about to embark on would be one with a very high priority. Dispatch was sending us to a residence about fifteen minutes away where a man had fired shots. He was still on the scene.

My partner and I immediately ran to our patrol vehicle and set out toward the location. Whenever we're enroute to a call such as "shots fired," the adrenaline rush from driving at speeds of 100 miles per hour or more is incredible. Aside from the rush I was getting while trying to get there quickly and stay in one piece, my mind began to entertain other thoughts, particularly about my family. What if something happened to me in the next few minutes? Did my family know I loved them more than life itself? Had I shown them how much they meant to me each day? I knew that anything could happen at these kinds of incidents, and that knowledge prompted me to think of those I loved. The anticipation and fear of the unknown caused me to want to call them, perhaps for the last time, to tell them I loved them.

My anxiety was quickly interrupted by the dispatcher's frantic voice telling us that the shooter was now at large. Then two minutes later, she informed us that the shooter was still on the scene. Our hearts pounded against our ballistic vests, thumping almost audibly with each update. My partner and I scanned the roadways and residences as we arrived. We saw no one. We cautiously made our way toward the back of the location, listening for any noises. As we approached the backyard, we saw a young male seated on the deck and an older male standing a few feet away.

"He's got a gun!" The older man yelled, as he pointed toward the other man seated on the deck. Having just arrived, we were unsure about what was going on. My partner barked out a command to the man on the deck.

"Show me your hands!"

No response. Upon closer examination we immediately realized what had happened and holstered our weapons. Blood was everywhere. Suicide.

Without going into detail, the scene could only be described as extremely graphic. The older man continued to franticly pace back and forth while telling us the younger one had a gun. We calmed the older man down and took him inside the house to investigate the situation further. We notified dispatch of our status and told her the scene was secure. Soon, investigators and crime scene technicians arrived at the residence to process the evidence and complete the appropriate reports.

While my partner and I discussed the tragic event with the older man, who turned out to be the victim's stepfather, the victim's mother approached us crying hysterically. She asked whether her son was okay. The mother began telling us that she knew her son was wrong, but that he was still her son and that she needed to know that he is okay.

At moments like this, my job is sometimes almost too difficult to bear. I stood there searching for the right words, but in this case there really were none. I waited silently for a few seconds as she asked one more time, "Where is my son? Is he okay?" More than anything else, I wanted to be able to tell this mother that her boy was still alive. Reluctantly, I told her as gently as I could that her son was gone. Instantly, I saw the horror and pain flash in her eyes, like a storm brewing on the horizon. I knew that nothing I said would release her from the hell in which she was then immersed.

She repeated over and over there was no way her son was dead. I recognized she was in shock, as any parent would be. Finally, her husband pulled her close to him and tried to assure her everything would be all right, but it wouldn't. Although this man had been close to losing his own life that night, he had to be strong for her.   He was.   After a few minutes, an ambulance transported them both to the hospital.

That night ignited a myriad of emotions in me, almost like a carnival ride with all of the highs and lows.   I had never experienced such a dramatic range of disparate feelings before. One minute I was laughing and joking with my partner; the next minute we were engulfed in a sea of despair.   We faced possible danger, and then we felt relieved knowing it had passed.   The harrowing ride to the location, barreling along as quickly as we could toward the belly of the beast, reminded me not to take my family for granted.   I had felt such a profound need and love for them, one that I had never felt before.

Afterward, I felt sad for the parents.   The stepfather, his life threatened by the boy, felt fearful that he himself would not survive.   Yet witnessing his stepson commit suicide will be forever etched in his memory.   And the mother, her regret that she was unable to save her son; the grief of losing a child, will be her constant companion.   So sad, so frustrating.

I know the parents could never have anticipated what had just happened, and I don't know if there were any contributing factors, such as alcohol, that led to this final catastrophic confrontation.

Whether some choose to believe it or not, when police officers respond to calls like this one, those calls do have a lasting effect on us.   Our duty is to protect and to serve the people in the communities where we work.   Often, that means finding ourselves in harm's way, running toward the danger when most people choose to run away from it.   On the outside, we have to be in control of our emotions, but on the inside, those feelings sometimes wreak havoc upon us, constantly trying to overrule what we know to be the proper course of action.   These constant highs and lows sometimes change our lives forever.

Seeing death, witnessing violence, and being exposed to

man's inhumanity to man can have a ruinous effect on an officer's physical and mental health. Police work is a vocation rather than a job—it's not for everyone. However, if one is able to withstand the dark side of what we sometimes encounter, it can be the best job in the world.

Jacquelyn Williams

is a senior corporal with the Dallas Police Department. She has served eight years with the department and has held her current rank for the past four and a half years. Jackie has enjoyed her time on the job and her position as field training officer. Although the training process is sometimes difficult, she finds it rewarding to see her former recruits at work and to discover a bit of herself in each of them.

Jackie is the mother of one child, and is very family oriented when not at work, spending all of her time with her daughter. They are very active, always looking for something new to do. Jackie and her daughter have several hobbies, but Jackie tends to steer her child toward sports as she feels staying active ensures a healthy and prosperous life. Jackie feels she has accomplished many things in her life, but considers her biggest is being a wonderful mother. She realizes having a great career enables her to provide for her child.

Jackie takes her job very seriously, understanding that she is protecting and serving the citizens of Dallas. Her main focus is staying safe and alert while out in the field so she can go home to her daughter at the end of the day.

7

I Want My 4400

by Jacquelyn Williams

One night I was dispatched to an address from which 9-1-1 hang up calls were being received. The dispatchers constantly tried calling the number back; each time they did, someone answered, but the only thing the operators heard was loud music playing in the background. The resident would then call 9-1-1 back and hang up again. This went on for a while before I was finally dispatched to investigate. The police don't take these calls lightly, nor do we brush them off as pranks. History has shown that some victims are only able to dial 9-1-1 for help, unable to speak to the operator lest their attackers hear them.

I was assigned as a trainer this particular night; my partner was a female officer who was on her last phase of training. We arrived at the call location, and as we approached the door we heard loud music coming from inside. I knocked on the door, and a young male soon opened it. He stood there and said, "If you don't have my 4400, then you need to leave." He turned around and slammed the door shut. We knocked once again, but before we had a chance to say anything, he did the same thing as before. We knocked a third time, and once again he came to the door, but this time he had some papers in his hand, which he threw outside. As he had done twice before, he turned around. However, this time before the door closed we saw him jump over something that was lying on the floor.

"Did you see what I saw?" I asked my partner.

"Yeah, he's naked from the waist down!"

At this point, we surmised we were probably dealing with a mental health patient and wisely decided we needed assistance. We got on the radio and called for cover. It took a while before anyone responded so we sat in our squad car to keep an eye on the house, still uncertain about what may have transpired inside. Once our backup arrived, a team of three male officers and a sergeant, we advised them of the situation; we all approached the residence together.

At this point, it was a case of déjà vu. Just as had happened before, we knocked, the young man came to the door, screamed he wanted his 4400, and then slammed the door shut. This happened two more times, and the last time we rushed inside, tackling him after he opened the door. Once inside the apartment, we were hardly prepared for the scene we encountered.

Blood covered the walls and floor. Moving into the kitchen, we saw the floor was also covered in blood. The walls in the kitchen, the front room, and up the stairs were all stained crimson.

"What happened here?" The thought that the man may have killed someone inside this house crossed my mind. "Let's go upstairs," I said to the recruit. As we proceeded up the stairs, we discovered even more blood in the bedroom and bathroom.

"Look!" I heard my partner say. The recruit had spotted something in the bathtub, which she thought might be a body, and she ran out. We later found that it was only a blanket that was also covered in blood, but nobody was found in the residence.

We went back downstairs to join the other officers who were trying to talk to the man to ascertain what had happened, and who or what was the source of all the blood we had seen. All he kept saying was that he wanted his 4400, and that we messed up the orgy he had been having with a couple of women. He then proceeded to make inappropriate remarks to the sergeant. As we were talking to the young male, we noticed he had the numbers, 4400, written all over the walls and on the television.

"I'm calling paramedics," I said. "We need to have this guy examined." A short time later, they arrived and began to assess the man's condition. They discovered he had severe blood clots, one of which had probably broken the day before. As the medics were attempting to wrap his leg, the man got up and began running through the house causing more blood to fly all over the place. Somehow, the paramedics determined he might be bipolar, so we took him into custody to transport him to the hospital and have him examined at the psych ward.

"Hey look at this," I said to the others as we were leaving the apartment. It was a piece of paper hanging on the door which read "Please help me!" We transported him to the hospital and completed our paperwork for the night. After dealing with that call, my trainee and I both had a better understanding of how mental health patients may sometimes act and how their pleas for help can be mysteriously disguised as something else. We also realized that regardless of how the assignment is dispatched, expect that it can be anything other than what the original call was.

The very next day I responded to a call of a burglary in progress at that same location. I figured someone had broken into the apartment since the homeowner was in the hospital. Before I or any of the other assist units arrived, a shooting call was broadcast. I thought someone must have shot the burglar. However, once we stepped inside the location, to my surprise the same guy I transported to the hospital yesterday had already been released, and he was at it again. Note: Law enforcement cannot forcibly commit anyone against his or her will. The evaluators at the psych ward apparently felt he was not a danger.

The other officers spoke with him, and he told them he had not called the police and that he was okay. The officers left the apartment, and the man slammed the door. We all cleared from the scene and about five minutes later another shooting call came over the air. I did not respond back to the call location, but I was later told the young man had been arrested for 9-1-1 abuse.

Myra James

joined the Hamilton Police Service, Ontario, Canada, in 1988 and is a crime manager at Division 30. During the past 23 years, she has been assigned to general patrol, motorcycle unit, breathalyzer technician, vice and drugs investigator, patrol sergeant, crowd management unit, Crime Stoppers Coordinator, Sex Crimes Unit, and Criminal Investigation Division. She is a charter executive member and Immediate Past President of the Ontario Women in Law Enforcement Executives, an organization that was established in 1997. Since 2000, she has also been on the Board of Directors of the International Association of Women Police and has attended their annual training conferences for the past 18 years; she is currently the 2nd Vice President.

Myra is consulted nationally on a variety of issues and pursues opportunities to assist others who have limited resources. She is an advocate for equitable treatment of women in law enforcement. In 2005, she received the mentoring award from the Ontario Women in Law Enforcement and the IAWP. She was humbled to receive the Hamilton Woman of the Year award from the Status of Women Committee as well. For the past 17 years, she has been a member of the Stoney Creek Rotary Club and recently accepted a position on the Hamilton Status of Women Committee.

On a personal note, Myra has been happily married to Rick for 30 years. They enjoy traveling internationally as well as riding their Harleys. Myra has a background full of unique experiences, such as oatmeal wrestling, sky diving, and her recent role as Assistant Transportation Venue Manager for the 2010 Vancouver Olympics. Additionally she enjoys woodworking and has played ice hockey for the past 35 years. She is always looking for new adventures to add to her inventory of life experiences.

8

A Year That Changed My Life

by Myra James

Less than five months after an off-duty confrontation with an offender who had just murdered my cousins, I found myself involved in another critical incident. It was back in 1991, which was a tough year for me; I was only three years into my career with the Hamilton Wentworth Regional Police in Ontario, Canada. Now we are the Hamilton Police Service after the province mandated community amalgamation. I'm in my twenty-third year of municipal law enforcement and ready to share the details of my experience. The names of officers involved have been changed to protect their identities.

August 14, 1991, dayshift at the Mountain Division in the overcrowded small briefing room was like any other day, commencing at 6:45 a.m. and concluding at 6:45 p.m. Acting Sergeant Bates led the briefing and conducted roll call. He shared details of a suspect wanted on a Canada-wide warrant for murdering two young woman, one in Burlington and one in New Brunswick. The majority of the officers recorded some of the information either in their duty books or clipboards, which is what I did. I remember specifically the Ontario license number 222 LED attached to an older model 1982 Toyota Corolla. The suspect's home address was a short distance outside the Hamilton jurisdiction, a place called Caistorville. His in-laws lived in a small community called Dundas, which was in the western portion of the county. My beat assignment for the day was 721, which was known as one of the busiest beats in the division. Geographically, it incorporated the area along the escarpment with an ideal view of the tip of Lake Ontario and often the CN Tower in Toronto on a clear day. Of course, the smoke stacks from the steel companies in our city were always in view, a less than desirable sight. Following the briefing, I remember thinking how unlikely it would be for me to encounter the suspect.

Typically, when I go 10-8, the code for "in service," I am immediately dispatched to a call for service. Several of my colleagues have time to grab a coffee and maybe a donut at the local Tim Hortons, which was only a stone's throw from the Mountain Division. I could count on one hand the number of times that I'd have an opportunity for coffee at the commencement of shift. Twenty years ago, the calls for service first thing in the morning were for overnight entries into cars, property damage, motor vehicle collisions, and follow up reports from the previous night.

It was a nice clear day, sunny and, fortunately, not too humid. The calls for service were steady, however, I found myself with sometime later in the afternoon to conduct some pro-active patrolling in and around Concession Street, which paralleled the edge of the escarpment. Shortly after 4 p.m. an all-car bulletin was broadcast to all three divisions of the police service. Details within the broadcast included similar information we had received on the morning briefing with the exception of the new developments. The suspect had been reported to the police as being in the area of his residence near Caistorville, perhaps en route to his in-laws' home in Dundas.

To navigate that journey would involve driving right through the streets of the Mountain Division, but not anywhere near my patrol area. Since I wasn't on a call for service, I volunteered to respond from Concession Street southerly to an area where I thought he might travel. I was heading for Rymal Road, which is a major east/west roadway about two miles south of my patrol area. Because there was a lapse in time from when the information was called in and when it was dispatched, I was not optimistic about the potential of locating the suspect. In my mind, it was likely that if the suspect took Rymal Road, he would be well west of my location by the time I could set up a covert location to observe the traffic. I stepped up the speed a bit, engaged no emergency equipment, and headed south on Upper Wentworth Street, which was a north/south major roadway that linked Concession Street with Rymal Road. Upper Wentworth Street hosted Limeridge Mall, the largest shopping mall in the city and a popular destination for young and old. Additionally, numerous city transit buses had designated stop zones on the inner perimeter road of the mall.

Initially, I was the only one who informed the dispatcher of my intention to head south on Upper Wentworth Street. I knew in my mind that other officers in the process of completing some paperwork would set that aside and be responding even though they didn't verbalize their intentions on the radio. That's what it was like; we were a team known as "C" squad, and we always had each other's backs. Little did I know what I was about to encounter as I drove that cruiser south on Upper Wentworth approaching Limeridge Road.

The traffic volume was light on the four lane roadway as I stopped for the red light at Limeridge Road. To my surprise, I saw a dark brown Toyota Corolla on the opposite side of the intersection heading northbound. There was car in front of him so I couldn't see the license plate; however, the male driver matched the description of the suspect who had been described by Acting Sgt. Bates that morning. As the light turned green, I maneuvered the cruiser through the intersection and did a U-turn in order to pull in behind the suspect to confirm his license plate number. Indeed, it was the suspect's vehicle.

My heart began to race, my mind cluttered with thoughts of apprehension strategies, but I wanted to remain as calm as possible. I took some deep breaths, reached for the police radio microphone, and informed the dispatcher that I had located the suspect vehicle with one male driver. I described the driver, and then the dispatcher requested any available units to respond to the area of Limeridge Mall. One of the thoughts that crossed my mind was, "What would I do if he stopped the car and took hostages?"

I continued the deep breaths and followed the suspect east on Limeridge Road to the entrance of the mall where he turned left into the massive parking lot area. With every turn or change in direction, I updated the dispatcher who had to remind other officers not to use the police radio. Our code was 10-3, which everyone knew related to no radio transmissions. Colleagues from "C" squad responded from all over the Mountain Division; I could hear their sirens and prayed they would arrive soon. Criminal investigation detectives and other officers also verbalized their responses, which interfered with my on-going communications about the direction of the suspect's travel.

I knew all of the officers responding would likely be thinking about our policy and procedures prohibiting high speed pursuits and ramming suspects' vehicles. I was only three years out of Police College so the policy was fresh in my mind. Fortunately, the suspect did not initially flee at a high speed. As I followed him into the mall parking lot, which wasn't too busy, I was certain he was aware of my presence. He weaved in and out of parked cars and up and down some of the lanes between the parked cars. I told the dispatcher, "He's playing games." In hindsight, the dispatcher may have wondered what I was talking about. Her calmness in maintaining control of the police radio transmissions had a positive effect on me. It helped me stay focused and to speak clearly so my colleagues would know where we were in the massive parking lot.

Eventually the suspect drove to the perimeter road, which had several city bus stops, stop signs and lanes that led to other large buildings adjacent the mall. I was really nervous following the suspect north along the perimeter road past the people standing at the bus stops. Our speed was about 20 mph, and I did not have any of the emergency equipment activated yet. The suspect took a left turn from the perimeter road into a large grocery store parking lot where he actually stopped for a woman pushing her shopping cart from the front of the store. At that point, all I could think about was, "What if he stopped and took her hostage?" After all, he had murdered two women and was capable of anything.

He continued driving past the Fortinos grocery store and then went west to Mall Road, which is where I recall encountering my first back up officer, Constable McElroy, who had less time on the job than me. I was relieved at his arrival and the anticipated presence of many of my colleagues. We took Mall Road a very short distance south and linked back onto the perimeter road of Limeridge Mall. The suspect was still driving slowly when he entered the perimeter road where he made a sudden left turn back into the large parking lot area. Constable McElroy then took the primary position behind the suspect, and I continued to transmit our direction and location. According to our policy and procedure, the second police vehicle in a pursuit is responsible for the radio transmissions.

The suspect started to increase his speed a bit as we followed him east across the parking lot where he re-joined the perimeter road on the east side of the mall. It was on the east side that the suspect would have a visual on the responding units. Acting

Sergeant Bates was monitoring our location and had a position in a parallel row in the parking lot. Strategically, it was a good option, for the suspect stayed on the perimeter road, and the Acting Sergeant would have been in a position to ram him. We knew ramming was in non-compliance with our policy, but the procedure may have been in the best interest of the situation.

Spontaneously, Constable McElroy and I activated our emergency equipment followed by the other officers who were behind us. The suspect's speed increased as he rounded the curve on the perimeter road on the south end of the mall and continued past the designated bus stop zone area. I could see people standing at the bus shelters, wondering what was going on. Suddenly I could see the suspect lift something up in the car, but I couldn't tell what it was. By then he was going over 40 mph northbound when he hit another grey car on the perimeter road and lost control of his vehicle. He hit a concrete boulevard and completely sheared off a tree that was in the boulevard before his vehicle came to rest.

Dust and some debris from the suspect's car was flying around as all of us brought our police vehicles to a prompt stop and we exited with guns drawn. At the time, we were carrying Smith and Wesson .38 specials, six shot revolvers, with two additional speed loaders on our duty belt. About six of us ran toward the suspect's vehicle. The only thing the dispatcher knew is that the acting sergeant had broadcast there had been a TA, which several of us, including the dispatcher, were not familiar with. It had been a term the member used while he was employed by a neighboring police agency. TA is a term used for traffic accident.

The police radio was silent as we raced to the suspect's vehicle to find him motionless with a .22 calibre rifle lying in the front seat. Some of us thought perhaps he was playing possum, a term used for a person feigning unconsciousness. Officers provided gun drawn cover while two other members pulled the suspect from the car. I went to the passenger side front window, which was either open or broken, pulled out the rifle, and secured it in the back of one of the cruisers. None of us knew if the suspect had actually shot himself or lost consciousness from the collision with the boulevard and the tree. There were no obvious signs of an entrance or exit bullet wound. I'm sure the one to two minutes of silent radio activity seemed like an hour to the dispatcher who was eventually updated with the details at the scene.

The emergency medical services were requested for the suspect who lay unconscious and handcuffed. Once the dust literally settled, one of the officers made a comment about the vehicle the suspect struck prior to the collision with the boulevard. The small compact grey car with a young woman and children was stopped about 150 feet from south of our location on the perimeter road. I ran back to her vehicle and saw that she still had a death grip on her steering wheel. She had no idea what had just transpired, other than the fact her car was hit by a brown Toyota Corolla at a high rate of speed followed by multiple police vehicles that were lit up like Christmas trees.

The acting sergeant assigned a member to complete a motor vehicle collision report, and the scene was roped off with police caution tape. Bus service into the mall was suspended for several hours. The media were upon the scene almost immediately. Emergency medical services provided medical intervention at the scene for the suspect who was eventually transported to the closest hospital, which happened to be on Concession Street on my beat. One officer accompanied the EMS with the suspect to the hospital while the rest of us participated in a complete grid search of the area the suspect travelled in the parking lot and perimeter road.

I recall being totally drained of energy, but I joined my colleagues on the grid search, which produced zero results. It took hours to complete the search. At one point, the Acting Sergeant informed us that the provincial SIU, Special Investigations Unit out of Toronto, would be responding to interview us and inspect our service guns to ensure we did not discharge them at the suspect. It was policy that if some type of significant physical injury to a suspect may have been a result of police action, the SIU was deployed. I had never been exposed to them and was anxious about how the whole process would transpire. Did I require a Police Association representative? I questioned myself about whether I had done anything wrong.

By mid-evening, several hours past the time of our regular duty shift, the SIU arrived and interviewed the officers from the Limeridge Mall scene. They inspected our service guns and confirmed there were no discharges. I finished my shift that day shortly after 10 p.m. and went home, exhausted physically, emotionally, and mentally. Once in my home with my husband of eleven years, I remember being relieved and comforted by his presence. So many thoughts went through my mind about what could have happened that day. I didn't sleep that night and had to report to work again for 6:45 a.m.

Upon my arrival at the station, the nightshift officers wanted a play by play of the events of the previous day. They also informed me the suspect had succumbed to his injuries from a self-inflicted .22 round to the head. He died shortly after 3 a.m. At the morning briefing, the Acting Sergeant commended me publicly, as well as the responding officers. Collectively, we debriefed the events of the previous day which included my comments about the calm demeanour of our communications dispatcher. Later, I submitted her name for commendation.

Following the briefing I was asked to stay in the station and wait for the arrival of another Special Investigation Unit member who wanted to conduct some follow up with me, as well as record a video of the actual route I travelled when following the offender. Again my anxiety was elevated, and I felt as though I had done something wrong. I was sleep deprived and had no appetite. The whole event brought back horrific memories of my cousin's murder on March 21, 1991. I think my commanding officers may have wondered if I was still in the throes of post-traumatic stress from March, as they demonstrated their concern and encouraged me to seek support from our Employee Assistance Program. My friends, family, and colleagues provided plenty of support so I never did seek EAP.

The SIU investigator, Gareth, arrived mid-morning on the 15th and we discussed the sequence of events again, followed by an actual drive around Limeridge Mall. He made me feel very comfortable and didn't seem like the type of SIU investigator my colleagues had referenced in the past. I spent about two hours with him and then returned to my patrol beat for the balance of the shift. Following our shift that day, "C" squad went to our club for choir practise, which for us was a way to wind down following two emotionally charged shifts. Even though I was exhausted and sleep deprived, I didn't want to miss our informal social time together. Fortunately my husband understood the importance of choir practise and was my pillar throughout this ordeal.

Eight months later the inquest took place in Hamilton, and seven individuals were granted "standing" at the event that lasted fifty-two days. It was declared the longest inquest in the history of the City of Hamilton. As a result of the inquest, one hundred and twenty-five recommendations directed police services across the province to change many of their policy and procedures regarding sexual assault and domestic violence investigations.

Looking back, these types of incidents are a learning mechanism for law enforcement. Debriefings are imperative for everyone involved, including our communications operators. I was fortunate to work with an exceptional group of men and women from "C" squad on the mountain. Many were veterans, such as Charlie and Mark, who I continue to value for their experience and knowledge. Just as important, were my friends and family who supported my emotional roller coaster throughout this entire ordeal. I will be forever grateful!

Nikki Tezak

of Castle Rock, Colorado, is a seven year veteran of the Palmer Lake Police Department. The first woman officer in the department, she was promoted to patrol sergeant in 2007, thereby becoming the first female sergeant in the department's history.

She began her career 18 years ago as a reserve deputy in Canon City, Colorado. Nikki became a detention deputy and then the jail investigator and was eventually promoted to patrol deputy. She married a sergeant within the department and opted to change her career path, joining the Colorado Department of Corrections. She quickly realized corrections was not what she wanted and applied for another Sheriff's Department position, starting over as a detention deputy. Nikki quickly moved up in rank because of her prior experience and soon became an investigator. Working as a deputy sheriff meant an election cycle every four years. Not wanting to endure that uncertainty again, she joined the Palmer Lake Police Department.

Nikki has worked as a hostage negotiator on the Fugitive Apprehension Team and Emergency Response. She has been recognized for assisting with the apprehension of an escape prisoner and by the Denver Bar Association for her efforts in saving the lives of 56 starved horses. She was Officer of the Year in the Tri-Lakes Area, in 2005 and 2007, and received a Chief's Commendation for the successful apprehension of a kidnap suspect. Recently, she was awarded the first ever Distinguished Service Award Medal for her leadership in the aftermath of the sudden death of her good friend, the Chief of Police.

In her spare time, Nikki can be found with her family, friends and dogs. She enjoys reading, crafts and making floral arrangements for weddings and Christmas. She recently began taking more time for herself and enjoys 3-mile walks. After 18 years she is able to leave her worries at work and enjoy her free time.

Kidnapped

by Nikki Tezak

The Palmer Lake Police Department in Colorado consists of a Chief, four full-time officers, and six part-time officers. This tiny contingent protects all 2,800 residents of this small town, which is located in El Paso County.

As part of my duties on July 11, 2007, I was driving to deliver a felony case filing to the El Paso County District Attorney's Office. The DA's office is located 25 miles south of my jurisdiction in downtown Colorado Springs. As I was driving, I overheard a call for service involving local deputies who were looking for a four-year-old child who had just been kidnapped within the county.

I completed my delivery to the DA's office and then started my drive back to Palmer Lake. While I was en route, dispatch aired a BOLO (be on the lookout) describing the kidnapped child by name, age, and physical descriptors. The suspect was also described and was said to have been seen driving a stolen, white, Volvo truck. The truck was further identified by its license plate number, Department of Transportation registration numbers, and specific business information, which was written on both doors. The alleged kidnapper was supposed to be heading to either Denver, Wyoming, or northeast El Paso County.

Since I was going to be driving north bound on Interstate 25 on my way back to town, I wrote as much of the information down as I could, knowing this was a very likely path the suspect would take. While I was writing, I drove past the turn I needed to make that would bring me back to I-25. It meant that I had to continue driving north on Nevada Avenue in Colorado Springs to get back to the interstate.

Dispatch continued supplying updated information on this developing incident, advising that our wanted man had numerous felony warrants and giving us the alias he may be using.

I came to stop at a red light on Nevada Avenue and East Jackson Street.   Directly across the intersection from me, heading south bound, I observed a white semi-truck in the left turn lane stopped for the light as well. I looked at the license plate number—it matched the number I had written on my notes. As I looked up at the truck, I saw a little boy stand up in the passenger seat of the semi.

Could this be the vehicle in the BOLO? I sat there wondering if I had the license plate number wrong, questioning my notes, and wondering what are the odds this truck is indeed "the truck." I called a deputy working on the case and asked him to provide me with more details. Deputy Scott Aldridge told me the license plate information was correct and said the writing on the doors were the distinct initials of the business.

The light turned green for the semi, and as he turned in front of me I confirmed the rest of the truck information located on its cab. Completely in shock, I told Deputy Aldridge that I had the suspect in view. I then hung up on him and called dispatch advising them of my location. Here is where the story gets confusing. The dispatcher assigned an officer from another town located next to Palmer Lake, which is the normal practice due to the proximity of both agencies. The assigned officer, however, had to confirm the location where I was. Once he did, he told dispatch that there had to be another agency closer to me than he was.

Since I was not in a lane in which I could easily turn from to get behind the suspect, I lost visual contact of the suspected vehicle for a moment.   However, once I turned around and headed in the same direction as the truck, I found it one block over from our original location.   The vehicle was now pulled over at North Weber Street, and the suspect began to step out of the truck.   He looked at my marked patrol car, and as I got closer, he began walking rapidly toward an apartment building. As I drove past the apartments, he watched me very closely while opening an apartment door.   I advised dispatch of his location and then drove out of his sight.   I checked the numbers on the truck, making sure they were in fact the numbers given by dispatch, and then turned my patrol vehicle around so that I was facing the front of the semi.   I stopped about a car length in front of it to make it appear as though I had left.

I saw the little boy in the front seat standing up, so I advised dispatch I had a visual on the boy.   While providing this information, the suspect began walking back to the passenger side of the truck.   At this point, I had to disconnect with dispatch; I had to ensure that no harm came to the child.

I stepped out of my vehicle and ordered the suspect to step toward me, while keeping both hands in plain view.   I asked him his name; he gave me the alias aired by dispatch.   I then asked if he had identification, he said he did not.   I told him I needed to see documentation confirming he was the person he claimed to be, and he said he only had a card that with his driver's license number handwritten on the back.   He said it was in his pocket.

Since I could see there were no bulges in the pants pockets, I ordered him to slowly reach in his pocket, get the paper, and then hand it to me.   The man looked to be in his early to mid-thirties, and the actual suspect's year of birth would make him thirty-one years old. He handed me a small check cashing ID card which was written by hand too. The ID indicated his year of birth was 1966. That would mean he was forty-four years old—I could plainly see he was not that old.

After I ran the information through dispatch, they confirmed he was definitely our wanted suspect. By now there were at least a couple deputies and a lieutenant headed my way, as well as the Colorado Springs Police.

Questioning the suspect again about his identification, he started getting jittery and rambled on asking questions like, "Why is Palmer Lake here," and, "Why are you here? Did someone say I couldn't have my nephew?" I asked what his nephew's name was, and the suspect gave me the same name as the kidnapped child. When the suspect began to reach for the passenger door, I ordered him to step away from the vehicle. Since I was not familiar with this part of town and didn't know when my back-up might arrive, I attempted to keep the suspect calm for as long as possible.

At this point the child stepped out of the semi and I asked him his name. He gave me the same name as that of the kidnapped child. To keep him out of harm's way I allowed him to get back inside the cab. He appeared very scared and attempted to hide under the semi before opening the door to get back inside.

I had the suspect step approximately twenty feet from the semi and made him sit on the curb. This made the suspect more nervous, and he started looking around, again asking me why I was there. He told me to call the child's mother to verify he had permission to take him, and he got up off the curb and attempted to walk back toward the driver side. At that point, I told him I was there for the child. I placed him in handcuffs and walked him back to my vehicle.

El Paso County Deputy Aldridge and Colorado Springs Police arrived on the scene minutes later. Deputy Aldridge thanked me for my efforts and assistance and then took over custody of the suspect. Prior to leaving the scene, El Paso County Lieutenant Cliff Northam, arrived and spoke with me regarding my participation. He thanked me for capturing the suspect.

Although I was directly responsible for the arrest of the perpetrator, I had no further involvement with the case or any contact with the little boy or his family. However, I have learned that the suspect is currently an inmate at a prison in Colorado. He received four years for kidnapping and three years for motor vehicle theft. He was also wanted for other crimes, making his total sentence 27 ½ years.

Pamela Starr

is a sergeant and 15-year veteran with the Dallas, Texas, Police Department. Prior to joining DPD, Pam was employed as a police dispatcher at Travis County Sheriff's Office in Austin, Texas and worked as an Emergency Medical Technician in Austin, giving her a total of 22 years in public service. She is currently certified by the State of Texas as both a Master Peace Officer and an Emergency Medical Technician.

Pam earned a Bachelor's of Social Science from Southern Methodist University where she focused on Sociology and Criminology. She also studied at Texas Women's University, ultimately earning her Masters in Women's Studies with a focus on women in leadership and government.

Pam has worked in uniform as a patrol and bicycle patrol officer. She worked undercover in the Narcotics Division, worked in Training as a firearms instructor, and served as a detective in the Background Investigations Unit. She is currently a sergeant in patrol, working Dallas' Central Division. Her interests include physical and tactical training, especially for females, and feminist studies. She is married and has two dogs.

Pleasing Mr. Dunbar

by Pamela M. Starr

Bicycle patrol units in most urban districts are tasked not only with crime prevention and response to criminal complaints, but also with fostering community-police relations. Because of the large concentration of citizens in a city's central business district, bicycle patrol squads have the opportunity to interact with a wide range of people, personalities, and problems. Their visibility and lack of a barrier, the squad car, makes them approachable and uniquely noticeable. Outside of police duties, the job is largely public relations oriented. As a recovering tree-hugger and social butterfly, an assignment riding a bicycle in downtown Dallas was my dream job, allowing me to spend duty hours outside while connecting with people from varying walks of life: business owners and the homeless share the streets of Dallas during the day. Experiencing the myriad sights and sounds, problems and concerns of the central business district (CBD) made that assignment my most rewarding to date.

I worked that duty for approximately seven years. During that time, I provided services that citizens typically expect of their police force: responding to 911 calls, providing directions, and answering crime related questions. Burglaries, robberies, and assaults were not uncommon in the CBD, and there were some fun times riding code three through urban areas. Dallas' downtown population grew by twenty-two thousand or more on weekdays, and the availability of other peoples' property was too good for some people to pass up. Although many of the calls I responded to were property-crime related, the most common call in downtown Dallas was a Signal 8, intoxicated person.

The homeless population in Dallas, with little else to focus on, tends to drink to fill their time. Dallas is split into wet and dry areas. Downtown Dallas is wet. As such, the homeless, with nowhere else to go, congregate around liquor stores. They panhandle for money, and when the cost of a forty ounce beer is reached, they immediately spend it on the elixir they hope will cure their ills. Whether the drinking itself is the problem or people drinking is an answer to their own problem is not always clear. However, what is clear is that when these individuals pass out among the business class in downtown, police officers are called to resolve the problem.

One of the intoxicated individuals I consistently dealt with downtown was a man named Donald Dunbar. Sober or drunk, he was a pleasant person who was always willing to share a smile and a story. Mr. Dunbar had been struck by a bus several years prior, leaving him partially paralyzed. His inability to walk limited his chances at stable and rewarding work. Without the ability to support himself, Mr. Dunbar began using alcohol to alleviate the woes he suffered daily. Jobless, he eked out a living on Social Security funds. Of course, his idea of living was to drink, and the best place to do that, apparently, was downtown Dallas.

Each month, when Mr. Dunbar's Social Security stipend arrived, I knew I would find him drinking, drunk, or passed out in the area around the municipal court at Harwood and Main Streets. There is an approximately three-foot high marble ledge around the building on that corner. Directly cattycorner to that ledge is a small store whose profits are made primarily from the sale of alcohol. It is a convenient corner for Donald, who struggles on crutches to the liquor store to get his bottle and then returns to the marble, tree-sheltered ledge to tie one on. Save for the accumulated empty bottles, the ledge is a pleasant place to pass the day people-watching. On one Signal 8 call, I met Mr. Dunbar on this corner and left him with no doubt about the lengths to which Dallas police officers were willing to go in support of the city's inhabitants.

On this particular day, I discovered Mr. Dunbar unconscious on his favorite corner. While awaiting the paddy wagon for transport to a detoxification facility, I began frisking him to ensure he was not carrying any contraband or weapons. For much of the search, he remained unconscious, lying on his back on the sidewalk. He was dead weight as I rolled him left and right in an effort to empty his pants and jacket pockets. During a search of his right front pants pocket, I found a pill bottle containing his anti-seizure medication. It was a typical prescription bottle—amber in color, about three inches in length and one inch in diameter.

Having become familiar with Donald, and thus his medical history, I was not distressed to find medication on his person, and I continued my search. After extracting that bottle, I moved on to his left pocket. Because David's jeans were so dirty and tight, I was able to ascertain he had property in this pocket as well. In typical anti-Terry Frisk fashion I manipulated the property in an effort to establish its identity and to maneuver it to the top of his pocket for easier removal. Donald was under arrest for public intoxication and, according to policy, I was searching and removing his belongings so that the book-in process at our detox facility could be streamlined.

In his left pocket, I felt what I believed to be another pill bottle. The size and shape of the object was similar to the first bottle, and I figured Donald had traveled downtown with his full medicine cabinet in tow. I started working on moving the bottle toward the top of his jeans. The task proved more difficult than I anticipated, and I became frustrated at my inability to remove a simple piece of property. Manipulating the bottle through his clothing, I was able to get my hand below the bottle and push it toward the top of his pocket. My goal was to force the property to expose itself at the lip of his pocket so I could remove it without placing my entire hand inside.

As I said, his jeans were old, dirty and tight, causing me to work on that damn pill bottle for a good four minutes. Up and down, up and down, trying to get the cursed thing out of his pocket and into my property envelope before the paddy wagon arrived to carry him away. Drunk, homeless people do not smell particularly pleasant in the heat of a Texas summer, particularly after they have urinated on themselves. Becoming increasingly frustrated at my lack of success in removing the bottle, I cursed at Donald under my breath. "Damn it, Donald! Come on! We have to stop meeting like this. I am hot and need you to come on!"

The entire time I was muttering at Donald to come on, I was working on that damn pocket with the pill bottle . . . up and down, up and down. I tried to remove the bottle without success. Again cursing under my breath, I looked at Donald's face. To my surprise, he had awakened from his unconscious state and was staring at me with a huge, lopsided smile. His eyes occasionally rolled in his head, but he refocused on me and smiled even wider. I smiled back, oblivious to what had caused his sudden bout of consciousness and pleasure.

I fleetingly wondered what it felt like to be homeless, with few options, and having constant contact with the police. I did not know if I could keep a positive attitude under the same circumstances, but I was glad that Donald had found a spot that allowed him to be happy in such troublesome conditions. Continuing to work on that pocket, I looked at his face again and found him still smiling. Being a good officer, and using deductive reasoning, I soon discovered the reason for this radical change in his demeanor. I was shocked!

Having had no luck moving the pill bottle from his pants I eventually forced my hand into his jeans to remove it. To my surprise there was nothing in the pocket. What quickly became evident was that Mr. Dunbar was in a turgid state! To my dismay, the pill bottle was actually a piece of David's anatomy, and my repeated attempts to remove it from his pants caused it to grow.

I yelped, I think, and immediately yanked my hand from his pocket as I recalled using the word come several times in my mini-tirade. Glancing around, I searched the area for witnesses and cameras. With hands balled in fists at my side and my face flushing, I fully realized what I had just done. In full police uniform, in the middle of a busy downtown street, I had just given a hand job to a passed out homeless person—I freaked! Donald continued to smile.

I still wait for the images of that day, captured on a hidden camera of some nearby business, to show up somewhere, perhaps at my retirement party or during a news story exposing the exploits of the force. Maybe even in an envelope sent to my grandmother. I lived in fear for a year after that arrest. My anxiety over being discovered has waned over time, even though the images of Donald's blissful face have not. I doubt Mr. Dunbar remembers that day, but I have no doubt he speaks highly of female bicycle patrol officers and the extreme lengths they are willing to fulfill the city's mission statement. That statement asserts that the police department will "Increase citizen satisfaction" and "Provide assistance at every opportunity." In his mind, I am sure Donald believes there is no limit to what the city of Dallas will do to foster community-police relations.

Sandy Smetana

Dover, Delaware, became a police officer in 1982 with the Baytown Police Department in Baytown, Texas. She served as a patrol officer and field training officer (FTO) for 6 ½ years. She left Baytown and joined the City of Dover Police Department (DPD) in the fall of 1989, working patrol and serving as an FTO. Sandy worked various assignments, including: Patrol, Detective Division, Planning & Training Division, Community Policing Unit, Youth Unit and Hostage Negotiating Team. She was certified as an instructor and a master instructor. Promoted several times, she retired as a platoon sergeant in charge of a platoon of officers in the Patrol Division. She was the first female in the Dover Police Department to reach the rank of sergeant, and the first female officer to retire from the department. During her career she earned a Bachelor of Arts Degree in Behavioral Science, and a Master of Science Degree in Administration of Justice from Wilmington University.

While employed at the DPD, she was honored to become a Nationally Credentialed Law Enforcement Officer, and received her certificate from then US Attorney General Janet Reno. Sandy also received several awards, including two Police Chief's Commendations, Officer of the Quarter in 2002 and Class A and Class B Commendations. She is a Lifetime member of Mid-Atlantic Association of Women in Law Enforcement (MAAWLE) and a Lifetime member of International Association of Women Police (IAWP). Sandra is also a member of the Fraternal Organization of Police (FOP) and has held several offices in her local FOP.

Sandy has two sons who are now following in her footsteps by giving back to the community. Her oldest son is a volunteer firefighter and her youngest is a Military Police Officer with United States Army Reserves.

First Shooting

by Sandy Smetana

I remember dreading receiving that call for the first time – the one where someone has been shot. How would I respond? Could I handle it? Would I be able to hold myself together while looking at the blood and gore and still be effective as a police officer?

One night I finally got my chance. I responded to a call of shots fired at a new apartment complex on Garth Road, in Baytown, Texas. One person had been wounded. I responded with other officers, and each of us rode in single cars. Back up was usually only two or three minutes away. We arrived, I can't remember which of us got there first, and found a white male lying in the open doorway of downstairs apartment A. There was a small amount of blood coming from a tiny wound in the victim's back, near his spine. He was yelling and crying like a baby. Then I saw that he was bleeding from his right hand as well. He told us he had been shot. I looked, but didn't see anything real bad – just a small amount of blood on his back and the same on his hand. Then I saw he was bleeding on his other hand as well. When the ambulance arrived, the crew found no other wounds and then transported him to the hospital.

We soon learned what happened. Two guys were playing cards in apartment A. The girlfriend of one of the guys slipped out of a bedroom window and went to meet the shooting victim, who lived in apartment B. The two had sex while the woman's boyfriend was playing cards in the apartment they shared together. It seems the boyfriend and the woman's lover didn't like each other. After having sex, the lover decided to take a shower.

The boyfriend and his card-playing friend decided to pick on the lover in apartment B, unaware the girl was in the lover's apartment. They went to the lover's apartment and saw that his motorcycle was parked on the patio. They knocked on the door. The girlfriend saw her boyfriend and his partner at the door and panicked. She told her lover that her boyfriend was at the door, and she quickly slipped out the window, never allowing her boyfriend to catch even a glimpse of her.

The woman's lover grabbed a towel and wrapped it around his waist. He told the two guys at the door to go away. They yelled at him and refused to leave. Fearing for his life because of past encounters with the woman's boyfriend, the lover grabbed a gun from a nearby table. The two guys outside knocked over the lover's motorcycle, which caused Lover Boy to exit his apartment, wearing only a towel and nothing else. He pointed the gun at the two guys, who immediately took off running. Meanwhile, the girlfriend, ran to her own apartment and climbed back through her bedroom window.

When the two guys took off running, Lover Boy, towel around his hips, chased them and began shooting. He shot the boyfriend in the back first, and then in both hands. As you might guess, the shooter's towel fell off as he was running and firing his weapon. The gun the shooter had, a .22 caliber, explains why the wounds were very small and caused little bleeding.

When the incident was all over, I reflected on my first shooting – a naked man with a gun chasing and shooting another man. Very little blood and no gore. Whew, I made it!

Traci Ciepiela

works at the Texas County Sheriff's Department for Sheriff Carl Watson. Texas County is a rural county in South Central Missouri. The sheriff's department is located in Houston and is the largest county in the state.

Traci grew up in Western New York, just outside the city of Buffalo. She originally started a career in radio news, working at stations in Buffalo, New York, Iron Mountain, Michigan, and Jefferson City, Missouri, before leaving for the ranks of law enforcement, a decision she says was the best one she ever made.

She has worked in law enforcement for 12 years, in both city and county jurisdictions. Traci holds a Master's Degree from Columbia College and is all but a dissertation from a Doctorate in Philosophy. In addition to the Sheriff's Department, she also works for Western Wyoming Community College as an Associate Professor, Kaplan University, Phoenix University Online, and Everest University Online.

Strange Behavior

by Traci Ciepiela

I have been told that all good redneck stories need to start the same way. "So there I was," working the night shift at the Sheriff's Department. It had been a busy week already as I had gone on a number of strange calls, including looking for a dead body in a location that was described as an area near railroad tracks, reported by some tweaked out meth-head who had been awake for about a week and found a need to start confessing to murder while at a psychiatric ward. The tweaker claimed he left the body near railroad tracks and a road. It had already been hot in Missouri that week, so I figured if there was a dead body out there I would have been able to tell pretty easily. I didn't find or smell a body that night, so I figured that if we eventually found a body near there we would at least know who to go question about it. On this occasion though, the call wasn't a dead body, another entertaining experience was waiting for me this evening.

I received a phone call at my desk as I had just come into the office to eat dinner. The person on the other end of the line identified himself as a detective from the neighboring sheriff's department, and he needed to let me know that something strange was going on. As I looked around the deputy's office and realized that no one else was around, I knew strange had become my calling that week, so I asked the detective what's up.

He informed me that a woman had been reported missing in

yet a third jurisdiction earlier that day. Her mother, though, had received a phone call shortly before he called me. The person on the phone wouldn't identify herself but indicated the mother should round up her entire family, drive only a red car, wear only cotton clothing, bring no identification with them, and expect to have to stay for a long period of time. The directions were apparently relayed to this woman, to the detective, and to me, and of course the directions led right to the center of the county where I was on duty. Now the instructions definitely piqued my interest, so I headed to the location that the directions indicated to see what in fact was happening.

While en route to the location, a call came into 911. Although the specifics were awfully confusing, from what I could piece together the missing woman was at the location where I was heading, she had brought children with her, and she was irritated. It's never a good combination when kids are involved in anything, so other deputies and I stepped up the response to what we would discover to be a strange situation indeed.

Upon arrival, I was ushered into a room where the owners of the house were. On the bed in this room was a woman lying with her arms around the necks of her children. When I arrived, she simply said, "Thank you for coming."

Well, I thought to myself "Cool, she is happy I am here." We often don't get that kind of response, but what was odd was that she never got up, didn't sit up, and didn't stand up. She just lay there on the bed with two children, who we later determined were two and four years old.

The woman looked at me and asked, "Do you know the one true lord, your savior Jesus Christ?" Now, when this question is asked, typically there just is no good way to answer it, whether it's someone knocking at your door in the middle of the day or strange people lying on a bed with two children.

"Sure," I said.

She announced that now that we were all there she had

something to read to us. Considering I had already called for an ambulance, we had some time to wait so I told her to go right ahead and read away.

The woman pulled out a Bible and opened it to Revelations and proceeded to read a paragraph. When she finished she looked up at me and said, "Do you understand?"

Not wanting to agitate her further, I tried my best to paraphrase what she had read. Apparently, my summation was right on target because she ultimately sighed and said, "Yes!" I knew right then and there that something had just broken inside her head. Apparently what she believed is that her second born was the "second coming." Apparently the little boy was only still alive because while she was giving birth the devil didn't eat him. She thought we should be very excited that he was there and that his name was Nathan, and he was two.

She continued to read to us while I tried to keep her children occupied. Unfortunately, while keeping the children happy I managed to help them break the frame of the bed, for I was allowing the kids to jump up and down on the bed. Could be one of the reasons kids shouldn't be jumping on beds. I apologized to the owners; they assured me the bed wasn't of that much value, even though it appeared to be antique. We ultimately discovered the house where this woman called from was one where she just showed up and announced to the owners that, "God had prepared the house for her to stay for the next 1,023 days." That would be a long time to have a guest, but the owners didn't really know this woman to begin with. They had met her once approximately twenty years ago, but it isn't like they had ever kept in touch. The owners of the house didn't have a clue what to think of the situation either.

Ultimately, I made an effort to get her to understand she needed to leave with us. She eventually agreed, but first we had to pray with her. I felt at this point I was going to do just about anything to get this woman out of the house peacefully. I told her to go ahead, but she refused until all parties in the room agreed to hold hands. So the other deputies and I stood there holding hands until the woman closed her eyes. I was planning to handcuff her immediately if she refused to go, but she followed through with her promise to leave with us. As I got outside, we learned that somehow the ambulance had been cancelled so we decided to transport her and her kids in my patrol vehicle.

The child car seats were arranged, but she insisted her son had to sit on her left side. We had to rearrange the car seats. As I asked if she had any shoes to put on since the driveway was just a bunch of rocks, she informed me, "Every step just reminds me that I am on God's path." You would never catch me walking on those rocks, God's path or not.

As we got ready to go, she announced the dog had to come with us. There was a dog running around the house, and I assumed the dog belonged to the landowners. Apparently not. Neither did the dog belong to this woman. I was finally able to determine she had dognapped the animal from a friend where she started out earlier that morning. I asked for the friend's phone number, and just as I thought she was about to give it to me, the woman told me, "She'll know to come."

Apparently some kind of divine inspiration was going to let the dog's owner know we had found her dog. Eventually, the dog was transported in another deputy's car. I ultimately was able to track the dog's owner through utility records of the city where the dog lived. It was a good thing the police department had access to those records.

On the drive to the hospital I asked about playing some music, but she refused to listen to anything on the radio. I asked her if she was hungry, and she insisted she couldn't have anything but water for the next 1,023 days.

Giving up on her needs, I focused on the kids, afraid she was starving them. She relented a bit and said they could have something small when we got to where we were going. Oddly enough she never asked where we were taking her. We also didn't offer up that information. We just promised not to take her to jail. Of course, she seemed to believe we had been sent by God, and she was told by angels we would be there to help her, so at least she trusted us.

Upon arrival at the emergency room, the doctor on duty was very impressed with my diagnosis of something breaking inside this woman's brain. He of course wanted to do his own diagnosis, but he did appreciate my efforts. The paperwork to confine this woman for treatment was awfully quick to fill out and the judge agreed that thinking she had given birth to Christ was probably enough to warrant a stay at a hospital.

After the kids were handed over to the appropriate state agency, we managed to contact the woman's mother to take custody of the children. The woman was sent to a secure facility, but as the mother was about to take her grandchildren home, she proceeded to tell me her daughter had to stay away from her husband because it was an abusive relationship.

I took the bait and I could have kicked myself as I asked how she knew that.

"God told me."

I wanted to put fingers in my ears and yell lalalalalalalalala, so I could pretend I didn't hear what she said.

The state agency determined the grandmother was fit to take the kids that evening. We didn't have many other options since the kid's father didn't have a car because his wife took off with it, and it was now sitting at the house of the people she didn't know in the middle of the county where I was working.

After everyone was gone, I took the opportunity to let all the other investigators involved in this case know they owed me a dinner. They each called back the next day just to hear the roundup of events that had taken place. Afterward, they all agreed to buy me dinner.

Shannon Leeper

is a Master Police Officer/Detective with the Lenexa Kansas Police Department, a suburb of Johnson County, Kansas. She began her law enforcement career 13 years ago. She has spent more than 6 years in the Investigations Division, working a caseload focused on crimes against children and on sexual assault and domestic violence. Shannon is a tireless advocate for women and children in her community and works closely with Sunflower House, a child abuse prevention center. In 2010, her efforts were recognized when she received the honor of Child Advocate of the Year for Johnson County, Kansas.

Shannon may be small in stature, but she has been described as a pit bull when dealing with suspects. That said, she makes sure to leave it all at the door at the end of each day. She is a firm believer in putting God and family first, cherishing time spent with her ever-so-understanding husband and two precious girls. Seldom is she seen without a camera in hand, hence her nickname The Paparazzi. She finds photography and writing therapeutic escapes from the daily grind. Those who know Shannon best will recognize the mantra she borrowed from Mark Twain: *"It's not the size of the dog in the fight. It's the size of the fight in the dog."*

One Good Shot

by Shannon Leeper

So, there I was, trying to stay warm inside my patrol car on a frigid night in Kansas. It was a Sunday, but my "Friday," which was typically a good thing after a long week on the evening shift. I worked the 38th district, a fairly rural and quiet part of the city back then. If things went as planned, I would stop a few cars, respond on a minor disturbance, work an accident or two, and be back at the station by 10:50 p.m. By 11:05 p.m., I would be on my way home.

I hadn't been out of the field training program and on my own for more than a month. I was a rookie in every sense of the word, but hoping not to let it show. That is, until the call came out.

"Unit 338, respond to an injured deer at 83 and Mize. The callers are standing by."

There it was, the call I was dreading—an injured animal. I would be responsible for taking care of it, a euphemism for euthanizing the deer. Oh, and with an audience. Perfect. Let me preface this story by saying I am not a hunter. In fact, I spent the first week of firearms training with duct tape over one eye of my shooting glasses, after being labeled "right handed, but left eye dominant." I realized how absolutely ridiculous I looked to everyone around me, especially the firearms instructor who came up with that helpful tape idea. I know duct tape can fix just about anything, but that was a stretch. I am certain he thought that would be the last of me at his gun range. I admit I was terrified when I realized that I needed to build up that eye muscle and learn to shoot without the tape. I surprised quite a few people when I mastered it and became a pretty good shot. In fact, I began to enjoy shooting as long as live critters weren't my target.

Regardless, I always knew the day would come when I would have to shoot an animal, so I reluctantly put my car in drive and headed west towards Bambi. I hadn't made it a mile before an officer jumped on the radio offering to handle the call for me. I am sure there were a variety of reasons for his offer, the last one being genuine concern for my psychological well-being. I figured out, early on, that my male counterparts liked to have any excuse to shoot at anything.

I politely declined his offer because I refused to let anyone else handle a call that was my responsibility. I also knew I had to prove myself as a new, female officer, but that didn't stop me from frantically typing a message on my laptop computer to the 35 district officer. This particular officer was a seasoned cop, but I knew he wouldn't make fun of me because he was new to my department. At least, we still had the capability of using instant messaging. I was grateful for that. It allowed me to send a covert message without anyone hearing it or, hopefully, knowing about it afterwards. My message was simple: "Hey, what's the best way to kill a deer?"

His response was equally as simple: "A shot to the base of the neck. One, if you're good."

My sergeant at the time overheard the radio traffic and realized I was on my way to discharge a firearm within the city limits for the first time. He was responding with a deer tag to claim the animal for some lucky citizen. I wasn't a big fan of the deer tag program because it ensured a crowd would be standing by anxiously awaiting my arrival. There's nothing quite like an audience witnessing a first time of anything, much less my execution of some helpless creature.

Upon arrival, I pulled to the side of the two-lane road, and parked behind a couple of trucks and a car. I hadn't even made it out of my vehicle before being flagged down. Little did I know, the first person to greet me would be a District Court judge—and an unpopular one at that. I also had no idea he was an animal activist of sorts, who was horrified that someone struck a deer and didn't stop to render life-saving treatment. Remember, it was a Sunday night with frigid temps and icy roads. And there was a judge asking me what animal rescue center I would be transporting the deer to. Of course, he had to mention that he was a Lenexa resident and taxpayer, as if I should thank him for my last pay raise.

At first, I thought someone was playing a really bad joke on me. After all, did it look like I was prepared to load a deer into the back seat of my car? Moreover, did I look trained to triage Bambi until I could find someone experienced in deer rehabilitation? I am fairly confident the expression on my face said it all before I even opened my mouth. I am also sure that moment sealed my fate for future trials in that judge's court, but that is a story for another day.

There I was, a newly trained officer, worried about taking the deer out with one good shot, and a judge demanding that I do SOMETHING immediately to save the animal. Meanwhile, my sergeant was miles from my location with that ever-popular deer tag.

To give you a better appreciation for my stress level, I had the kind of snot running down my face that freezes before you can do anything about it. All the while I'm trying to explain tactfully that a rescue mission wasn't in order and fielding questions about whether or not Bubba could "dress" the deer right there on the side of the road. At that point, I didn't even think I would be able to wrap my frozen finger around the trigger, and I couldn't figure out why Bubba was using the word dress in the same sentence with deer.

It felt like time was frozen just like the surrounding landscape as I waited for permission to destroy the deer. The poor thing was trying to stand and run off, all to no avail. He slowly slid down the snow-packed embankment and onto the edge of the road.

I knew what had to be done, so I got on the radio and let my sergeant know it was time. Fortunately, the judge decided my cruel and unusual punishment of doing nothing was far too much for him to bear, so he left. Bubba and another guy were on my heels, hoping for that prized deer tag like it was the state lottery. An antsy child meant one guy couldn't stick around any longer, so that left Bubba as the last man standing. I promised him I would hold the tag, so he could drive a mile or so down the road for his hunting truck, which I didn't fully understand until I saw the big chain and hook attached to the bed.

I had a small window of time and needed to move quickly, before my audience returned.

As I began my approach, Bambi locked eyes with me. Her injuries were severe, but limited to her legs. That meant she was well aware something bad was about to happen. Unfortunately, I had a real problem with the persistent eye-contact. I had to formulate a plan and fast. I drew my duty weapon and kept it by my side, as if that would ease the animal's fear of the unknown. I wasn't able to get in position because she could turn her head darn-near all the way behind her. Like I said, I had a real problem with the whole eye-contact thing, and I didn't have the heart to pull the trigger with those big, brown eyes staring back at me.

I began running circles around Bambi, slipping and sliding on the icy ground, trying to disorient her. Finally, I was out of breath, and she was too dizzy to find my face. She looked straight ahead, and I tip-toed up behind her. Then it was over, with one well-placed shot, just in time for Bubba's return. I was actually pretty proud of my tactics when it was all said and done.

Afterward, I sat in my car, took a deep breath, and went back in service. A minute later, I received a follow-up message on my laptop asking how many times I had to shoot Bambi. "Just once," I told him. His response was, "Really? I was only kidding. It usually takes me two or three shots." My comment back to him: "Guess I am just a good shot."

I admit, I am still not a hunter but I have put my fair share of unfortunate creatures out of their misery since that day. While I may have devised some down-right hilarious tactics to get the job done, it always ended with one good shot.

Kathleen A. Ryan

is a retired, 21-year veteran police officer of the Suffolk County Police Department on Long Island, New York. She worked in Patrol, Public Information, and Crime Stoppers. She is also a breast cancer survivor who volunteers with the American Cancer Society and Crime Stoppers of Suffolk County, Inc. She lives on Long Island with her husband, their two children, and their nephew.

Kathleen has written a true crime memoir and enjoys writing short/flash/crime fiction, and personal essays. Her work has appeared online at A Twist of Noir, Misfit Salon, Flash Fiction Chronicles, Nanoism, Terrible Minds, Six Word Stories, and in print in The Southampton Review; Six Sentences: The Love Book; Six Sentences: Volume III; Hint Fiction: An Anthology of Stories in 25 Words or Fewer, edited by Robert Swartwood; and Discount Noir, an e-book edited by Patricia Abbott and Steve Weddle.

Her website and blog can be found at :http://www.kathleenaryan.com; she also blogs with fellow NY Sisters in Crime http://www.womenofmystery.net.Twitter @katcop13. E-mail: katcop13@gmail.com. Kathleen is also a member of Long Island Sisters in Crime, Mystery Writers of America (New York chapter), and the Public Safety Writers Association. She has won three writing awards from PSWA for Creative Writing and Flash Fiction.

The Watcher

by Kathleen A. Ryan

In 1989, during a day tour in my third year of patrol in the Suffolk County Police Department, I received the kind of 911 call that typically does not end well—the one concerning an elderly resident who hasn't been seen in a while. I met with the caller in front of the cottage of Emma Brown (all names have been changed to protect confidentiality), a 75-year-old divorcee who lived alone in a residential neighborhood of East Northport, Long Island. The complainant did not possess a key to the house, nor did she have any contact information for Emma's next of kin.

The concerned neighbor took me to the side of the house. "If you look through the window, you can see her lying in bed, but she's not moving," she said.

Beneath a partially-drawn shade, I observed what appeared to be a person sleeping in a bed. I tapped on the window and then checked the front and back doors, but there was no response. I used my portable radio to request a supervisor.

When I heard the voice of Sergeant Lenny Smith, the epitome of a salty cop, crackle over the airwaves, I realized my regular supervisor was probably on vacation. "Whaddya got?" he asked. I was surprised he didn't say, "Kid" at the end of that question.

"Sarge, I've got an apparent natural inside a residence, but it's secure. Can I break in?"

Sergeant Smith advised, "Ten-four—with minimal damage."

In the rear of the home, directly above the doorknob, I broke a small corner of a multi-pane window. I reached in and unlocked the door. As I entered the kitchen, I detected the pungent odor of a kitty litter box that needed changing. Brown paper bags and groceries lined the counter top, as if someone had stopped in the middle of putting them away.

I surveyed the single-story home to see if anything was amiss. I saw nothing unusual, although I did notice several cardboard boxes stacked in the living room near the front door.

As I walked into the bedroom, I anticipated a strong odor, but there wasn't one. I leaned down and touched her neck, searching for a pulse, but her body was cold and stiff. I felt sad for this woman who had died alone in her home; I only hoped her passing in her sleep had been painless.

I returned to the neighbor who was waiting patiently outside and confirmed that she'd been right. I gathered the necessary information for my report and thanked her for looking out for her neighbor and for contacting the police.

I asked the dispatcher to contact a PA—physician's assistant—to respond for pronouncement.

Sergeant Smith met me at the scene. The smell of cigarette smoke clung to the uniform of the bespectacled man with a comb-over. He had a leathery look about him. I wondered if I could determine the number of years he had been on the job by counting the lines on his face —sort of like checking the rings on a tree to see how old it is.

He picked up the phone in the kitchen. "I know Emma's family," he said, as he dialed a number.

He reached an answering machine. In his gruff voice, he said, "Yeah, Danny? This is Lenny. Your ex-wife's dead," and he hung up the receiver.

I tried not to reveal my stunned reaction upon hearing this inappropriate message. I figured he must know Emma's ex-husband fairly well to leave a message like that. I had delivered several notifications before, but they were usually made in person and always with a great deal of compassion. (Of course I'll never forget the story a New Jersey homicide detective told me. He rang the doorbell to a home in which the television was blaring. In the gentlest manner possible, he said: "I'm sorry to tell you this, but your son's been shot and killed in a drive-by shooting." The man's face fell into his hands as he sobbed. However, his tears were interrupted when he heard the jingle for the lottery drawing. He whipped out the lottery tickets from his shirt pocket, spun around, and checked his numbers.)

When the PA showed up, I led him to Emma's bedroom. It is routine, of course, to check the corpse for obvious signs of foul play. The instant he flung back the covers to expose the body—surprise!—a screeching cat sprang out. Letting out a few colorful words, we both jumped. I don't know who was more frightened, the cat or us.

Sergeant Smith asked me to notify Emma's sister who lived just a few miles away. "She lives above a bar in Greenlawn with a bunch of senior citizens," he told me.

At the sister's residence, I met several seniors who were gathered in a communal kitchen. I learned that Abigail was out but was expected to return shortly.

"Is this about her sister?" one of the female residents asked.

I paused, wondering how anyone could possibly know about Emma already. "Yes, it is," I said, slightly puzzled.

"Oh, she already knows," she said, as if my visit was unnecessary.

Even more confused, I insisted, "I... I... don't think she does."

"Well, isn't this about her sister, Charlotte, who died last week?"

"Charlotte? Last week? I didn't know about that sister; I'm here about another sister—Emma!"

Abigail returned shortly thereafter. I calmly broke the tragic news to the poor woman. I extended my sincerest condolences over the loss of her two dear sisters. But if I thought the surprises of the day were through, I was wrong.

After arriving home after work, I recounted the day's events to my husband, Joe, who said, "You won't believe this, but I delivered those boxes you saw in Emma's living room. Her sister, Charlotte, was a long-term tenant in one of my father's apartment buildings."

"You're kidding."

"After Charlotte passed away last week, my father asked me to bring her belongings to Emma's house. I placed them in the living room near the front door. Oh, and I know Emma's ex-husband, Danny. He does plumbing work for my father. We knock back a couple of beers at the Laurel Saloon every now and then. He's probably gonna need one after hearing that message today."

As I lay awake in my own bed that night, I thought about Emma's cat, and wondered why he'd hidden under the covers. Had he sensed that she was in trouble? Was he protecting her? Was he waiting for her to wake up? I recalled how my own childhood pet, Catsy, used to behave whenever I cried. No matter where Catsy was in the house, she'd come running. She'd affectionately, persistently, brush up against me, sensing my sorrow and comforting me. Her soothing behavior never failed to improve my mood.

In the summer of 2007, I had the privilege of attending a Memoir Writing Workshop at the Southampton Writers Conference, taught by the master himself, Frank McCourt. While the participants were gathering one morning, someone mentioned a news report about a cat that predicted patients' deaths at a nursing home in Rhode Island.

Upon hearing this news, I shared the story of Emma Brown and her loyal cat that had hidden beneath the covers.

Frank sat at his desk, listening.

"You have to write that story," he said.

Oscar the cat had lived on the third floor of the Steere House Nursing and Rehabilitation Center in Providence, Rhode Island. Oscar would sniff and curl up next to a patient during the last hours of the resident's life. He correctly sensed the deaths of more than 25 residents who suffered from Alzheimer's and Parkinson's disease. When the staff realized the pattern, they were able to contact a patient's family, enabling them to see their loved one before he or she passed away.

Oscar was honored with a plaque in recognition of his compassionate efforts. The animal behavior specialists interviewed for the story believed it possible that cats smell some chemical that is released before death, or that they can sense when their owner is upset or sick.

Perhaps that was why Emma's cat was under the covers as death quietly called for Emma, and why Catsy soothed me as a child whenever I cried. This was what I also found comforting: that at the very least, Emma and I both knew the comfort of a warm and snuggling cat when we needed it most.

Gwen Grimes

has been a police officer for more than five years. She is an avid outdoorswoman and loves to spend time off-duty, enjoying the benefits of living in the great state of Alaska. Officer Grimes has dedicated her life to her family and to law enforcement, always ready to respond and take action when needed.

Those Darn Bears

by Gwen Grimes

It was dark, and the thermostat registered twenty below zero. The heater in my truck hummed softly, as the wind howled, stirring snow into swirling mesmerizing patterns across the frozen ice road as I drove my patrol truck toward a call out for "grizzly bears in the dumpster." I could see how one could freeze to death on the open tundra, just by watching the beauty of the crystal white snow spinning around, northern lights glowing overhead while engaged in their captivating deadly dance across the heavens. One could easily get lost in this glorious trance and drift off to an eternal sleep.

I had to shake my head to focus on the call. Don't get distracted. Focus. Shotgun? Check. Cracker rounds? Check. Bean bag rounds? Check. Slugs? Check. I was ready, mentally checking off the tools I'd need for this call. I'd handled countless bear calls, generally harmless, always exciting.

The snow was blowing hard, causing me to squint to see twenty feet ahead of me. It helped to switch off my headlights, turning the glare of the falling snow down to a dimmed visual that gave me another ten feet of visibility.

I rounded the corner of the building, the lights from the hotel dimly seeking their way through the dark and snowy night. The dumpsters were about fifty yards behind the complex, well away from foot traffic, creating a barrier between the workers, tourists, and the bears. This barrier, however, never stopped the workers from becoming "tourists," running out with their cameras taking photos of these massive creatures to send home to their loved ones thousands of miles away.

Tonight was different. It was 2:00 a.m., and it was just me and the bears in our own little showdown. No cameras, no tourists, just the three of us. I saw the two brothers rooting around on top of an overly-full dumpster. The pair was well known in the area, always traveling together. They were about two years old, and we'd tracked them since they were cubs.

I watched them for a moment in the windswept snow. Bears are beautiful animals, large massive bodies covered softly by the falling snow. They hadn't seen me yet. I took a moment to appreciate their beauty and then realized I had a job to do. No bears are allowed in this area.

I activated my overhead light bar and switched on the siren, changing it to several different bursts to startle the bears with sight and sound tactics, as I drove aggressively toward the dumpster to intimidate the bears. This tactic normally causes them to turn tail and run for the river. That night they must have been hungry; they didn't budge. The larger of the two bears lifted his head and looked at me like he was annoyed with my presence. I backed my car up and charged again, shifting the siren as I advanced. Both bears looked up and then resumed eating.

My two carnivorous friends were getting conditioned, which was not good. Once a bear is conditioned to human interaction, the danger level increases for both species. We carry cracker rounds for our shotguns, basically, a really cool firecracker shot out of a gun. Once fired it travels up to several hundred feet and explodes. I've fired many cracker rounds over the years, and I know they are never completely reliable. Some explode close, some far, and others don't fire at all. Tonight I loaded several crackers in my shotgun and racked a round in the chamber.

Backing up to give myself some effective distance, I opened my door and stepped out, taking aim just over the dumpster. I wanted the crackers to go off right over their heads. I was a little too close, but it's a risk I'll take, even if they go off fifty feet past them. The rounds are loud enough to scare them out of the dumpster.

I fired the first round; it popped, igniting the fuse as it spun out of my barrel toward the bears. I felt the wind blowing and watched the cracker, like a tracer in the night, fizzle out and go black just beyond the bears. Okay, I fired two more rounds, each had the same effect. The wind must be blowing out the fuses. The bears don't even realize anything has been shot at them as they continue foraging in the bountiful trash atop the dumpster in the continuing snowfall.

Changing my tactics, I drove closer. I wanted the next round to sting. I maneuvered myself about twenty feet away from the dumpster and loaded a bean bag round into the chamber of my shotgun. *This will get their attention,* I thought. My overhead lights strobed in the night, creating a lucid, peaceful calm, while my spotlight illuminated the massive beasts against the black night sky. The falling snow, picked up by fierce winds, spun and twisted, causing me to pause and focus on my sights. I locked onto the largest bear's front left shoulder. *This will knock the wind out of him and send him running.*

I took a deep breath and then began to exhale slowly. As the last bit of breath exited my lungs, I began my trigger squeeze and concentrated on my sights. I watched as the scene unfolded in front of me in slow motion. I felt the hammer drop, causing the gun to kick into my shoulder, and as I started to rack the next round, a slug, I watched the grizzly swing his massive head toward me. I saw his eyes and watched the fur in the center of his forehead explode as the beanbag round hit him square in the center of his head. It all happened in milliseconds, but seemed to take several seconds. This was the "matrix moment" most cops experienced when adrenalin dumps into your system and time seems to stand still. Events move forward in slow motion, and your vision becomes crystal clear.

The bear stood and reared back from the enormous impact. He had to have been at least seven feet tall. Reeling from the brunt trauma of the beanbag shot, he toppled backward off the top of the dumpster. The other bear quickly jumped down and ran off into the night. Suddenly, I returned to real-time and racked the slug in my shotgun, prepared for a charging angry bear.

Nothing. As the wind continued to punish the landscape, building snow drifts that allowed my lights to reflect colorful images, I got back into my patrol truck and left the door cracked open so I could get out and shoot if necessary. I slowly drove forward, edging my way toward the dumpster where the massive best had fallen.

Immediately, I saw his crumpled body lying still behind the dumpster as I slowly drove forward to assess the damage. My mind started spinning. *"Oh shit, I've killed him!"* Dreading the required paper work, I shook my head, wondering how I would explain this one to the Chief.

However, before I got lost in my thoughts, the bear suddenly jumped up and shook his enormous body like a dog shaking off water. He turned on his paws and sprinted away into the night. I swear he looked back over his shoulder at me as he ran off, probably wondering what kind of beast had just rocked his world. I chuckled, while thanking God for my good fortune and then cleared my shotgun for the next call.

Back at the station, I told my partner about the incident. We shared a good laugh and went about our business. Later that night, we got another call for two bears in a dumpster, but near a different hotel. My partner responded to that one. When he returned, he had a smile from ear to ear so I asked him what was up.

He told me he had driven up toward the bears and there were hotel workers everywhere, all of them within twenty feet of the bears in the dumpster. They were taking photos and standing in a large group in the parking lot, oblivious to the danger presented by two large grizzlies. The workers were so engaged in taking photos that they put themselves in a potentially deadly situation. I never understood why anyone would think that these wild animals were harmless.

My partner initiated his light bar and revved his engine as he raced toward the dumpster across the parking lot. As soon as he hit his siren, the bears about shit themselves and couldn't get out of the dumpster fast enough. They tumbled ass over elbows out of the dumpster right near the crowd of people trying to get away from the massive flashing white beast that had just charged them while making a hideous shriek. The workers ran in every direction, trying to get out of the way of the startled bears that eventually ran off into the blackness of the night. The workers returned to the safety of the hotel, shutting their bear proof doors against the danger they had just witnessed.

As my partner told his story, he was laughing so hard he had tears in his eyes. He said, "You should have seen those bears! I know that one of them had to be the one you hit in the head. He must have told the other one what happened to him because I've never seen bears move so fast. And then watching those idiots taking pictures run for their lives . . . priceless!"

We shared a good laugh at the expense of the hungry bears and the foolish workers. My partner's experience became one of his favorite stories to tell in cop circles, and always ended with everyone laughing. The story has become somewhat of a legend and lives on to this day.

Eidolon Schreiber

is the pen name of a rowdy, but good-hearted beat cop. Eidolon has worked the mean streets of one of the largest police departments in the state of Texas for six years. Because of a recent conflict with the command staff of her department, anonymity is required at this point. Eventually the issue will be resolved, at which time Eidolon insists on selling the movie rights to this epic battle to Director Quentin Tarantino.

Thursday

by Eidolon Schreiber

1 300 hours. The 9-1-1 dispatch received a call to the Mosaic building. A woman, dressed in all black clothing was sitting on the ledge of the 18th floor, her legs dangling over the edge.

My partner and I headed that way, maneuvering the squad car down the one-way streets around the high rise apartment. We passed two other squad cars, the officers looking intently at the face of the massive building. Only one car was actually assigned, the rest crept nearby, waiting to see what might develop. Only the unit assigned to the call is tasked with the report if things went bad. The best way to avoid getting roped into a cluster is to be nowhere near it. However, the best cops are adrenaline junkies and love a good story. If something wild happens, you don't want to miss it. Hollywood spends billions of dollars trying to duplicate the craziness cops see every day.

We circled closer until it was too late. We were assigned the call.

"Bravo 198, the sergeant is calling for an element to block the south sidewalk. Are you available?" The dispatcher knew we were available for assignment, and she could see our little car icon on the map on her console. The computers in dispatch showed everyone's location in real time. We were already sitting on the south. We could not avoid it.

"10-4"

We posted up.   Looking upward, we tried to spot the possibly suicidal girl.   I counted eighteen floors up from the ground, so I'd know where to concentrate my attention.

While those of us on the call had attempted to be stealthy and low key, it was too late.   The pedestrians in the area soon figured out why we were there.   Clusters of civilians gathered and stared, straining to see what we were looking at, and to get a glimpse of some real world drama, rather than the tinsel town version of it.

Some dared to ask us what was going on.   Others whispered, as if it might be a secret just between us and them. Some called from across the other side of the sidewalk without even slowing their pace.   I related what little I knew, but totally down-played the situation.   Some cops don't give out any information.   They just look stern and tell onlookers to move on. I prefer to tell them a softened version of the truth.   It satisfies their curiosity, and I believe it reduces the chance of panic developing.   The absolute worst scenarios form in people's imaginations when they don't know what's going on.

As I stood at my post, scanning the windows of the upper floors, a woman in a cluster of heavyset black women in colorful business attire yelled to me from across the DART rail tracks. "Oh, Lord! What's goin' on?"

I called back, "We got a call about someone on the ledge, but I haven't seen anything. It's probably nothing."

The women looked skyward, truly fearing a body might be plummeting toward them at that very instant.

"I'm gettin' outta here!" one yelled, and the group quickly stepped down the block, cackling and chattering like hens. I smiled and shook my head.

Suddenly, a flash of movement caught my eye. It was a figure. On the ledge. The 18th floor.

Well, I'll be damned!

The figure came away from the open window and sat Indian

style, right on the edge, but it was a male, not a female.   I broadcast this new development over the radio as I scrutinized his movements.

He sat so close to the edge that I was able to see that he was wearing a white t-shirt and blue jeans.   I broadcast the description of him and his clothing over the radio.   After a good minute or so, he finally realized that the building was surrounded by cops and crept back to the window.   He didn't go back in immediately; he had a cigarette to finish.

Little did he know, our forces weren't just outside the building, but we were organizing on the inside as well.   Not only did we have an apartment manager with a master key, we also had a guy up in the parking garage across from the apartment getting intel from the construction workers.   The worker said lately kids have been sitting on the ledge every day.

About the time our smoker went back inside, officers were gaining entry through the front door to greet him.   Now I really had something good to report to the onlookers to ease their fears.   "It was just a guy taking a smoke break."   I told them with a smile.   They look relieved, and we rolled our eyes as if to say, "Good grief!"

I knew there may be more to it, since the original call was about a female, and we still hadn't found her.   Nevertheless, right now everything seemed okay.

The radio crackled, "Bravo 198 to my partner."   The two of us had split up early in the call, and I ended up with the group that made it into the apartment.   The front line.

I moved my mouth closer to the mike and keyed it, "Go ahead."

"Can you secure the car and then come up and search a couple?"

"10-4."   I was just about to pull the squad car forward to open up the street anyway.

Soon I was marching across the DART rail toward the front

door of the Mosaic, looking very official. After all, there were citizens around and everyone was watching to see what the police were doing.

As I entered the building, I realized I couldn't get on the elevators without a fob. It seems ridiculous that some buildings are so secure that even cops can't get inside.

I radioed for help, and in less than a minute, an elevator door opened and a very pretty, friendly looking blonde girl smiled and beckoned for me to come inside.

For the life of me, I can't remember what we chatted about, but I'm sure it was mindless at best. Neither of us was too concerned about the situation, since it was all but finished. Nothing bad was going to happen.

The sergeant was waiting in the hall for me. "Hey, Schreiber, this way." I followed him through the open door of the apartment.

Officers dotted the small apartment, casually looking around at the furniture and décor. The guy from the ledge sat handcuffed on the couch, and two girls were sitting in chairs. All eyes were on me as I entered the room.

All three detainees appeared to be in their early twenties. At first glance, they seemed attractive, but that impression can be quickly disproved when seen through the prism of an experienced eye. The three looked like they each had a case of mild acne. Nothing out of the ordinary for a young person, right? But I knew the truth immediately. They were hooked on methamphetamine.

My friend, Annie, used to shake down prisoners at the Garland jail. She told me that meth is a toxin, and the sores are caused by the body literally trying to push it out through the skin. I believed it.

I've also heard, from other sources besides Annie, that once a person is hooked on meth, the brain chemistry becomes so altered, that one is never completely free of the addiction. I believe that also. How else can one explain the poor souls that keep smoking it, even as their body rots away? When they look into the mirror, they must be able to see that their teeth are decaying and falling out, their skin is blotching and tearing, their hair is falling out, and their weight is dropping dangerously low. Nevertheless, they continue to smoke it.

I called to the dark-haired girl to come over to me. "What's your name?" I asked sternly, as she walked across the room. It's wise to use a person's name when speaking with them, they always respond better.

"Sara," the girl answered.

I could tell Sara was nervous, but was trying to remain calm, and cooperative. We probably wouldn't have any trouble from her. There weren't any pockets in her hootchie-cut sweat pants, so I checked the waistband. She was wearing flip-flops, nothing to search there. I pulled the trucker cap from her head and checked the lining—nothing.

All that was left to search was her bra. I unzipped her hoodie, and reached in bare handed. A lot of cops are germ phobic and won't touch anything without wearing gloves. I was a nursing assistant for six years before becoming a cop. My hands have touched some disgusting things. As long as your skin is intact, most everything can be washed off. My choice not to wear gloves had a purpose. The contraband most often hidden in a bra is drugs. Cocaine comes in tiny, delicate baggies, and I've seen female officers miss up to ten baggies because they couldn't feel through the rubber gloves they were wearing. One baggie of cocaine is a felony. It's not something you want to miss. Moreover, the cop who conducted the search in the field gets a bad reputation if their arrestee is found to have contraband on them once they are searched at the jail.

I did a sweep of one of her bra cups, and as I moved my hand to the other one I noticed that the sores weren't just on her face; they were all over her body.

"What is all of this?" I asked, and gestured toward her chest.

"It's a fungal infection.   Well, it started as a bacterial infection, but the doctor gave me the wrong medication and it got worse."

"Ohhh . . . kay," I offered.   "Don't move."   I called back over my shoulder to her, as I ran to the sink.

"I'm sorry.   I guess I should have told you.   I wasn't thinking."

"It's all right."   I said, as I began the surgical scrub up to my elbows.   "How contagious is it?"

"Not very."

"You mean as long as I don't have any open cuts or wounds?"

"Yeah," she replied.   "As long as you don't have any cuts. I'm so sorry."

"It's okay."   Thank God for my medical background, so I knew what I was dealing with.   I knew that one of the guys in the room was super paranoid about germs, and I figured he was probably going out of his mind about now.

I took Sara into the bedroom, away from the guys, and searched her.   Actually, I let her search herself, while I stood about three feet away.   I had her lift her bra and turn out the pockets of her jacket.   I sent her back out and called for the blonde girl to come in.   I didn't know if she had the same condition, but I wasn't taking any chances.   I had her search herself while I stayed at a safe distance.   When I was done, we sat them down in chairs that were lined up in the living room. Our guy was still in cuffs.

I heard one of the cops mention something to the sergeant about a forgery detective calling back.   I glanced around the room and saw a laptop on the couch.   It was sitting wide open with the image of a Texas driver's license filling the screen.   The girl in the license photo wasn't any of the girls in the room.

Ah hah.   Now I understood what was going on.   We had

stumbled across a bigger fish than I'd thought.

I stood in the doorway of the bedroom, guarding our suspects. Less than two feet away from me was a huge fancy wooden dresser. The top drawer was half open, and I could see a notebook and a stack of credit cards. I wanted to go through it, but I fought the urge. Did we have a legal right to search yet? "The fruits of the poisonous tree" is a familiar legal phrase to cops. Anything seized in an illegal search may be thrown out in court. We had to do things right. I looked back toward the living room. I tried to ignore the drawer, but it was practically calling out to me. If I were a dog, I'd be whimpering and squirming around. I looked back toward the living room and tried to push it from my mind. There was movement in the kitchen. The cops were beginning to search. *We were in. Thank God!*

I pounced on the drawer and found all sorts of treasures: people's credit cards, three Texas driver's licenses with different information but with a picture of the guy we had in cuffs, and pills floating loose among all the clutter. By the time I separated out the contraband from the socks, scraps of paper and other junk, I figured I had enough evidence for a couple of felonies and at least one misdemeanor.

"Schreiber!" One of the cops called from the living room.

"Yeah."

"She needs to use the restroom." I stepped into the open doorway. The blonde girl just glared at me, hatred burning in her eyes. Sara squirmed a bit in her seat, giving me a pleading look.

"C'mon." I said and motioned for her to come with me. Sara scurried to the bathroom, and I followed, closing the door behind us. She ran water in the sink and sat on the toilet. She was still acting nervously. I'll bet she didn't expect me actually to accompany her inside. Maybe she was hoping to flush some drugs or other contraband. She had no idea about how much evidence we already had. She could have flushed everything in the bathroom and the adjoining closet, and we'd still have more than enough to charge her.

I decided to take advantage of this opportunity. She was cut from the herd. It is far easier to crack someone under questioning when they are alone.

"It's just you and me now, Sara. No one can hear us in here. Tell me everything you have in this apartment, and we'll see what we can do about goin' easy on you."

She tried to look confused, like she had no clue what I was talking about. She stuttered, but never gave me a real answer.

"Come on. You didn't notice that your man was making fake IDs on the computer?"

"Well, yeah, I knew he was playing around with it, but he never prints them out. He's very artistic."

I didn't have a reply for that response. It was much too idiotic.

"Ok, forget about him and the forgery. He's done."

"What?" She looked shocked. "Even if he never used the IDs?"

"Yeah. Possessing identifying information of three or more people is a felony. He's at least good for that charge. Plus, he's on probation." One of the interesting items found in the dresser drawer was the business card of the guy's probation officer.

Sara was either playing dumb, or she really was dumb. I suspected that she was probably a little of each. I would need to lead her gently in the right direction.

"So, it started as a staph infection? That can be very contagious."

She looked surprised that I knew that, for she hadn't mentioned the actual name of her condition.

"Yeah. I work in a bar…"

"Ewww. That's probably where you picked it up. You can pick up a staph infection from surfaces, and there's no telling what kind of cooties people are dragging into a bar."

She was warming up to me because I was showing concern for her. "Yeah, right! It wasn't that bad at first. I went to the doctor, and she prescribed a really strong antibiotic. It threw everything out of whack. I went back to her, but she wouldn't listen to me, told me to finish taking all of them."

Fifty percent of doctors finished in the bottom half of their class.

"It just kept getting worse, and then it spread. It's a fungal infection now. I usually never miss work, but I missed three days last week." She was not only talking, she was rambling. I pretended to listen, as I looked around the bathroom for possible hiding places. I was going to search this bathroom as soon as I got her out of here.

She sat on the toilet and told me all about her condition and the alternative treatments that she'd tried. When she was finally finished on the toilet (I don't think she even did anything), she tore off some toilet paper and wiped her ass. Then with the same wad of paper she wiped her cootch, threw the paper in the bowl, and flushed. My guess is that with better hygiene and laying off the meth, her health would quickly improve.

"So, how long have y'all been together?"

"About six months." The way she said it made it sound almost like a question, like she wasn't sure.

"How long have y'all lived in this apartment?"

"Only since the first of the month. He just moved his stuff in from storage. That's what I was trying to tell you. If there's anything in here, it's old. We just haven't been through everything yet."

I guess she thought that was a defense to possession of illegal drugs, drug paraphernalia, fraud evidence, and stolen checks and IDs. I'm sorry your honor, we just hadn't cleaned in a while. Oh, well in that case, all the charges are dropped, and you are free to go.

She stood in front of the sink and scrubbed with some antibacterial soap. At least she was washing her hands.

"Look, this ain't my first day on the job. I know y'all are on something, I'm just trying to figure out what that something is."

She stammered. She was trying to deny my allegation, but she just didn't have anything intelligent to offer. I gave her my patented "don't bullshit me" look, and raised an eyebrow. "Weed?" I knew what they were up to was much worse, but it was a starting point. Most people would admit to smoking pot.

"No, no."

"Meth?" She just stared at me with widened eyes. I could tell she wanted to deny it, but she knew that I knew.

"Well, we used to do it, but we don't anymore."

"So there's no meth, no pipes, no nothing in this apartment?"

"Well, maybe, but it's old. I've quit. If y'all find anything, it's just been packed away. I haven't thrown it out yet."

"So you haven't done anything in this apartment since you moved in?"

"Oh no, not since we got the puppies. I would never do anything around them."

Oh, shit, we wouldn't want to corrupt the puppies. All jokes aside, I caught something subtle in her answer. She hadn't been smoking here.

"When was the last time you smoked?" My question was direct, and she had no way to dance around it.

She hung her head. "Two days ago." At least she was catching on that lying to me wasn't going to fly.

"So you did it somewhere else?"

"Yes, at a friend's house. I told you, I don't do anything around the puppies." There she goes with those damn puppies again. One of the cops had put the puppies in the enclosed patio off the living room. They were really cute, but they probably didn't care whether or not Sara smoked meth as long as she remembered to feed them.

We returned to the living room. The guy in cuffs looked at Sara sheepishly, as if the cops' investigation was all a big, ridiculous misunderstanding.

In the drawer, I had also found a handwritten letter. It was sent to him while he was in jail. It was from his "baby mama." She was pleading with him to tell her where their relationship stood and for him to help take care of their child. Even if he didn't want to be with her, she would still bail him out. She just wanted him to be in the baby's life. When it got to the part about all the broken promises to his daughter, I had to put the letter down. I wondered if Sara knew about the baby. I'm sure she's heard his screwed up version, the one where somehow he's the victim, and it's all a big mistake. Moreover, I wondered how the poor kid was going to turn out.

I surveyed the living room. The search was going well. We had two piles, one for fraud, and the other for drugs. A plastic storage bin had been commandeered for all the fraud evidence. A large printer/laminator was too big to fit inside, so it sat beside the bin. The cops had been through most of the living room, but the coffee table looked undisturbed. I took that as an invitation.

A tin had been pushed to a back corner of a shelf. Ingenious hiding spot, guys. Of course it was filled with burnt meth pipes, a plastic baggie with a huge chunk of crystal meth, a blow torch of a lighter, and some more pills. I left the lighter and hauled the rest of it to the growing drug pile being housed in a large manila envelope, and then went back to the coffee table. I intended to return to the bathroom to search, but this spot was just too good to pass up. Besides, we had cops flipping the bathroom and the closet. Well, they could have it.

A stack of books sat on the bottom shelf. On top was *Masters of Illusion*, a book about Salvador Dali and other surrealist painters. *At least the guy had good taste.* He really was artistic.

There were paintings hanging on the walls that he had painted. They were actually pretty good. Too bad he was using his talent for evil. Under the book, there was a notebook. The pages were filled with personal information of various people. Stuffed into the pockets, were pawn tickets, property and vehicle titles, account applications, and a huge stack of checks. There were at least a hundred checks, all filled out, and all from different people.

A hundred different people. A hundred lives destroyed by this low life. I thought about all of the phone calls. *We haven't received your payment, so now you owe an additional $30 for the late fee. But I swear I mailed it last week!* I thought about all the people working hard, thinking everything's fine, until the day they check their credit report. I thought about all the letters, the hours, the effort and the stress of trying to repair the damage. A thief is probably the worst type of person, and an identity is just about the worst thing one can steal.

I was finally satisfied with the coffee table and looked around to see what was left. It looked like we were about done. I walked over to the sergeant and the forgery detective who had arrived to supervise.

"Looks like we've about got it all," the detective said. "Me and my partner will put the drugs in the property room. One of the cops is coming with us, he'll get the forgery stuff. We'll call you with the property tag number. Did you want to try to charge the girls with any of it, or just let Narcotics sort it out?"

The apartment was in Sara's name, so legally, she could be charged. The stuff was mostly the guy's, so he could also be charged. We already had plenty on him, so it would be overkill to tack on all of the lesser charges.

"She's the one that signed the consent to search; she's been very cooperative. You can just log it in as Found Property, and if Narcotics wants to file, they can." The detective clearly did not give a damn about arresting Sara. That worked for me. It was close to the end of the shift and I wanted to go home on time. Dope arrests took a couple of hours to process.

Officers escorted the guy out of the apartment in handcuffs to be transported to jail. There was some last minute maneuvering with getting some car keys out of his pocket and returned to Sara and retrieving some cash that had been taped to the bottom of one of the dresser drawers, so she could pay rent. How did I miss that in my search? She may as well keep that money because she was as good as evicted. One by one the officers shuffled out of the room, doing one last scan to ensure nothing was missed. Then, it was just me, the sergeant, Sara, and the blonde girl.

"I hope this has been an eye opening experience for y'all," I said as I looked at both girls. "Today is your lucky day. He's going down for a long time. You've been very cooperative, so we're not going to charge you with anything. You realize that since this is your apartment, you could have been charged with all the same stuff—as an accomplice?"

Sara nodded. "Yes, thank you for not arresting us." Her voice was cracking. Good.

"As for the drugs, we're going to log them into the police property room. We're going to list all three of y'all, and there's a possibility that Narcotics will file a warrant at a later time. So don't be surprised if that happens." It most likely wouldn't. Narcotics had bigger fish to fry, but I had to put some fear in the girls. Sara was starting to lose it. Tears welled up in her eyes. The blonde girl still glared at me.

"Now let me tell you something, I've dated my share of losers . . ." I began. The sergeant shook his head and tried not to let the girls see him laughing as he walked out. He knew what was coming. I was going "Dr. Phil" on their ass.

"Have you ever been arrested?"

The blonde girl shook her head. Sara shook her head vehemently. "No ma'am. Not for anything serious. I got a

DWI a couple of years ago, but that's it."

"No man is worth catching a felony. I know how they can sometimes be charming," I said. "They can tell you what you want to hear. But no man, No Man, in this world is worth screwing up your life and going to prison."

Sara nodded in agreement as her mouth twisted and tears began pouring down her cheeks. I thought I even saw a nod out of the blonde girl. My lecture was mostly for Sara because she seemed to be a good person. Her life had just taken a wrong turn down the wrong path. If the blonde girl could stop hating me for just a minute and listen to what I had to say, she might make some changes in her life as well.

"Now, let's have a chat about the drugs." By this time, Sara was sobbing. I knew seeing all the police in her apartment, and going through all of her possessions was a very stressful experience. I also knew that she had come close to being arrested. That was stressful too, but this was not the time to get soft: I had to finish her off. Sometimes you have to hit absolute rock bottom, before you are able to pull it together and build yourself back up. Trust me, I've been there. Not quite this bad, but I'd been there.

"Now I'm not trying to preach, and I'm not trying to insult you, but y'all look like crap. Y'all are torn up. How old are you?"

"Twenty-four." Sara wailed and went back to sobbing uncontrollably. The blonde mumbled a number in the early twenties.

"Y'all need to quit the meth, it's tearing you up. You are both young, beautiful girls, but I took one look and I could tell you were on it. If you don't do something now, rehab . . . something, you're going to look like you're old and haggard before you hit thirty. Now, you're both grown, and you can do whatever you want as soon as I walk out of this room, but I pray that you will listen to what I'm saying." With that, I gave up and walked to the door.

I stopped and took one more look back. The blonde girl just sat there, but it seemed that some of the anger had left her expression. It even looked like maybe she was thinking about what I had just told them. Sara continued to sob, but I could tell that she agreed with me and knew that I was right. Knowing what the right thing is and actually doing it are two different things. What happens now in their lives was completely up to them. I left and pulled the door shut behind me.

The sergeant was waiting for me by the elevator. He was still chuckling.

"I practically saw your finger come out to wag at them." He laughed. "Mama was coming out."

I cracked a smile too. "Somebody's got to straighten these babies out." We rode the elevator to the ground floor.

"Good job, Schreiber," he called over his shoulder as he headed toward his car.

"Thank you, sir!" I yelled at him as I jogged across the tracks.

I jumped into the passenger seat, and my partner began to drive away. "Damn, I'm hungry. What do you want to do for lunch?"

Sandy Smetana

of Dover, Delaware, became a police officer in 1982 with the Baytown Police Department in Baytown, Texas, where she served as a patrol officer and field training officer (FTO) for six and a half years. She left Baytown and joined the City of Dover Police Department (DPD) in the fall of 1989, working patrol and serving as an FTO. Sandy was assigned to: Patrol, Detective Division, Planning & Training Division, Community Policing Unit, Youth Unit, and the Hostage Negotiating Team. She was certified as an instructor and a master instructor. Promoted several times, she retired as a platoon sergeant in charge of a platoon of officers in the Patrol Division. She was the first female in the Dover Police Department to reach the rank of sergeant, and the first female officer to retire from the department. During her career she earned a Bachelor of Arts Degree in Behavioral Science and a Master of Science Degree in Administration of Justice from Wilmington University.

While employed at the DPD, she was honored to become a Nationally Credentialed Law Enforcement Officer and received her certificate from former US Attorney General Janet Reno. Sandy also received several awards, including two Police Chief's Commendations, Officer of the Quarter in 2002, and Class A and Class B Commendations. She is a lifetime member of Mid-Atlantic Association of Women in Law Enforcement (MAAWLE) and a lifetime member of International Association of Women Police (IAWP). Sandra is also a member of the Fraternal Organization of Police (FOP) and has held several offices in her local FOP.

Sandy has two sons who are now following in her footsteps by giving back to the community. Her oldest son is a volunteer firefighter and her youngest is a Military Police Officer with United States Army Reserves.

17

The Motorcycle Gang

by Sandy Smetana

I responded to a fight at a local bar in Baytown, Texas, that was frequented by members of a motorcycle gang. That said, the gang members usually outgunned us and carried guns in their boots as well as knives. At that point in time, we carried Veratcom radios. The radio on our belt had to be put into the console in the car to work.

I was the first officer on the scene of a fight and saw 20 to 25 motorcycles parked outside the club. I also saw a familiar three-wheeler that I knew belonged to a member of the gang who was known to always be armed. I got out of my car and pushed the button to release the radio so that I could put it on my belt. As I went to put the radio on my belt, I missed, and watched in horror as it fell to the ground, breaking into about a hundred pieces. I looked over and suddenly realized that about thirty gang members had also watched my radio fall and shatter.

There I stood, outnumbered and outgunned. I looked at them; they looked at me. What to say at a moment like this? The first thing that came to my mind was, "I guess I'm f***ed."

When the bikers heard that, they broke out laughing, erasing any tension that may have existed between us. We chatted until my backup arrived, lights and sirens screaming, because they couldn't raise me on the radio and thought the worst. (We had no cell phones in those days.) My accident with the radio not only broke up the fight, but it also broke the ice as well. They could have easily destroyed me and everything else.

I later became a Field Training Officer and used this incident as a training tool for new officers. The lesson was to treat people with respect, and they will treat you the same way. I didn't get smart with these guys, and I joked about my misfortune. They, luckily, took it in the way it was meant, respectfully, and returned that respect back to me.

Donna Roman Hernandez

 was born and raised in Newark, New Jersey, and served with the Essex County and Caldwell Police Departments in Northern New Jersey during her 28-year law enforcement career. She was the first female police officer in the Caldwell Police Department and the first female to hold the rank of Captain in the West Essex area of Northern New Jersey.

Donna is a Domestic Violence Police Specialist, a Domestic Violence Response Team Trainer, a Sexual Assault expert, and a Domestic Violence Trainer with the New Jersey Division of Criminal Justice, Office of the Attorney General. Donna is the creator and host of a monthly broadband police talk radio show "The Jersey Beat" that features guests discussing police topics (www.thejerseybeat.blogspot.com).

Captain Hernandez is the founder of Violence Intervention and Prevention Specialists (VIPS). In addition, she is a board member with the New Jersey Governor's Advisory Council Against Sexual Assault and serves on the Law Enforcement Advisory Board with the New Jersey Coalition Against Sexual Assault. She volunteers countless hours educating students and training law enforcement officers about domestic violence, sexual assault, and bullying.

Donna is the President and owner of Blue Force Films, LLC, a film/video production company based in New Jersey and specializing in police documentaries, dramas, and law enforcement training videos (www.blueforcefilms.com). She is an award-winning author, composer, public speaker, independent filmmaker, and director. Donna directed and produced her own documentary memoir, "*The Ultimate Betrayal: A Survivor's Journey*," that exposes the 35 years of domestic violence in her family and chronicles the abuse inflicted by her father, a former peace officer. This documentary has landed her a string of international and domestic film awards and is being used as an awareness training video by schools and colleges, domestic violence/social service agencies, police departments, criminal justice agencies and the FBI National Academy Library.

Afraid To Tell

by Donna Roman Hernandez

I am Donna Roman Hernandez, a former Police Captain from New Jersey. I was born and raised in Newark, New Jersey, and served 28 years in law enforcement with Essex County and Caldwell Police Departments.

We are all vulnerable to crime; it can strike any one of us, including cops. I survived a near-death assault on June 2, 1991. Almost twenty years later, I am still haunted by the memories of this attack perpetrated by my own father, a former court constable, who owned three handguns, two rifles, and frequently slept with a firearm underneath his pillow.

My father was a highly decorated WWII Navy veteran and post-war court constable who carried a gun, a badge, and a family history of domestic violence. He and his siblings were physically abused by their mother, and my father continued the generational cycle of abuse within our family.

I realized my childhood dream in 1990 when I was sworn to duty as a Police Officer with the Essex County Police Department in Newark, New Jersey. I was one of four female officers employed in the more than 250 officer police force, and we patrolled the county parks, roads, and bridges within the 21 Essex County municipalities.

My father tried to kill me twice; once by strangulation and the second time with a firearm. I protected and hid my family secret of child abuse and domestic violence perpetrated upon me throughout my 28-year law enforcement career.

I was a "woman in blue" hiding black and blues from body bruises, scars, belts, and healed marks underneath my police uniform, guarding when and how I changed into and out of my clothes in the police locker room.

Domestic violence is a pattern of coercive domination and control based on or supported by violence. It is a global widespread epidemic that affects women and men, all socioeconomic groups, races, cultures, and professions like law enforcement.

No one knows precisely how often domestic violence occurs or how many people are affected because incidents like mine go unreported, misreported, and are often times hidden in divorce statistics, medical reports, school records, and police and government documents that disguise the information.

I never felt responsible for the abuse, but I was understandably depressed and confused during and after being abused. I wanted the violence to stop, but didn't want the daughter-father relationship to end. Love, family, shared memories, and a sense of commitment are hard bonds to break to end our biological relationship. As odd as it sounds, I loved my father but hated his behavior.

At least one out of every three women around the world has been beaten, coerced into sex, or otherwise abused in her lifetime, with the abuser usually someone known to her. Victims are betrayed by the people they love and trust.

Most people wake up from their nightmares. I was forced to live mine daily, growing up facing a journey not meant for young children. Parents are supposed to protect their children from dangers that threaten them, to ensure they can grow in a safe environment surrounded by love and stability, and to lead by example. This is not what happened in our house. On a regular basis, I viewed examples of what not to be.

My father preyed on all of us, thriving on our vulnerability, compliance and fear. Violence was the oxygen that sustained him. His intentions were cruel and premeditated, his actions criminal. I knew the odds were greater that I would be killed in my own home, rather than as a cop working the streets.

*****

Childhood is a formative time, and the early and constant exposure to physical and psychological violence had devastating long-term effects on our lives. It wore on me daily and severed the sibling bonds between me, my sister, and brother.

Our house didn't have a spooky exterior children dare each other to approach. It wasn't surrounded by iron bars and walls. There were no hardened beds, cells, or windows that were backed with steel to keep us there inside. It had a white picket fence, a manicured lawn, a garden filled with roses, and an exterior American flag displayed year round.

To all I met, I was just as free as they themselves were, but that's because my chains were invisible, no one ever saw or knew what kept me there. Unbeknownst to all, my father was the gatekeeper, and we were his prisoners.   He avoided detection and prosecution because we feared him. He provided the only income for our family, and we were dependent on him.

During my law enforcement career, I handled and responded to hundreds of calls/incidents of domestic violence and was the commander of my police department's Domestic Violence Unit. I arrested and prosecuted batterers for the same acts I allowed my father to perpetrate upon me. I wore my image armor well and never let anyone know what I faced daily in my home.

How could I expect my fellow officers to believe that I allowed my father to abuse me when I could not believe I allowed him to physically, mentally, and emotionally harm me?

My academy training taught me how to defend myself and others tactically, but I felt helpless to stop my father's behavior.

My quest had always been to live a normal life, violence free, but how does this happen in a dysfunctional household with the ever-looming potential of lethal violence? For me, fear of when the violence would happen was worse than the actual acts of violence. I spent lots of time and energy protecting myself from facing what I'd been through. Mentally and emotionally, I played the abuse down every way I could.

*****

The generational and cultural cycle of domestic violence existed in my family for three generations. I wasn't fortunate enough to have grandparents to confront my father or comfort me with unconditional love; they died when I was a toddler. All my maternal and paternal relatives witnessed the abuse, but no one stepped up to stop him. My mother created somewhat of a safe space for me whenever my father was out of the house, which wasn't often.

His verbal abuse was non-stop. He argued with my mother constantly about everything, always attacking her self-esteem. My mother medicated herself with Xanax, cigarettes, and alcohol. She told me that blacking out was better than enduring the daily verbal abuse.

My medical doctor discovered bruises on my body during annual physical examinations. I begged him to stay silent, and he did because he knew my father was capable of killing all of us. I slept with sleigh bells on my bedroom door knob so I could be alerted if he tried entering my bedroom while I slept.

One sunny Saturday afternoon in the summer of 1991 my father almost succeeded in murdering me . . .

I arrived home from attending a Saturday criminal justice class at Rutgers University in Newark to an argument between my parents in the kitchen. However, this argument sounded different than the others. My mother was screaming that she had enough, couldn't take it anymore, and was leaving.

I was shocked, stunned, but happy to hear her utter the words "I'm leaving," for she had never before said she would leave my father. I wanted to sprint towards the kitchen, but felt frozen, like my feet were sinking in quicksand. My police gut instincts were telling me this argument was heading towards a physical confrontation.

I walked through the dining room and entered the kitchen where I saw my mother with a cleaver in hand charging towards my father who was standing against the kitchen wall. My mother had blood in her eyes and intent in her hands. As she raised the cleaver to attack my father, my police instincts kicked in. I intervened and knocked the cleaver from my mother's hands. It fell to the floor under my feet: however, that didn't stop my mother from attacking my father, scratching and wildly punching at his body.

My mother was out of control, fighting back for the first time, finally defending herself and her children from this monster, and I was in the middle of the fight. I felt the physical power from my mother's tiny, 4'11" body as she struggled to be freed from my grasp as I tried to separate the two combatants. Her voice was hoarse, but her words cut like a knife "You son of a bitch, I hate you, I hate you, and I want you dead. No more, I'm not going to take this anymore."

I made a rookie tactical error when I turned my back to my father to shield my mother and he reacted, cat-like, spun me around, grabbed me by my neck, lifted me off my feet and banged me onto the kitchen table with such force that it took my breath away. Then he mounted and straddled me, channeling all his anger and hate into his mallet-like, destructive hands, strangling me with a vengeance.

Our eyes locked, and we became one. His eyes were

bulging, his mouth frothing, and I felt mine doing the same. I knew my father's intention was to kill me first and then my mother, to hang her from the pipes in the basement, the ones near the furnace, as he had threatened to do so many times before. Ironically, I felt at peace floating above my own body, ready to leave this life. In my haze of serenity, I saw my mother repeatedly hitting him, trying to pull him off me and screaming "Stop, stop, you're going to kill her!"

Her voice embodied a determination to save my life, the life of her last born, the child she called "Baby Doll," her co-survivor. Her determination propelled me into police survival mode as I realized I loved my mother more than life itself, and if my father killed me she would be next. I would not allow him, the enemy, to end her life. I was a cop who was academy trained to save lives, and now I was going to save us.

For the first time in 32 years, I fought back with an infusion of power from the heavens above, punching and kicking my father with all my will and desire to live. One of my punches was to his center mass on his open heart surgical stitches causing him to release his grip on my neck. Miraculously, I had the energy to slip off the table, hit and stun him again, and scramble away.

My mother was screaming, "Run, Donna, run." With my father in pursuit, I staggered through the dining room, and then the parlor, rounded the corner, and made it up the twelve carpeted stairs to my bedroom where I retrieved my .32 caliber snub nose revolver.

As he barreled up the stairs ready to finish the job, we simultaneously met at the second floor landing. I drew my revolver, cocked it, and pointed it at his head, and, in that moment, a moment I had subconsciously planned for, as he looked down the barrel of my gun, he knew I meant business. In that instant, I was in control of him and what happened next. With my finger on the trigger I was ready to gain my freedom and end his. I told him "You will never touch me or my mother again." I would no longer accommodate myself to his brutality.

A few days later, Mom and I went to her doctor's appointment and never returned to that house of horrors. Several months prior, I had rented an apartment, furnished it, and developed a safety plan for us to escape. Shortly thereafter, my mother filed for divorce.

But this isn't the end of my story.

*****

Four years after my mother and I escaped, and after my parents' turbulent divorce, my mother encouraged me to make amends with my ill, wheelchair bound father, and I reluctantly agreed to see him. I wondered had he changed?

After arriving at the house that I vowed never to return to, I noticed my father looked frail, unkempt, and was a skeleton of the full-bodied abuser, master manipulator I feared. After minutes of uncomfortable forced small talk, the monster was resurrected; he blamed me for taking his wife away from him, cursing and ranting that he was good to me and my mother and how nobody loved him. I felt compelled to ask him why he physically and emotionally abused me. He denied doing any of that and portrayed himself as the victim.

After a second pissed off rant, he wheeled away from me and went into the dining room where I heard him mumbling and struggling to open something, possibly a drawer. My police instincts told me not to go into that room, to stay put, close to the front door, close to freedom. I knew his capabilities. After several minutes passed, I heard the sounds of bullets being chambered into a gun. One round . . . two rounds . . . three . . . four . . . five. I knew my father had loaded a gun and was plotting, desperately wanting to be successful this time, the final time, to end my life.

He hadn't changed. He was lethal. I knew him well, this man who had given me life. He was capable of only one behavior—violence—he was a batterer, a manipulator, a perp. I was no longer willing to be his victim, to allow him ever again to be in control of my life, or to end it, his way.

I doubt he heard me ease open the front door, back out with my pistol in hand, ready, just in case this time I had to pull the trigger to end his misery. I didn't look back. I couldn't look back. I wouldn't go back. I wasn't that little girl anymore who feared the monster inside that house.

A wound can't heal until the glass is removed. Years of checking in with a counselor helped me deal with my own demons, to realize that I did nothing wrong to deserve my father's abuse, and to learn how to let it go. Forgiveness is an easy word to say; it falls quickly from our lips. However, living in forgiveness and moving on is difficult.

*****

My mom died on September 2, 1997. After her death, I found letters she wrote about the abuse she suffered. Nine months following her demise, I went to my father's hospital bed where he lay semiconscious, close to death. I bent over him, whispered in his ear "I forgive you, but I will never forget," and quickly left there feeling relieved that he would never hurt me again.

I was afraid to tell my story, but not anymore. I survived the ultimate betrayal and I know there are other women in blue who suffer in silence like I did.

Marilyn Edwards

was born in Dallas, Texas. She is a nine year member of the Dallas Police Department and is assigned to the Neighborhood Policing Unit. Marilyn can be found on any day patrolling the streets of Dallas. She is married to Darrin Lee and has two sons, Ryan and Isaiah. She holds a Bachelor of Applied Business Administration from Dallas Baptist University. Marilyn is also a 21-year veteran of the United States Air Force Reserves (ret.). She served several tours throughout the United States and abroad, including a tour to Balad Air Base, Iraq, in support of Operation Iraqi Freedom.

Marilyn believes there is a divine order to everything. For her, that order is God, family, and country. She is an active member of Antioch Fellowship Missionary Baptist Church. She loves the Lord with all of her heart. One of her favorite passages of scripture is Psalm 46:1 "God is our refuge and strength, a very present help in trouble." She believes God has been gracious to her and that there is still more work for her to do. She is a volunteer with the Dallas Police Department's Military Assistance Program, an all-volunteer group that sends care packages to the deployed officers and friends of the department. Working with this program is her way of continuing to serve, despite being retired.

Marilyn enjoys traveling, working out, reading, and spending time with her family.

God and Country

by Marilyn Edwards

When I joined the Dallas Police Department in 2002, I was a single parent, mother of two. I knew that it would be difficult to be a good parent and juggle the profession. However, I had no idea of exactly what was forthcoming. I had a strong support system in place, so I figured it would be a lot easier. My mother assisted me when I had to study long hours and work shifts that were nontraditional. She was my support system. She was battling terminal cancer, yet through all of the chemotherapy, she managed to assist me with my children so that I could accomplish my dream. She lived long enough to see me graduate the Dallas Police Academy in August of 2002. She also had an opportunity to see me complete my field training and become a bona fide police officer.

Shortly after I completed field training, my mother died in April of 2003. That's when my whole world turned upside down. The support system I thought I had in place came tumbling down. I thought I would surely lose my mind. I was working deep nights (11 p.m.-7 a.m.). I would have to drive from Northwest Dallas (which was the station that I was assigned to) all the way to Cedar Hill, Texas, to have my son at school by 8:00 a.m. Somehow, we made it every day.

In addition to the Dallas Police Department, I am a 21-year veteran of the United States Air Force Reserves. In 2005, my reserve unit was called to active duty. Can you imagine being told that you will have to leave your children for a year just after getting some sense of normalcy after the loss your mother (who was their caretaker)? Nonetheless, I would not do anything to bring dishonor to my family's name, so I deployed to California for training and then on to Balad AB, Iraq.

What a life-changing experience .My children and I had to improvise, adapt, and overcome. My new support system became my fiancé (who would later become my husband) and some relatives and friends. My children, who were sixteen and eight at the time, both started acting out due to the separation. I was the only parent they were accustomed to, and they were unsure if they would ever see me alive again. Ryan, the oldest, started skipping school and doing things he normally would not do. Isaiah, the youngest, became very angry and had several fights at school. Again, I thought I would surely lose my mind. I was half a world away, and my children were being sacrificed. I believe faith in God is what carried me through. I talked with them and assured them they were going to be okay. I was emphatic with them about their mother coming home—no matter what.

In Iraq, the days were long. I thought my Dallas Police Department family had abandoned me in a sense. At the time, there was not a system in place for officers who were deployed. I can count on one hand the number of officers who wrote me or sent care packages while I was deployed. That has since changed. I am an avid member of the Dallas Police Department Military Assistance Program (DPDMAP) because I don't ever want another officer to feel like I felt. We volunteer our time and send care packages to deployed officers. I consider it an honor to have had an opportunity to experience what life was like in a combat zone. In Balad, Iraq, I served in the 332 Air Expeditionary Wing, which is the same wing the famous Tuskegee Airmen served in. I am, therefore, a third generation

Tuskegee Airman. I have an experience not many officers can claim. I know what it is like to serve my country in a combat zone and on the streets of Dallas.

I tell everyone that I love my job as a police officer. I get a front row seat to life every day. Although I am a neighborhood patrol officer, on any given day, I can be found answering calls. As a neighborhood police officer, I serve as a liaison between the department and the community. I assist the citizens with crime prevention techniques and I attend career fairs at schools and in the community.

It's been nine years now, and my children have grown up. Ryan is twenty-three and Isaiah is fourteen. I don't so much worry about the obstacles that may come my way. I have learned to trust that God will work things out for my highest good. I continue to work varying hours and different days off. My husband and children are never certain I will return home when I leave each day. However, I serve proudly. Life as a police officer has not been easy, but it has been worth it.

Gloria D. Spencer

joined the Dallas Police Department at the tender age of 21, shortly after graduating from Stephen F. Austin University. For the past 35 years, she has learned life's lessons from her law enforcement experience. Gloria has been exposed to people and things she never envisioned. Ironically, police work was not her first choice as a career, but now she cannot imagine having done anything else with her life. She views things from a police perspective; it's embedded in her being.

Gloria has worked in several capacities within the department. Currently, she is a family violence detective. She also worked in patrol, personnel, training, and the gang unit. She was the original LETS officer, the department's drug and gang awareness program taught to elementary age students. Sadly, the program fell victim to budget cuts about two years ago.

In her spare time, Gloria likes reading and gardening.

20

Gunfight in the
Ladies Department

by Gloria Spencer

November 29, 1979, was a cold, windy day. It was about 10 a.m., the first shopping day of the Christmas season. Stores were packed with eager, enthusiastic shoppers. I was riding alone, for my partner, Robert Greenwald, was on his day off. The police radio crackled out a call to me and Officer Kenneth Beck. Officer Beck was also working solo. The dispatcher advised there was a disturbance on a city bus involving a white female. She had pulled a gun on the bus driver and demanded to be let off the bus. The driver let the woman, later identified as Kathy Mental, off at the Sears store located at Ross and Greenville. The dispatcher said the woman was wearing a tan trench coat and a green blouse and was last seen entering the Sears store. I was about six blocks away from the call location. I checked en route to the call. As I approached the intersection of Ross and Henderson where the store was located, I saw a squad car on the parking lot. Given that there appeared to be officers at the location, I made the decision to enter the store.

I entered through the north doors. Much to my chagrin, the store was crowded with white females wearing tan trench coats. I briefly stopped and looked around for any white female acting suspiciously. None of them were. Walking through the store, I began the search for my suspect. I was heading through the main isle of the clothes department, scanning the crowded store for my suspect. The cash register was located to my left about fifteen feet in front of me. There were people waiting to check out at the register.

Suddenly, my police radio came to life, and at that exact moment, I saw a white female in a tan trench coat whirling around with a wild look in her eyes. I immediately knew this was the woman I was looking for. Without saying a word, she reached for her pocket, placing her hand inside her trench coat. I had little time to react and no place to retreat to. I yelled at her, "Don't put your hand in your pocket!" I quickly decided my only hope was to rush her and try to keep her from removing the gun from her pocket. I ran toward her and was about two feet from her when she removed the gun from her pocket and pointed it in my face.

The barrel looked like a cannon! (It was later discovered to be a .22 caliber revolver). Just as she raised it inches from my face, I reached up and knocked her hand upwards. She fired one shot, and I saw my life flash in front of me. The shot was deafening. I literally heard it go over my head. The bullet was later located lodged in the exit sign above the rear door.

She and I engaged in a life and death struggle for possession of the gun. I recall thinking, "What did they tell us in the academy?" Instinctively, my training kicked in. During the hand to hand struggle, we fell to the floor. We flip-flopped several times. First she was on top of me, and then I was on top of her, back and forth. The struggle seemed to last an eternity; things around us turned in slow motion. I could hear people scampering and screaming as they hid behind the clothes racks. Despite the crowded store, no one came to assist me. As I for fought for control of the gun with a woman sixty pounds heavier and several inches taller, my mind said, *You can't give up this fight. Your mother cannot handle losing another child.*

Five years earlier, I lost my brother while he was swimming in Galveston. The undertow sucked him out to sea. I watched my dear mother struggle with losing her second child, her only son. The thought of her having to bear the loss of two of her three children gave me the will and determination to keep up the fight. Several times during the struggle, Ms. Mental pointed that cannon directly at my face. Each time I pushed the barrel away. She shot twice. Another bullet was later located at the checkout counter. The third one was never found.

After what felt like an eternity, I managed to fight my way back on top of Ms. Mental, straddling her as she lay on her back. I held her gun hand (right) down with my left hand and restrained her hand on the floor. She was screaming and yelling at me to let her go. She said if I let her go she would drop the gun. I refused. Instead, I removed my service revolver from my holster and placed it directly against her head, well prepared to pull the trigger.

When she saw the gun pointed at her head, she released her grip on her gun and let it rest on the floor, but still dangerously close to her hand. A man ran from behind the clothes and kicked the gun so that she could not reach it. Exhausted, I rolled her onto her stomach, holstered my service revolver, and proceeded to handcuff her. I had one cuff on when, suddenly, someone pushed me from behind, sending me sailing several feet across the room.

At that moment, I thought, *Oh no, I can handle one but I can't handle two*, as I was physically and emotionally spent and had experienced an adrenaline dump. I leaped back on my feet and saw, much to my relief, Sgt. Tommy Maddox leaning over Ms. Mental, completing the task of hand cuffing her. In short order, Officer Beck arrived to assist Sgt. Maddox. Then Captain Doug Sword arrived. I was drained and of little help to them, as I was trying to catch my breath and sort things out in my head. I later learned that Sgt. Maddox and Captain Sword were the occupants of the police car I saw in the parking lot when I arrived.

Things calmed down in the store. More reinforcements arrived, and I prepared to transport Ms. Mental to jail. All of a sudden, I felt a burning sensation in my left side that quickly intensified. I pulled up my navy blue uniform shirt to expose my white t-shirt and saw blood and a bullet hole in the t-shirt. At that point I realized I had been shot. An ambulance was ordered. Sgt. Gregory, a patrol supervisor at my station, asked if I could walk to the patrol car. I said yes. He made the decision to transport me by patrol car to the nearest hospital, which was about five minutes away. He drove Code 3 while I rode in the front passenger seat and operated the emergency equipment.

We arrived at Baylor hospital, and I was rolled into the ER, not having a panic attack but I was most certainly hyperventilating. Once the ER personnel got me to control my breathing, a thorough examination was performed. An entry and exit wound was located on my left side, waist level—a flesh wound. The ER doctor told me I was very lucky. He said if I had been shot three more inches to the left I would have been seriously injured or possibly killed. He also said three inches to the right and the shot would have completely missed me. I spent most of the day in the ER.

My partner, "Greenie," stopped by to visit following his court appearance. In his usual humorous manner, he teased about waiting until he was off and "going out and getting shot." I also had many other visitors, including the chief of police Glenn King. Also, my then boyfriend, who became my husband, and later my ex-husband, made his way to the hospital by flagging down two officers driving down the street. My dear mother, who unwittingly gave me the strength to fight, came to visit the following day. She lived three hours away and had to make arrangements for transportation, for her vehicle was not reliable. I dare say I am living today because of her prayers. She passed away many years ago. She never once questioned my chosen profession.

I later learned Ms. Mental had a documented history of mental problems and had been in and out of mental institutions. She was hearing voices on that eventful day. However, I must admit I find it interesting she was not so mentally disturbed that she didn't respond by dropping her gun when mine was pointed at her head. It was discovered she had a box of 150 bullets in her purse.

Marta Bell

is a lifelong resident of Indianapolis, Indiana. She graduated from Manual High School and continued her education at Indiana University, Bloomington. She graduated with a double major in criminal justice and public affairs. Upon graduation, she worked for the Bloomington Police Department. Marta is now a 28-year veteran officer with the Indianapolis Metropolitan Police Department, where she is a detective assigned to the domestic violence branch. She is professionally trained in investigating domestic violence and intimate partner stalking.

Marta is the mother of two daughters, and considers motherhood one of her greatest accomplishments in life. She is a member of Oasis of Hope Baptist Church, Alpha Kappa Alpha Sorority, Inc. and Not To Believers Like Us.

Marta is a survivor/thriver of domestic abuse, and considers it a blessing to be able to teach across the states as well as in her community, conducting workshops on domestic violence, single parenting and empowering women. By sharing her story, she hopes to be the voice that helps others avoid abusive situations.

She enjoys reading and writing poetry, singing and traveling. Marta is an aspiring author.

One Voice,
Many Faces

by Marta Bell

On April 24, 1987, officers were dispatched to a domestic disturbance. Arriving at the scene, they were told by dispatch that an ambulance had already been there and was headed to Community Hospital with the victim.

As the officers made their way to the hospital, dispatch called them again and told them to beware because the alleged suspect of the domestic disturbance might have a weapon and may also be on the way to the hospital. When the officers arrived at the hospital, the medical staff advised them that the woman had an injury to her hand from a gunshot wound, which she said was the result of an argument with a relative over who would care for the couple's four month-old child overnight.

Upon interviewing the victim, the police officers observed a fresh gunshot wound to her right hand. The woman explained she had worked a night shift and had to be back at work the next morning and had allowed her sister to take the child for an overnight stay. When the child's father came home, he became upset and angry that no one had asked for his permission for the child to leave the house.

A heated argument ensued and the child's father grabbed a

loaded gun and threatened to shoot her. When the man pointed the gun at her, she reached for it to keep him from shooting her in the face. During the struggle the gun discharged, the bullet penetrating MY right hand.

Yes, even though I am a police officer, I was the victim. That's my story. What's yours, or someone you know and love? No house is exempt. Domestic violence affects us all, directly or indirectly. Statistics show that a woman is beaten every nine seconds at the hand of an abuser. Not a stranger, but someone she has grown to love, trust, and depend on to protect and defend her. Statistics also show that it will take a woman being beaten an average of seven times before she leaves the abusive relationship and does not return.

When someone experiences violence in a relationship, they must get out. But leave with caution and realize that domestic abuse is about power and control, and the most dangerous and potentially fatal time is when you separate from your abuser.

After the injury to my hand, I knew that my child and I were in imminent danger so I moved in with a friend for our protection. Yes, I was the police. Yes, I carried a gun. Yes, I was trained to protect and serve. **NO,** I did not feel safe, to say the least. I felt disbelief. How could I have allowed myself to get into this type of situation? Believe me when I tell you I did not wake up one morning and decide that I would be a victim that day. The choice was not left up to me. If it had been, I definitely would have chosen differently.

What I did choose to do only empowered my abuser even more. I once again heeded the code of silence, pretended that my life had not been shattered, and I did not discuss what had occurred with anyone for more than ten years. Even my family did not know what my child and I were experiencing, and I was too embarrassed to seek help. Moreover, I actually didn't know to whom or where to turn for guidance.

*****

I should have felt safe since I was away from my abuser. He stopped calling and didn't know where I had moved. I was glad. I went to work every day and carried out the duties I was sworn to do: protect and serve the citizens.

But who was going to protect me? I knew I could and would protect my child. After all, that's what a good mother does, and I was a great mother. However, I didn't feel so great. I felt like a failure and questioned myself as to how I could have been so blind not to see who this man really was. Was I so blind, so needy, and so selfish to birth a child conceived by an abuser? What was wrong with me? Was I the cause of him becoming abusive? Did I do something to trigger him, to set him off?

On May 4, 1987, a supervisor of the police department was dispatched to assist me after I had called 9-1-1 and requested two district cars be sent. As the supervisor was en route to my address, I broadcast that I needed the district car 10-39, which is police jargon for immediately. A short time later, I advised that the subject involved was leaving the scene.

My abuser was back. Remember, I left the abuse and my abuser, but he had not left me or my child. He came back searching for us both. Abusers usually feel a sense of entitlement and don't like to lose. Abuse is about power and control, and an abuser cannot control what you cannot see, find, or have access to.

It had been two weeks since I had moved out of the residence I shared with my abuser. I had chosen to live with another officer, thinking I would be safe and out of harm's way. I thought wrong, and once again, the idea of any kind of peace of mind or safety was gone. My fear factor had elevated to a point that I was not sure the police department could protect me, and I knew mentally I could not function as a mother, a police officer, or a protector for anyone. Nevertheless, I pretended I could.

When the supervisor arrived to assist me, he must have thought I had lost my mind. I was on the telephone involved in a heated argument with my abuser. There was a police radio and a police service revolver lying on the couch in the living room. I was angry, disgusted, and victimized once again. I had already secured an apartment for my child and me to move into within the next week or so, but I felt my child's father knew this. But how? How had he found out where I was staying, and how did he have the audacity to come to another police officer's house and challenge me, knowing we were armed? Who had tipped him off?

I felt like I could trust no one, but I felt confident the officer I was living with had my back. We began to strategize about who would sleep at what time, and where, and with what form of protection. *Is this really happening in my life?* Everything I was experiencing seemed like it should be on a TV screen, not actually reality, not to someone like me. Victims, however, rarely look like victims.

I focused on healing from my injury so I could go back to work. The mental aspect of what I could and could not handle never really entered my mind; I was just going through the motions to get through minute by minute. Days seemed long and nights even longer.

Police are people too, and we experience the same problems as everyone else.

Melanie K. Draft

works as a road patrol/E-unit deputy paramedic for the Ottawa County Sheriff's Office (SO) in Western Michigan. The Ottawa County SO E-unit program has been providing police/paramedic first response to its citizens since its origin in the mid-1970s. The E-unit program has become a unique and valuable program, providing first line advanced life support care prior to ambulance arrival. Prior to joining the SO in 2007, Melanie worked for a private ambulance company in Grand Rapids, Michigan, beginning in 1998.

22

The Storm

by Melanie K. Draft

It was just after midnight on a very stormy May night. The call came over the radio as a three year old boy missing from an apartment complex. The first deputy on the scene responded in routine fashion, gathering information and conducting a house check that we all know to do in these situations. Nine times out of ten a call from a frantic parent or family member results in police arriving, checking the house, and finding the missing child sleeping under a bed or hiding in a clothes hamper.

The weather was bad. Wind and rain whipped the landscape, which was aglow in flashes of luminescent lightening and punctuated by deafening thunder. I just assumed this call would end in the nine times out of ten category. At the time, my youngest son was three years old, and I could not imagine him outside in this kind of weather. Shortly after the first officer arrived, he advised that he would need more help. Despite having checked the apartment and the immediate surroundings, the little boy was nowhere to be found.

I arrived on scene to find the boy's aunt and grandmother inside the apartment. The aura surrounding the situation was easy to read—panic. I saw it in their eyes and heard it in their voices. As a mom, I dread being in a situation where I wouldn't know the whereabouts of my three year old boy at midnight in the middle of a storm. My heart went out to this family, and I immediately thought of my own little boy at home tucked safely in his bed. I resisted the urge to call and check on him. We immediately devised a game plan utilizing the few resources and scant manpower we had at the time. Equipped with a rain coat and flashlight, each of us went our separate way into the storm in an attempt to locate the toddler.

My first instinct was to look in the bushes near the apartment, knowing children have a natural survival instinct. Next, I planned to search areas in the complex he would be familiar with: the playground and the office. After a few minutes of probing the bushes, I saw that the local fire department had arrived with extra manpower and lighting. Meanwhile, the wind was so fierce it hampered our ability even to walk, forcing us to bend over to make any forward progress. The monsoon-like rain limited the ability to see, almost as if one were looking through a waterfall. The frequent lightning strikes were akin to scary special effects in a horror movie. All I could think about was the little boy out in this weather. Alone. Scared.

The apartment buildings had two large retention ponds located near the entrance and separated by the main drive into the complex. While acting as drainage, they also gave the property an aesthetic appearance. One of them was near the office and the playground. I scanned the first retention pond where the fire department was setting up light towers, praying my eyes would not see what I had been conjuring up in my mind since I arrived. Nothing there.

I crossed the street to the other pond near the apartment office with my ear close to the radio, hoping for a voice to announce they'd found him and that he was okay. As I made my way down the muddy embankment, the light from my flashlight was inadequate to see across the pond in the cascading rain. I could not wait for the fire department to finish searching the other pond, so I stepped boot high into the water in an attempt to stretch my beam a bit farther out into the water. It was dark and murky. I took another step in the muck and it was then that the light captured what I dared not think about. Looking back, I don't know if it was actually the light from my flashlight or the eerie back light from lightning that had just flashed, but I saw as plain as day the little boy in his pajamas, floating face down about ten feet from me.

Shoving my flashlight in my back pocket, I started wading out to him. I got about waist deep and grabbed him. I had no idea how long he had been in the water, but he felt warm. My paramedic instinct kicked in immediately. I flipped the tiny lifeless body face up and opened the mouth. He was not breathing and had no pulse. I scooped him up and carried him to the bank of the pond where I could administer some chest compressions to help pump water from his lungs and open his airway. As I was making my way to the embankment, I tried to radio that I had found the boy and I needed help. I also wanted to request an ambulance for a drowning at the south retention pond. No one knew where I was or that I had found the boy. Unfortunately my radio traffic was not getting out, possibly because of the weather or because it may have just been submerged in the pond. Either way I was on my own.

I placed the boy on his back and gave some chest compressions. Just across the parking lot was my police cruiser with all the advanced medical equipment I needed: oxygen, intubation, and IV supplies and a heart monitor. I performed a few more chest compressions and then gathered the child and made my way to my cruiser. Halfway there I saw my sergeant heading back toward our vehicles. "Sarge, call an ambulance!" He saw I had the child in my arms and ran to help me while making the call on his radio. The limp little boy was placed in the back of the fire engine and we went to work. Within minutes an ambulance arrived and he was moved to the back of the rig. We immediately left for the hospital and continued to work on the boy during the trip. It was a short ride to the local emergency room where advance care continued. No effort was spared to save that precious little angel, but despite everyone's heroic actions and prayer it was not enough. He died.

I watched the ER staff work on the little body while he lay on that big gurney. He seemed so small in comparison and if I didn't know better, I'd swear he was sleeping, but in my heart I knew what the outcome would be even before I heard the doctor say it. "Time of death is . . ." Walking away I heard the sorrowful sounds of the little boy's family crying out as they learned the fate of their child. I glanced into the room and saw the boy's father fall to his knees, as if begging the doctor to take back the news he'd just given them. I thought about the somber reaction of the staff in the emergency room, standing quietly, looking to each other for comfort, and trying to understand why an innocent baby has to die. I walked away from it all, with a strange, yet vivid memory: hearing my boots squish from the pond water in them as I walked down the hallway. I suddenly realized how cold and wet I was, and all I could think about was that I have to get changed out of these clothes and get back to work. I again resisted the urge to call home to check on my own children. What I really wanted to do was go home and see them, touch them, and wrap my arms around them.

Back at the station, I found a dry uniform and boots and hit the road to finish my shift. To many people this probably seems warped or somewhat abnormal, but for me it was completely natural. Police officers develop their own defense mechanisms and coping strategies to deal with crises. Mine was to go back to work. What happened that night was tragic, but tragic things often happen in police work; but if we let them consume us, we wouldn't last very long before the horror takes over our mind.

At the end of the shift I changed into my jeans and tennis shoes and left "work" in my locker. I went home and became mom again. I made my way to both my son's bedrooms. Lying next to each of them, I was thankful they were safe and said a silent prayer for the family that had lost their little boy in the storm.

Amy Sue Michalik

 started her law enforcement career in 1998 as a police officer with the Atlanta Police Department (APD). She was the only woman on her watch, but it didn't take long for her to earn the respect of the men with whom she worked. In fact, it just took a punch in the nose. "Shorty White," as she became known on her beat, had a reputation for being a tough, hard-working cop.

In 2002, Amy moved from the APD to the Bureau of Alcohol, Tobacco, Firearms, and Explosives (ATF). As a special agent, Amy worked a variety of cases in the nine years since being hired. She has worked in Atlanta, Georgia; Miami, Florida; and San Bernardino and Glendale, California. She has taught new agents at the Federal Law Enforcement Training Center, been the Victim/Witness Coordinator and Senior Operations Officer in both Atlanta and Los Angeles, been specially chosen to work on two multi-agency Violent Crime Impact Teams (Miami & San Bernardino), and worked on the David Wilhelm Strike Force/Organized Crime & Drug Enforcement Task Force.

Amy developed health issues, causing uncertainty about her future in federal service. She began looking for other career choices and discovered the University of California, Los Angeles' Online Professional Screenwriting Program. With a renewed passion for life and a newfound love of screenwriting, Amy took the opportunity to transfer to the LA Field Division with ATF to chase her Hollywood dream.

Amy attends the University of California, Los Angeles in pursuit of a Master of Fine Arts in Screenwriting while continuing to work for ATF. She is a finalist in the 2011 NexTV Writing and Pitching Competition, with an original TV pilot she wrote called "SHOOT." Shoot is about celebrity/fashion photographer, Dallas Cooper, who at the pinnacle of her career must reluctantly fulfill her promise to take up the family's legacy as an assassin when her father doesn't return from a mission.

23

Earning My Stripes

by Amy Sue Michalik

In 2000, I was a snot-nosed FNG (f***ing new guy) for the Atlanta Police Department, assigned to Southwest Atlanta, otherwise known as Zone 4. Zone 4 borders each of the highest crime areas in the city of Atlanta. I was just a few months out of the academy. Back then we still had wooden batons, carried 9mm Smith and Wesson pistols, and patrolled solo.

I was dispatched to a signal 39/29 (information on a fight) and told to see the fire department upon arrival. The call sent me to one of the bigger urban housing developments in Atlanta called Allen Temple.

As I entered the development, I heard one of the other units very close to me raise dispatch and ask if I was sent into the Temple by myself. Dispatch answered affirmative and said he'd start with me.

When I got to the scene, I saw a large group of people, approximately fifty or so, outside of the apartment building and the fire department was struggling to keep them back.

Upon my arrival, the Fire Chief rushed up to me and yelled, "Arrest this man!" An angry mob of African Americans had surrounded the Fire Chief. I attempted to calm the group and ascertain what the hell was going on. People were yelling at me from every direction. Several times I had to scream above the voices to even be heard. A small African-American woman stepped out of the group and got in my face, screaming, "Officer, do you have children?"

I simply replied, "No I don't."

She counters, screaming, "I KNOW YOU DON'T."

As the crowd got rowdier, I chastised myself for jamming that damn 24" stick they call a baton into the door like everyone else. I sure could use it right about now. When the second unit joined me, we immediately took down the African American man the Fire Chief wanted arrested. While the two of us struggled with the man on the ground, the female who screamed at me earlier charged us, yelling "Oh no you don't!"

We nearly had the man cuffed so I jumped up to stop her from interfering. I grabbed her, pushed her backwards and said to her, "Oh no **YOU** don't.

I keep pushing her backward until her back was against the apartment building. She had a hold of my collar and each of us struggled for the upper hand. A group of approximately thirty women had surrounded us. At that time, in Atlanta the fire and police departments didn't always see eye-to-eye, so it was uncharacteristic for the Fire Chief to decide to help by trying to remove the woman's hands from my collar. When he got one of her hands free, she seized the moment to punch me in the nose.

At about the same time, the suspect got away from my partner, and out of the corner of my eye I saw them both running. Then I heard my partner tell dispatch that he was "Signal 20," which meant that he used his O.C. spray. I had to go help him. I shoved the woman against the wall and turned to see where my partner was. The woman's daughter, a young girl eight to ten years of age, came at me and jumped towards me, yelling, "Don't you touch my mommy!"

I simply stuck my hand out to stop her forward movement and said, "Don't touch me." I then took off running to find my partner.

When I finally caught up to him, I asked him if my nose was

bleeding. He asked me why, and I told him I was punched in the nose by the woman I was wrestling with. He balled his fists and screamed, "Where is she?" I thought a vein was going to pop in his head. I began to hear the sirens getting closer. By the time we got back to the scene, the troops had arrived, and we began hauling people into the wagon and got the hell out of there before we had a riot on our hands. At the time of the arrests, neither the women who assaulted me nor the man who got away from my partner was arrested.

My usual partner, when I was doubled up or on foot beat, was driving the paddy wagon that night. He slammed the back door of the wagon, causing the back window to shatter. We got the glass out of the wagon so none of the prisoners would hurt themselves and then "got the hell out of Dodge."

Back at the Precinct, my shift was over, and we handed over our vehicles to morning watch. A call came into the precinct that the woman was back at her residence. I ran out the door with two other officers on my heels. We jumped into a spare car and took off to go hook this bitch up. As soon as I walked into the door of her house, all I heard was, "Yeah, there's that cracker bitch cop." The guys stepped in, but I never even touched her after that except to search her. I smiled the whole time.

You might think the story ends here, but you'd be wrong. What the hell were all those people having conniptions about? As it turned out, there was still a small child inside the apartment. Apparently when drugs are your top priority, you forget how many children you have. The man, the woman and four of her five children got out of the house but they forgot the baby inside. I have the biggest heart of anyone you could meet, and if anyone would have told me a child was inside I would have gone in to get the child myself. Let me also say that the fire was quite small, started by some kids playing with matches inside an abandoned apartment, but the building was evacuated anyway. No adverse effects for the baby or anyone else.

The next day when I got to work, my regular partner and I were assigned to the paddy wagon and immediately sent off to pick up prisoners on a road block, known as Safety Check Point. By then, the stories had gotten around and more than a few people were calling me "Slugger." The supervisor at the road block handed me the tickets, and we began putting people in the back of the wagon. The sergeant wanted to hear all about my fight the night before. I need to preface the rest of this story by telling you that I'm 5'3" on a good day with the right shoes, and at the time I weighed 140 pounds. It was then that the sergeant also noticed the broken window in the wagon. My partner immediately seized the opportunity to spin a good story. With the wagon full of prisoners he looked at Sarge and said, "You heard what Amy did to the wagon last night, right?"

Sarge shook his head.

My partner said, "We were at that fire, and Amy got so pissed she brought over one of the prisoners and, BAM! Slammed his head into the window a couple times and, POW! The window shatters." I couldn't help but smile, but I didn't deny a thing, especially in front of the prisoners.

We drove the prisoners into the sally port of the jail, and I opened the doors to let them out. The man closest to the door as I opened it was about 6'5". He looked me up and down and said, "You're a feisty one, ain't ya?" And so the legend of "Shorty White" was born. I wouldn't get the nickname for another year, once I had my own beat. If you were to go to Southwest Atlanta and ask around, I'd be willing to bet they can still tell you Shorty White stories.

That was all it took with the guys I worked with, now they knew if they needed back up, I could handle myself. I was the only woman on my shift of twenty plus officers, working evening watch, 2-10 p.m. Unfortunately, I came under fire with all of the supervisors and was nearly written up for NOT hitting the woman back. I was sat down by both my female sergeants and counseled about not being afraid to hit someone because in the academy they filled our heads with all this liability stuff, and that maybe I was afraid to . . . blah, blah, blah.

I tried to explain over and over that it wasn't anything like that. I was surrounded by about thirty women, and my partner just took off running after his perp. Had I punched her back, I would have been on the bottom of a pile with back-up, well, who knows where. No one else was there; they don't know the circumstances or what was going through my head. I will forever maintain that I did exactly the right thing, given the circumstances.

The story has a very comical end to it. About a month later, I was dragged into Internal Affairs (IA) on a "Use of Force" complaint. Eight people went to IA to complain about me. With my union rep at my side I told my story, and when I finished not only was I exonerated, but I was basically told that deadly force would have been justified.

Karla Rodriguez

considers her life to be a message. Times were tough for Karla, growing up in a single parent household with many siblings. The family struggled with poverty, addictions and even just evolving. With bronze skin, almond shaped eyes, and dark hair, even body image was an issue for her. Everything from molestation to unfortunate circumstances marked her life and the lives of the people around her. Karla found a way to move forward and use her circumstances as the foundation for a passion for life.

Karla is a 16-year veteran of the Hartford, Connecticut Police Department and is considered an expert in gang violence. After being a patrol officer, she was promoted to detective and assigned first to the Major Crimes Division, and later to the Intelligence Division, which is assigned to investigate serious crimes related to gangs and firearms. Karla was promoted to sergeant and assigned to the patrol division. She later supervised the Street Crimes Unit. She is presently the supervisor of the Police Activities League (PAL), a job she refers to as "God's work."

Karla is also a certified physical fitness instructor and holds many other certifications. She is an active member of the Hartford Police Awards committee and an adjunct instructor at the police academy, outside police agencies and dance schools. She is the former President of the Connecticut Association of Women Police. She holds a B.S. in Business Management and a Master's Degree in Public Policy. Karla began a small business named Sudor Taino, based on the ideology of "Fitness and Life with Passion," one she considers to be the most valuable legacy she can foster in her 9-year old daughter.

In her late thirties and close to retirement from the police department, she describes her life effortlessly: a delicious partner, a budding daughter, an awesome support network of yummy family and friends, a blessed home, a rewarding job and a life with a purpose. Karla's goal is to contribute to the progress of humankind by continuing to touch the lives of everyone around her. For more info visit www.sudortaino.com

24

God's Work

by Karla Rodriguez

God has blessed me with so many things. I have been able to work for a city police department for 16 years, and remain in one piece. Even with the internal politics and rough streets, I have continued to evolve as a person. The calls for service, undercover work, homicide investigations, search warrants, task forces, gang expertise, community interaction, chases and proving myself, are exactly what I signed up for. All the on-the-job experiences make me who I am, and silences the naysayers along the way.

Working in the same city I grew up in allowed me to have, in some ways, an inside track. I knew where the bootleggers and hot spots were, and where they sold Icees on a hot day for only a quarter. I knew where the prostitutes gathered, and I knew how to spot the crusty men who came to pick them up. Growing up, I was shipped out to camp every summer so I wouldn't hang out with the wrong crowd. For the most part, that strategy worked. Deep down inside, I wanted to fight crime because I also knew so many good people who lived in the city and were vulnerable to the criminal element. In addition, I knew I would look hot in a uniform – you know the gun and the whole bit, it was me.

I have found love in my daughter and my ex-partner, and discovered how to love myself. I am a cop, but I am also a fitness instructor who sneaks in motivation and inspiration.

Yeah, that's right, motivation to always look my best and never forget where I came from and where I have yet to go. Having seen the dangers of alcohol and drug addiction has been my inspiration to stay away from them. Witnessing crime was my motivation to become a cop. Seeing what having no aspirations did to people, caused me to excel in school. Seeing how raggedy people look or how fake they can be, made me want to be real from the inside out. Watching women get passed over for a job, even if they are qualified for it, made me try to succeed all the more.

Women in blue must almost have to bathe in Vaseline to ensure everything that happens to them slides right off. And then another bath with sensuous smelling body wash to remove it. After running around to pick up my daughter, getting homework done, taking her to dance class and teaching at the gym, just maybe I will have a chance to do something for mama – like sit in my Zen room and meditate, or just breathe out the daily grind frustration. On most days, by the looks of me, my honey doesn't know what I have been through and I can concentrate on his exhausting day. It's the yin and the yang of life, and the same concept that applies to any relationship.

Keeping it fresh sometimes requires that I put on what I call "my off-duty gun belt." I always keep my gun on it, but I also include lip gloss, high heels, body spray, tweezers, hair products and matching undergarments. I really never hang up the off duty gun belt; I just select the tools that I need on it throughout the day. On the weekend (because I have most weekends off now!), I never take it off. With my close knit group of friends (more like sisters) and family, it's pretty easy to keep myself in check. We call ourselves the yummy girls, and we will call each other out if one of us steps out of line. The talk would go something like this, "Hell no, that was so not yummy and delicious!"

At least this gun belt doesn't weigh 40 pounds plus the

weight of my bullet proof vest. There's nothing like it on a hot day when the vest is riding up like a bad girdle, and the sweat is being rubbed in by it. Or that pain you get from wearing your gun belt during an eight hour standing post, pain that attacks you right in the center of your back and feels like labor! Who thought of those dark uniforms and tie? Certainly, not a woman. In most cases, a woman would make sure the attire worn by police officers would be multi-functional. You know, look good, be comfortable and provide an easier way for us to use the bathroom.

It's always comical when the arrestees try to pick you up. When you take them to booking and they are searched, you see that their socks have crusted to their feet causing a foul odor to emanate. Female officers are always tested, particularly someone who is five foot three and a half, like me, although, I feel strong and feel I have the command presence of a man who is six foot three. Eighty-five percent of being a police officer is learning how to communicate with the community. The other fifteen percent, well you might have to use some type of justified force. My field training officer gave me good advice to live by: "When you go in like a lamb, you are justified, if need be, to come out like a lion." This is when he started talking to me. Back then, training officers didn't volunteer for the training job, they were told, "You are training her." He didn't want to train anyone, let alone a chick, but after a serious bar fight where I stepped up to the plate, he and other police officers offered a wealth of knowledge about the job.

In the words of a famous lieutenant, cops are doing "God's work." With only one year on the job, I assisted a fellow officer in trying to get a man out of the car: he had just finished raping a 13-year old girl. In a nutshell, he wasn't going to succeed. I reached into the vehicle to get the keys out of the ignition and my arm got tangled in the steering wheel as he put the vehicle in gear and it began to move forward. I felt the gravel under my feet and thought, God, I am not ready to die. My partner grabbed my available arm and yanked me free, severing all of the tendons in my left arm. He saved my life, but he was hit by the vehicle right after he saved me. We both survived by the grace of God.

Can you imagine being in the middle of a parade in an undercover capacity to combat gun violence and somehow, nine people are shot? One of them, a known gang banger, dies in your arms. And another is a seven year old boy who is shot in the head. I watched a fellow officer take off his shirt and wrap it around the boy's head, carry him 100 yards to where I was standing in front of an ambulance. The EMT was in shock in the middle of the chaos, and I had to scream at her to get into the ambulance to care for the child. The same officer had to commandeer the ambulance to get to the hospital so the boy could be saved. Our training took over, but we could hardly deny feeling God's presence as we saw the vulnerability of people.

How about conducting surveillance on a perpetrator with a gun, surrounding him, and he winds up firing at the group of detectives? When I heard the shots ring out, recognized the cross fire and saw the bullet enter the hood of the undercover car I was ducking behind, all I could say was, "God, thank you for sparing our lives."

Today, as a sergeant I am in charge of nurturing the lives of inner city children, showing them alternatives to criminal activity. All of my work, degrees, experience, training and life to this point have prepared me for this work. I am ready to take this responsibility God has tasked me with. I am not afraid of being who I am a knowledgeable, experienced woman who believes we must show up in life motivated and ready to move humanity in a positive direction. I will remain a woman humbled by her life, one who is not ashamed to wear two gun belts; it is a legacy I will pass on to my eight-year old daughter, whom I love to pieces.

Violet Orchowski

was born and raised in Chicago, Illinois. In 1972 she began her career as a police officer with the Chicago Police Department. In 1994, after 22 years with the department, she retired. She and her husband, Jim Mikos, moved to Grayslake, Illinois, where she currently resides.

Violet has worked as an accountant, substitute teacher, and stockbroker. She is a member of the Exchangettes of Grayslake, the Prairie Patch Quilt Guild and she volunteers with the AARP Tax-Aide Program.

She enjoys traveling, gardening and walks with her dog.

25

How It Happened

by Violet Orchowski

When had it all started? When my Dad made Mom give the cap gun away? When I met the cops in the lawyers' office where I worked? When had the pieces started coming together?

How did I become a cop? It was a joke. I worked for a law firm in downtown Chicago. Occasionally, a police officer would come in, and, being the only secretary, we would talk. One of them mentioned I would make a good policewoman. Yeah, right. A twenty-seven-year-old female from the southwest side of Chicago does not become a policewoman—a secretary, nurse, or school teacher, maybe, but not a policewoman. I didn't even know who my alderman was, and if I had a thousand dollars I wouldn't use it to become a cop.

A few weeks after chatting with one of the police officers, I found a card on my desk. It was an application for the position of policewoman in the City of Chicago. Very funny. After shoving the card around my desk for a week or two, I actually read it. For five bucks I could take the exam. What the heck, why not see how the game's played?

I got tired of working for lawyers who were taking me for granted. So, on June 3, 1972, I took the written exam for policewoman. Then I got a job at one of the largest law firms in the city. I interviewed for the position of legal secretary, but they needed someone to input data for a computer program they had purchased. Seeing that I was working on a degree in math at Northwestern University in the evening, they offered me that position, and I accepted it.

My office was right in the corner, just past the partners' offices. They had recently allowed their secretaries to wear pantsuits, but they must have cringed seeing me in my denim pantsuit and other hippie styles. However, since no one in the firm wanted to do data entry and the billing had to get done, they tolerated me.

One morning, Miss Dugan, the Office Manager, called me into her office and told me to close the door. *Uh, oh, I'm in trouble.* "You've been taking exams." she said. One of the partners was reading the newspaper on the train that morning and saw the results of the Policewoman's exam (his daughter had taken the exam) and my name was number seven on the list.

I didn't know what to say. Just like the department to publish the results without notifying the parties involved. I was speechless. She pretty much told me to go for it. I told her I would think about it, and if I decided to follow up, I would give the firm two weeks' notice.

Well, in typical Chicago Police Department fashion, I received a letter on Wednesday, October 25, 1972, telling me to report the following Monday to be sworn in as a Probationary Policewoman. I took the letter to Miss Dugan. Later that day I was given my Christmas bonus (two weeks' pay) and their best wishes.

Classes were held at the old Training Academy at 720 West O'Brien Street in the heart of the old Maxwell Street market. It was a very old three-story building with warped floors and creaky doors. Rumor had it the building was used as a hospital during the Civil War; that wasn't hard to believe. It was like being back in high school again with various classes Monday through Friday and even a homeroom.

I'll never forget the restaurants and fruit stands – corned beef sandwiches at the Vienna Beef outlet store, steak tacos right off the grill, cafeteria style lunches at Manny's, and, of course, the Fannie May candy factory: Crenshaw melons, sugar cane, and St. John's bread. It makes my mouth water just remembering. Oh, the classes. Eighteen weeks of Reporting, Code of Ethics, Law, Sociology, Law Enforcement, First Aid, Defensive Tactics, Investigations, Rules of Evidence, etc.

One Thursday, they issued our gun permits and told us we had to have our weapons by the following Monday. I went downtown to Abercrombie & Fitch and picked out a .38 caliber Colt Detective Special. The clerk went to her manager, and I could clearly hear him say, "Tell her she can wait until Monday to pick up the gun for her boyfriend." I then went up to them and pointed out the permit was in my name, at which time they rang up the sale.

The shooting range was quite an experience. I doubt if any of us had ever discharged a weapon before, and you could tell. With the noise and gunpowder, we all left looking a little green around the edges.

We spent one shift in the Woman's Lockup at 11th & State Streets. Those jail bars are a lot more intimidating in real life. We had to leave our weapons before going inside with the prisoners. While learning the procedures, one prostitute told me, "That's okay, honey. I'll do that," as she was fingerprinting herself. She had more experience at it than I did.

While at the academy, we attended a talk about the St. Jude League. Other law enforcement agencies also attend the academy, so some of those officers were also in attendance. Sitting in front of me was a Cook County Sheriff's Deputy. Some law enforcement officers take extreme pride in their appearance – tailored uniform, sewn-in crease, etc. This particular officer was one of those meticulous dressers. However, when I looked down I noticed he was wearing a

Mickey Mouse watch – completely out of character. I lost it and laughed out loud.

After graduation on March 23, 1973, I was assigned to Area 5 Youth, located on the 2nd floor of the 14th District, the Shakespeare station, on the northwest side of the city. It seemed like all the police stations in Chicago were creaky, old, overcrowded buildings and the Shakespeare station was no exception.

We went in for roll call, got our assignments, mostly follow-ups from the districts, and started making calls. We worked at finding missing girls, investigating child abuse and/or neglect cases, and guarding female prisoners. Linnie Price and I, also a new policewoman, often worked together. We must have been quite an odd pair. Linnie was a single, black mother of two girls, slight of stature, who learned to drive to become a policewoman. I was a single, white woman, taller than average. But we worked well together. Area 5 covered the 14th (Hispanic, European immigrant), 15th (Black), 16th (middle class White), and 17th (Appalachian) districts. We even went into the Wooden Nickel, a notorious Native American bar looking for a runaway girl. We got plenty of stares, but they were polite to us.

One day as we were walking down the stairs, we encountered Tony, who had been in the academy when we were. He had an abandoned baby that he was turning over to Youth Division. The irony was that he and his wife had two children, but I had never handled children, other than at my godson's christening. And there he was, turning this child over to me. Fortunately, the placement was only until we could arrange placement with Children and Family Services.

We got a call to assist a domestic violence victim. It was a mother and young son who needed a place to stay. After many calls, the Salvation Army shelter had room, so we took them there. What a warm, caring atmosphere we encountered. The young boy was immediately attracted to the resident dog. The manager told us residents were families with children and stayed no longer than thirty days, at which time they got them into an apartment and into a job and/or training.

One of us got a warrant for a runaway girl. We went to talk to the mother and saw the girl running out the back. After a chase down the block she got away from us. However, after talking with the mother, we realized we were being used as bad guys and this was some kind of silly game mother and daughter were playing. When we got back to the station to type up our reports, we asked a couple of the male youth officers if they would assist us the next time we went to the house.

It was a quiet, rainy Sunday when we got a call from the mother that Sandra was at the house. The youth officers were available, so they went around the back with their unmarked car and waited for us to go to the front. Sure enough, as we talked to the mother in front, Sandra ran out the back, right into the waiting arms of the youth officers. The mother begged us to let her dry her off, to give her shoes, to talk to her, all to no avail. We had had enough of being played for fools. In the station, we tried to explain to Sandra all she had to do was finish high school. She would be an adult and she could go where and when she wanted. Of course, we got that typical teenage look that says, "Yeah, I've heard this all before".

We sent her to the Audy Home for juveniles, minus shoes, I might add. A number of months later, we went in for check-off roll call, and there was Sandra. The first thought going through my mind was, what kind of trouble is she in now. Thankfully, I didn't say it because she had come in to tell us that she had gone to summer school, was now in her senior year, and would graduate with her class. She thanked us for setting her straight. I was very surprised, to put it mildly.

Another time I got a call of "abandoned children." A baker had rented the back cottage to a woman with two children.

That morning, he heard a child crying for a long time so he went to investigate and found the children alone. As I and the patrol officers were removing the baby girl and toddler boy, the mother appeared. She was arrested and the children turned over to IDCFS (Illinois Department of Children and Family Services). About six months later, I was notified to appear at an adoption hearing. I learned the boy was sent to live with family in Puerto Rico. The baby girl was adopted by a couple from Des Plaines who were unable to have children. A happy ending to a sad story.

June of 1974 marked my thirtieth birthday. That year the department asked for female volunteers for a pilot program in the Patrol Division. Until that time, women did not work in patrol. While the policewomen assigned to the Youth Division wore uniforms and drove around in marked squad cars, the men wore plainclothes and drove unmarked cars. The men had to take an exam to become youth officers (detectives) and make detective pay. I decided to volunteer for the Patrol Division. My partner, Linnie, did not volunteer for patrol and stayed in the Youth Division. On our last day working together, she asked for our list of preferred eating places in the area, which I was glad to give her. My last assignment in the Youth Division was the 4th of July Celebration at Soldiers Field.

There were fourteen of us – seven policewomen and seven female recruits - who had volunteered. On July 8, 1974, we appeared at the Training Academy for two weeks of Patrol Function Orientation.

We had to have new uniforms, for our old uniform was a skirt and a beret with a button shield instead of the usual policeman's hat.

I was assigned to the 16th District – Gale Street, or the Jefferson Park station. It was a quiet district on the northwest side of Chicago. Obviously the department never anticipated having women in patrol. The Gale Street station was an old stone building with the locker room in the basement—exclusively male. Lockers were put into a small bathroom at the bottom of the stairs for us. One evening after checkoff roll call, I walked down the stairs and heard from the open door of the men's locker room, right next to ours, "Watch it, Orchowski's coming," and, "If she hasn't seen it by now, it's about time," to the sight of an officer's bare backside.

On July 25, 1974, I bought my house on North Mulligan Avenue in Chicago. Chicago police officers are required to reside in the city. When I went to Liberty Savings and Loan for the closing, one of their employees approached me and asked if I knew what I was doing. In those days, single women did not buy homes by themselves. In fact, on the closing papers I was listed as a "spinster" (a single female). How's that for an ego crusher?

Two burglary detectives were kind enough to volunteer to move me from my apartment in New Town to the house. It was an old common brick bungalow built in the 40s. Two styles were built by the WPA (Works Progress Administration): the Cape Cod and the Georgian. My house was a two-story Cape Cod. The rooms were all small by today's standards, although it did have four bedrooms. It was kind of a fixer-upper. In other words, it needed a lot of work, but it was a house I could afford. One day I was up on an extension ladder painting the fascia when an unmarked squad car pulled up and a detective yelled, "Isn't that taking women's lib too far?"

Another day I had been cleaning the kitchen, was exhausted, and just sat down on the floor and cried. What had I gotten myself into? Was this more than I could handle? With help from "Ace, the Helpful Hardware Place" and fellow officers, I eventually turned a house into a home.

Elizabeth Gibson

Columbus, Ohio, received her bachelor's degree from a Big Ten University and then went on to become a police officer with the Columbus Police Department (CPD).

She considers the day she received her letter of acceptance into the academy as a monumental one in her life because she is the only member of her family to enter into law enforcement. She has been serving with the CPD the past six years, five of which have been in patrol on the north side of the city.

In her spare time, Elizabeth enjoys competing in soccer and softball. She participated in a charity soccer game at MLS Columbus Crew Stadium to raise money for Get Behind The Badge, an organization whose purpose is to provide for fallen officers' families waiting for benefits from line-of-duty deaths. She cherishes time spent with her family and her two year old German shepherd.

Many officers have goals they want to reach throughout their career. She achieved one of her goals very early on in her career when she became one of only two female officers ever certified as patrol rifle operators. Elizabeth believes the keys to becoming a great police officer begin with a foundation of self-discipline, integrity, a strong work ethic, and confidence in knowing who you are as a person. She is confident that if you value these principles first, the end result will be a great officer.

Foot Chaser and Comforter

by Elizabeth Gibson

In five short years as an Ohio police officer, I have experienced many trials. Having to prove myself almost daily is a reality while working in a male dominated field. Male officers are taller, stronger, and faster. Most females are at a disadvantage in physical confrontations. However, we are able to talk and sympathize with most people, a trait everyone should develop in his or her career in law enforcement.

One cold winter night, I was working late in an inner-city precinct. I was dispatched to a burglary in progress. Several officers were en route, but because of the ice and snow covered roads, response time was slower than normal. A male officer and I arrived together and approached the house.

Instantly, we saw several individuals run out of the back of the house, and we gave pursuit. My partner officer ran after two suspects who stayed together; I ran after the third. All of us wound up slipping and sliding everywhere. For six long minutes, I pursued my bad guy between houses, through yards, and over fences for several city blocks. My heart was pounding and my chest burned from breathing in the frigid night air. Nonetheless, I kept the suspect in sight.

The fleeing felon spotted a cruiser approaching through an alley just to his south. He hid, waiting for the officer to pass, and then ran north between the houses—heading right toward me! Secreted between two houses, I patiently watched because the would-be burglar was unable to see me. Summoning my last bit of energy, I chased him down, tackled him in the snow, and handcuffed him.

Exhausted and defeated, the two suspects who ran from the male officer simply stopped when ordered. My sense is that because a female was pursuing him, my suspect assumed he could escape. Although it's hard to predict the outcome of a given situation, on that night running from a police "woman" was the wrong choice.

*****

One Christmas Eve night, several officers were dispatched to a report of an armed robbery and stolen vehicle. A description of the vehicle and the suspect was broadcast. In this case our suspect was a female. The transmission drew us in because females rarely commit armed robbery.

As officers saturated the area, one of us observed the stolen car at an intersection about a half-mile away from where the robbery occurred. Officers pursued the suspect who had stopped and then took off in the car again. I was driving the fourth cruiser in the pursuit when the suspect spun out and crashed into a guardrail. As is the case with many stolen vehicle chases, the suspect fled on foot. Keeping the female robbery suspect in sight, I pursued cautiously. We ran down a snow-covered ravine, through a creek, and back up the other side. I saw the woman emerge from the trees and into a clearing that was adjacent to an apartment complex.

Frightened and intent on escaping, she ran toward the apartments closest to her and disappeared between the buildings. I followed, carefully, and as I emerged from around the corner of the building, I saw her banging on an apartment door. With my weapon drawn, I ordered the suspect to stop and get on the ground, but she ignored my commands and took off running. She ran into the parking lot and tried to hide among the cars.

As I cautiously searched, I spotted the woman as she got up and began to flee again. I took up the pursuit and cut her off, finally tackling her like an NFL linebacker. Thankfully, another officer arrived to help handcuff her.

The moral of the story? Officers, male or female, need to have the drive, stamina and courage to chase after suspects who could be armed.

*****

As a police officer, the public expects you to be a mediator, counselor, nurse, problem solver, and miracle worker. Emotions can run high when a cop is dispatched to a location and find, more often than not, the circumstances are not the best. Charging into one of these less than ideal situations, like "Mr. Macho" with muscles bulging, is not always helpful. Being empathetic and showing people you care and want to help almost always solves the problem.

I was dispatched to assist a six-year-old child who was not breathing. When I arrived, paramedics had her in the back of the ambulance and were about to transport her to the hospital. I spoke with the mother who told me her daughter was autistic and had suffered a seizure. Once we arrived at the hospital, the mother further explained that when the little girl was younger, she had a traumatic childhood, causing her to have these health problems.

My cousin is autistic so I was able to sympathize with the woman, knowing what she was experiencing. This caring mother had no family in the area. She told me she was waiting on her neighbors to come to the hospital to comfort her. I had no idea how long that would take, but I waited with her. When her neighbors finally arrived, I left.

Several months later, I returned to that mother's house to see how her daughter was doing. I knocked on the door and the grandmother opened it. She did not know why I was there, but when the mother came to the door and saw that it was me, she started crying. She was grateful that I was following up on her daughter and for having spent time with her during that traumatic time. Her daughter was doing just fine, she told me, and she gave me a picture of her daughter who had just graduated from kindergarten. She invited me to watch the video of the graduation, and we took a few pictures while I was there. I thanked them, wished them well, and then left.

Encounters like this one lift the heart and reinforce the feeling that officers have chosen the right profession. One rewarding experience negates most of the bad ones and strengthens the faith that officers need to have that most people are basically good.

Part Two:

Dispatchers

Tired Dispatcher (TD)

is a blog writer with many years dispatching experience. Beginning as an Explorer Scout at age 16, TD has worked for the Highway Patrol, County Sheriff, City Police, and College Police into her 50s. Following her law enforcement husband around the state has given her an opportunity to work and experience large and small agencies, each having its own needs and quirks.

TD balances the stress of working hour upon hour, year after year, immersed in trauma and drama, by volunteering in her community. "If you're not part of the solution, you're part of the problem," is her mantra. By volunteering with the Boy Scouts, Lions Club, and a non-profit to benefit foster children, she has learned what it takes for her to cope with the pressure and strain in the career of law enforcement dispatching.

TD still loves the challenge of being the first back up for officers and the first line of help for citizens. She knows retirement will happen one day, but still feels she has much to offer law enforcement and the citizens she serves.

27

Musings of a Police Dispatcher

by Tired Dispatcher

Few people have any idea about the critical role dispatchers play in police work. They are usually treated like the ugly stepchild of the family. Frequently, they are Monday morning quarterbacked by people who have little or no clue regarding the stress dispatchers work under while being blind to callers yet hearing so much . . . sometimes too much.

I believe long serving experienced dispatchers develop a super power: extraordinary hearing. Not unlike people who have lost their sight, we don't get to use our eyes to observe the body language of someone who is nervous, lying, frightened, or hurt. But we do hear the nuances and different tones with our superior trained hearing that others would not. That unique ability has saved lives by bringing help when needed, as well as caught some callers who were not providing full information. I am very proud to be a member of such a special community.

In the following pages I will share some of the experiences that stand out in my mind during my many years of serving as a police dispatcher.

The Gall of Some People

Every so often, a single phone call makes you sit back in your chair and wonder about the gall of some people. Here's an example:

A female calls 9-1-1, screaming mad that her daughter's school is refusing to allow the child's father (her husband) to attend their daughter's junior high school graduation. Further questioning reveals the following: The father has been arrested for assaulting school staff on school grounds and damaging school property. In fact, he has an outstanding warrant for those charges.

I tell the woman, "Okay ma'am. So you want the school to reward his bad behavior at the very same place where he created the problem, just so he can watch his daughter graduate from junior high school, all the while knowing he has this warrant that is over a year old?"

Her reply, minus the dramatic sighs, yelling, and lack of non-cursing verbal skills, was that the school staff was being rude and unprofessional, and it just wasn't right. She even suggested to the school that they have their daughter graduate within the first half hour of the ceremony so the husband can leave early, rather than stay for the entire graduation.

Clearly this woman is living in la-la land to think a school is going to rewrite their graduation program to accommodate a man who has little self-control and who lacks ownership for his bad behavior by not satisfying the warrant.

The icing on the cake? The caller has her own outstanding warrant for . . . drum roll . . . assault and vandalism.

Cell Phones

Seems like everybody owns one, some of them are even advertised as being "smart." Too bad their owners aren't.

"9-1-1, what is your emergency?"

"Oh, you mean I can call 9-1-1 from my cell phone?"

"Yes, sir, just like your home phone. Do you have an emergency?"

'No, just wanted to know what I can do with my cell phone."

"9-1-1, what is your emergency?"

Baby babble.

"Hi baby. Where is mama? Say mama."

Baby babble.

"Say mama, baby. Where is mama?"

"What are you doing with my phone? Give it back to me."

Hang up.

Call back.

"Hello?"

"Hi, ma'am. This is 9-1-1. Your baby was playing with your cell phone and called 9-1-1. Is everything all right?"

"Lady, you crazy. He's only six months old. How he gonna call 9-1-1?"

"On many cell phones it is very easy to dial 9-1-1 by mistake. We just call back to make sure everything is alright."

"My baby did not call 9-1-1, and you're wastin' my time."

Hang up.

"9-1-1. What is your emergency?"

"My boyfriend won't let me see my baby."

"Is he there right now ma'am?"

"No. He left a couple days ago with my baby. I want my baby back."

"Ma'am, 9-1-1 is for life and death emergencies. Please call our non-emergency line."

"This is an emergency. He won't let me have my baby back."

"Is there a custody order ma'am?"

"A what? What for? I'm the mother. I'm here right now to pick up my baby, and he won't let me in."

"Is the baby his?"

"Yeah. So what? I'm the mother. I'm the one who takes care of him."

"We cannot take the child away from him. I suggest you go to the courthouse and file for custody."

"I want my baby back!"

"Ma'am, if you have any questions please call our non-emergency line. Better yet, head to the courthouse to file for custody, you don't even need an attorney."

"You have to do something or I will."

"Ma'am, please think before you do anything. Get yourself some legal advice."

"What good are the police if they can't help?"

Conclusion: The police were dispatched to that location to arrest the mother for assault and vandalism against the baby's father and his apartment.

Cell phones can be helpful; they're a great tool. At times I can't imagine living without mine, but I wish that most citizens would also be smart when using their smart phones.

Michelle Perin

 spent seven and a half years as a police telecommunications operator with the City of Phoenix, Arizona, Police Department. Married to a Phoenix officer, she gained personal insight into the dynamics of the occupation and its struggles. She holds a Master's degree in Criminology and Criminal Justice from Indiana State University and has been published in numerous law enforcement publications including *Law Enforcement Technology*, *Law & Order* and *Police Magazine*. She writes two monthly columns for *Officer.com*, one on communications/police life and one on juvenile justice. She currently works at Jasper Mountain, a psychiatric residential treatment facility for severely traumatized children. Michelle enjoys spending time with her two adolescent sons, watching ice hockey, volunteering at the local ferret shelter and playing her bass.

Best Wishes!

28

A Dispatcher, a Wife

by Michelle Perin

Marc Todd Atkinson was murdered on March 26, 1999. Gunned down sitting in his car, on a clear, balmy evening in Phoenix's West Side.

"You have an officer down," the man yelled into the phone. "He's shot! There's another guy chasing the shooter. He has a gun too."

My fingers flew over my keyboard, adding the information into the already expanding 9-1-1 call screen.

"Which direction did they run?" I asked, my voice sounding far away, as if echoing through fiberglass batting in my head. I felt like I was projecting my voice, and it bounced back at me through an ocean of maple syrup. The man on the phone had the same skills, his voice distant and foggy as he described the shooter's clothing.

"He's dead you know," the man on the phone said into my ear. "Your officer, he's dead."

My mind wanted to shut down upon hearing those words. I had been a police telecommunications operator for just under a year, and this call was my worst nightmare. I couldn't produce enough saliva, and my tongue felt glued to the roof of my mouth. Pounding waves replaced gentler ones, our voices flowed through, and my stomach lurched in time with the rhythm. My mind turned to pictures of my own husband. Three years had passed since the night he took the oath, and I pinned his badge on him. As the man on the phone continued to give me updates, my mind continued its journey away from this situation. Only my fingers continued to do their job.

*****

"Michelle, I need you in radio," my supervisor's words came over the same shoulder her hand softly rested on. I quickly clicked off the 9-1-1 phone, stripped off my headset, and shoved all my papers into my black canvas dispatch bag. I completed cross-training several months ago and was on my own in radio, but I still felt butterflies every time I plugged in.

"Take the console behind Teresa and pick up Channel 12 for her," she said, as I passed by the supervisor's console, crossing over to the radio side of the room. Three sets of eyes watched me as I went.

The tone hit me right away like a wall of glass. All the voices rising into the air had the urgent professionalism of an emergency situation. Good dispatchers enter into crisis mode well, their voices becoming a steady, calm and controlled monotony of commands washing over the flurry of officers engaged in a crazy, often violent situation in the field. The voices are a link, a security blanket wrapped around the officers reassuring them, promising them their pleas will be heard and their needs met.

I walked into the blanket of voices hearing only one side of the conversation, echoes of my memories helping fill in the words on the other side.

"Hey, what's up?" I asked putting my bag down and plugging the other end of my radio headset in the console behind Teresa. I adored Teresa. She had taught me many things both on-duty and off.

"I'm moving Channel 12 traffic to Channel 2."

I reached over and punched the button for Channel 2 on the

giant black board displaying dozens of buttons, each a link to a group of radios and officers on the other end. I was now live.

"Channel 2 is now open for regular Channel 12 traffic," I said, depressing the pedal under my bare foot. My black high heel rested beside the pedal and I spread my toes out enjoying the freedom under the desk. Teresa echoed me at my back, "All regular Channel 12 traffic switch to Channel 2. 422I, your traffic remains here."

My brain processed the unit number and a voice burst into my ear.

"T357, run a plate?"

"T357, go ahead," I said, trying to reassure myself Teresa was in control, and things would be okay. She was a good dispatcher. I punched in the vehicle information my motor gave me and repeated back what ACIC/NCIC popped up on my screen.

A steady stream of requests followed the first one and filled my time. Officers had been waiting to run routine information as the emergency traffic took over Channel 12. Officers made request after request. I gave information to unit after unit, my ears focused on their voices, their needs in the back of my mind while I screamed for an update on 422I. Finally, a lull in traffic occurred, and I turned towards Teresa's screen. My eyes scanned the long list of officers in red, all Code 6 in South Phoenix.

"422I?" Teresa asked. "422I, do you copy?"

Teresa stood up and yelled towards the supervisor's console.

"There's something wrong with the radios."

Sitting back down, she repeated, "422I, you're cutting out. What's your current status?"

I watched her stare at her screen, her forehead crinkled in concentration, her fingers poised over the keyboard.

"Damn it," Teresa said, slamming her hand down on the desk. Involuntarily, I jumped in my seat. I nervously twirled the white gold band with the sapphire solitaire encircling my left ring finger.

"What the hell's wrong with these damn radios?" she yelled. "422I?"

The radio supervisor walked up and stood beside Teresa now. "What's wrong?" she asked.

"700F for info," Teresa's words faded into the background as the voice in my ear took precedence.

"700F, go ahead."

"I need you to run a subject for me."

"10-4 go ahead."

"Last name...Martin...common spell...First name is Jere..., John... Mary..."

"700F, you're cutting out. Try it again," I said, exasperated.

"...they're following a suspicious vehicle, the driver on his cell phone. The car just keeps driving around the block. This is the third time around, and the damn radio keeps cutting out," Teresa said, her voice echoing behind me as I waited for 700F to clear again, the radio silent. My eyes glanced over at the memo sitting on the desk.

Individuals living on the South Side have declared war on the police. Several known gang members have made statements they will shoot any officer they see. They have mentioned Marc Atkinson's death and said they will cause as many deaths as they can.

"422I, copy," Teresa said, her voice dropping even further into crisis-response mode. "Going all call," she yelled into the room.

My blood chilled. 422I was a two-man unit, and going all call meant they were in serious trouble. Neither man riding 422I was prone to hysterics or asking for back-up when they could handle the situation on their own. I was familiar with their style of policing, and it was gritty, matching the hardness of what they experienced in South Phoenix. I knew this personally. One of those men was my husband.

"Shots fired at an officer 48th Street and Hidalgo. Switch over to Channel 12," Teresa's voice filled my ear as well as every headset and radio in the city. She quickly dropped all frequencies but her own.

"For units responding, 422I is at 48th Street and Hidalgo, southbound, following a 1980s beige Lincoln Continental. Their last transmission stated they were being fired at from between two cars. Unknown if the person in the car is firing as well," Teresa updated the responding units. I noticed the tightness in my chest and consciously released the air in my lungs. I sucked some back in, but it lodged in the same place, as if my ears controlled my breathing and were afraid any noise would make them miss something.

"422I, update?" Teresa asked.

"422I?"

"422I?" Desperate exasperation crowded from behind the wall of her controlled monotony.

"Shit."

I heard a batch of static crackle in my ear and then a hollow emptiness. Two dispatchers from different sections of the room stood at the same time, "The radios are down," they each yelled.

The supervisor's phone rang. She picked it up, listened then shouted back, "Towers down. We're off the air.

I looked down at my hands and made myself loosen them. My palms each had four indented moons. I turned toward Teresa. She turned toward me, her eyes sympathetic.

"He's going to be okay," she said softly. "I've prayed and he's going to be okay."

*****

A week later, I stood in our little kitchen in the house we had picked out together. It was our first home, and we were so proud to have been able to buy a piece of the American Dream.

We spent hours poring over paint colors and carpet swatches and tiny pieces of granite and tile. Excitement permeated the apartment we lived in as we waited for our house, our new home to be finished. Never had we felt more in love than when he put the key in and unlocked our front door for the first time and led me and our small son inside.

Now I stood there surrounded by our burnt sand walls, butter cream tiles, and misty morning countertops pouring cereal into a bowl for our four year old son. The sun was out. The sky was blue as usual. I dropped the slates of the white mini-blinds and shut out the cheeriness and the reminder of how life goes on. No matter what has happened--no matter how deep the sorrow or how badly you want the world to stop and let you off, it just keeps moving forward even when you don't want it to.

"Can I have one of these?" asked the little, blue-eyed, tow-head sitting shirtless at the round oak table. I snapped out of my reverie and tried to focus on him. He pointed at the bouquet of cookie flowers the Phoenix Law Enforcement Association had sent over to the house the day before.

"I want the car one," he insisted, reaching for the one shaped like a patrol car, his father's badge number inscribed on it in black frosting.

I reached over, grabbed the little car, and handed it to him. A big smile spread over his face, and he clapped his hands together while his eyes wrinkled in delight. *Wow, he really wants this cookie.* I wish simple things could always bring this much joy. I hoped our son would always hold on to the simple pleasure of a cookie. He waved the little car in the air and giggled. A voice sounded over my shoulder right before a soft kiss brushed my cheek.

"I want the badge one for breakfast," my husband said, reaching over and ruffling the hair on his son's head before taking his seat at the table. He giggled again this time while smashing as much of the patrol car into his mouth as he could. "Of course," I said, taking the badge cookie out of the bouquet. For a moment, my eyes rested on the message written on the card, *Thankful you weren't hurt. All your friends at PLEA.*

Thankful. We all were.

Tired Dispatcher (TD)

is a blog writer with many years dispatching experience. Beginning as an Explorer Scout at age 16, TD has worked for the Highway Patrol, County Sheriff, City Police, and College Police into her 50s. Following her law enforcement husband around the state has given her an opportunity to work and experience large and small agencies, each having its own needs and quirks.

TD balances the stress of working hour upon hour, year after year, immersed in trauma and drama, by volunteering in her community. "If you're not part of the solution, you're part of the problem," is her mantra. By volunteering with the Boy Scouts, Lions Club, and a non-profit to benefit foster children, she has learned what it takes for her to cope with the pressure and strain in the career of law enforcement dispatching.

TD still loves the challenge of being the first back up for officers and the first line of help for citizens. She knows retirement will happen one day, but still feels she has much to offer law enforcement and the citizens she serves.

I'm a Hero Too

By Tired Dispatcher

As much as our local newspaper loves to slam our police officers for every real or imagined slight, they have also been known to acknowledge the good work of these men and women in blue. However, I do wish that dispatchers were remembered and thought of as heroes too.

Imagine sitting in a windowless room surrounded by padded walls that lack any real color and contain a few scattered photo enlargements of outdoor scenes to complete the décor. Imagine also that just three feet away there is another person seated at a console, both of you in chairs not designed for around the clock use. Each of you stare at two or three computer screens in front of you while listening to hour upon hour upon hour of crying, complaining, whining, confusion, panic, pain, fear, anger, drunken conversation, lectures on how to do your job, demands that you do something, language barriers and accents . . . well, you get the picture.

Despite these working conditions, we dispatchers must soothe hurt feelings and extract information from minds not fully functioning due to combinations of alcohol, drugs, fear, and confusion. We're expected to answer questions, many of which should be asked of someone with a legal background (but we're cheaper), give directions, play nursemaid, marriage and/or mental health counselor, phone information operator. . . well, you get the picture.

When working the radio we sometimes deal with an unending list of calls for services that are waiting to be dispatched. Between twelve and seventy officers may be listed as present on my screen, and it is my responsibility to keep them safe and know their location at all times. Officers who are so focused on what they are doing in the field are sometimes not paying attention to the dispatcher, who is also trying to assist twenty other officers. They may continue to talk to the dispatcher or demand more information be researched, while she is assisting another twenty officers and also dispatching calls for service. Trying to understand what the officers are saying while they eat their mikes or yell into them is difficult, and at times we must ask them to repeat because they are speaking much faster than my one hundred plus words per minutes typing skills can keep pace with.

Citizens treat us like nitwits because we tell them we can't do what they are asking. Often the citizens simply do not understand how law enforcement cannot solve overnight a problem they created over years of refusing to deal with an issue. Citizens feel that because we are public servants, our job is to cater to their needs and wants, reasonable or not.

Some officers treat us like we are below their stations in life, that we are only there to satisfy their needs and wants. Some believe that it is our job is to simplify their lives by getting all the necessary information before they arrive and know instinctively what back up or additional equipment is necessary. They think we should have the ability to read minds and know what is happening out there in the field. And heaven forbid a "thank you" or "well done" be uttered more than once or twice a year.

Our supervisors have no problems burdening us with additional responsibilities or cutting back to minimum staffing. They are quick to criticize and very reluctant to praise and acknowledge good work. Thank you's and well done's are even more foreign from that quarter.

Because I put my heart and soul into my job, demonstrating patience, tolerance, intelligence, and skill, interspersed with occasional tears, hour after hour, makes me a Hero, too, dammit.

Not on My Watch

Every so often there is a call that reminds you why you are here and why you love this job.

On this particular day, I played an important role in preventing a woman from committing suicide. She called 9-1-1 to let us know she was preparing to step in front of a train that was due shortly at her chosen location. The woman knew the train schedule and approximately how fast it would be traveling. She called because she wanted us to know so that we could respond quickly and clean up the mess, for which she apologized, so others didn't have to see it or come upon it unexpectedly.

The caller was very matter-of-fact in her demeanor and spoke very calmly. She explained why she felt that ending her life was the best thing to do, how taking too many pills hadn't worked; they just made her sick. Cutting her wrists only gave her some additional scars. Yes, the train would definitely be the fastest and easiest way to do what she felt she needed to do.

I knew I couldn't let that happen; I couldn't fail this woman. Somehow I kept her on the phone, kept her talking. It was probably not my winning personality, but rather my training that took over and allowed me to talk her down until officers arrived on the scene and ensured that she got the help she needed. I recognize that there is a good chance, a very good chance that she will eventually make good her desire to end her life.

Nevertheless, it didn't happen that day on my watch.

9-1-1 Calls

One frustrating waste of time, events we regularly handle as emergency 9-1-1 dispatchers, is dealing with those 9-1-1 calls that aren't emergencies. You know the ones I'm talking about, those 9-1-1 callers who say "Oops, misdial," or the people who give their little kids the cell phone so the kids can push buttons and ruin the hearing of the dispatcher answering the phone as the keypad tones blast in their ears.

I love those callers who, when you call them back to confirm everything is okay after a 9-1-1 hang up or abandoned call, argue with you and demand to know why you're bothering them. Do they honestly believe I am so bored that I dial numbers randomly just to accuse them of falsely calling 9-1-1? How many of you have had this call?

Me: *Hello. Hello.* (Over an open 9-1-1 call)

Caller: Hello? Is there someone on this phone?

Me: *Hello. This is* _____ *Police Department. We received a 9-1-1 call from this cell phone. Is everything okay?*

Caller: Oh my. Yes. Everything is okay. I put my cell phone in my purse/bag/briefcase/backpack (choose one), and it must have accidentally dialed out. I could hear voices yelling "Hello," Was that you?

Me: *Yes sir/madam (choose one again). I am trying to confirm if there is a problem.*

Caller: Well, clearly it was an accident. I just said I heard voices coming from my phone and was answering.

Me: *Yes sir/madam (never mind). I understand about the voices you hear from nowhere. (Okay . . . it is my dream to respond like that.)*

Domestic Violence

This is a hot button for me. My mother was a victim, and I was a victim too of child abuse.

We get calls almost daily from women, and occasionally men (increasingly so), about valid complaints of domestic violence, ranging from pushing to assault with a weapon.

Recently I took a call from an adult son calling on behalf of his mom. She couldn't call us herself because Dad had ripped the phone off the wall, making it impossible for Mom to call for help. She uses a walker to get around, due to the physical damage inflicted upon her from multiple beatings and abuse by her husband over the years.

I won't go over the psychological issue of why women stay in such relationships. My mother did; this caller's mom continues to as well.

What angers me is the lack of prosecution of this "man" (and I hate to use this word for such an addlebrained/dimwitted member of the Homo sapien race) by our County District Attorney. And not just one DA either. According to premise history, this man has been arrested numerous times for domestic violence, spanning at least three different DA terms.

In our state, a victim (not all domestic violence victims are women) does not have to file a complaint like they did during my mother's era. If an officer observes physical evidence of assault, the suspect is arrested and can then be prosecuted without the victim needing to testify. When this law was enacted, a lot of law enforcement and victim advocates danced happily in the streets.

However, for some reason our County DA has a problem following through on prosecuting domestic violence suspects. A quick online search of the County Criminal Courts shows a very high percentage of cases seem to be plea-bargained down. This particular man has been arrested numerous times, yet spends little county jail time and goes home to repeat the cycle.

I wonder how many people convicted of domestic violence are actually in our prison system. This perpetrator should be one of those inmates who enjoy the rent free, first run movies, superb medical and dental coverage, and free gym equipment access residence provided by our state and funded by my tax dollars. But for some reason our County DAs just let him go home again and again with only a slap on the wrist.

Super Power Hearing

If you dispatch for any length of time, you develop a very special super power. Over time, your hearing enables you to read the subtle verbal messages from callers, a superior skill that comes from experience. Since we don't have the opportunity to read the person's body language by observing a caller, something an officer is able to do, we hear differently.

I recently took a 9-1-1 hang up call. When I called back to confirm everything was okay, following our policy of having the person on the other side of the call confirm their address and phone number, I heard a male on the phone sniffing and muttering, saying a child had made a mistake. However, when I asked the man about the child, he replied that the child was already gone. Furthermore, the man didn't know the address and phone number.

My antennae immediately went up. The man's demeanor and avoidance, as well as his constant repetition of the phrase, "It's a mistake," set off an internal alarm in me that had been forged through years of experience. It told me that something was off center and needed attention. A call for service was created, and officers were sent. I sent a note to the responding officers that something sounded hinky, and so they said they'd check it out.

Lo and behold, what did officers find, but a domestic violence situation with the suspect male trying to hide from officers. He was in violation of a restraining order and on probation, so this visit by the police meant a pair of silver bracelets were gifted to his wrists and a free ride to the county jail where he was booked. A return to the state funded country club to complete his original sentence loomed ahead of him, all due to domestic violence and assault.

The officers were very good about not shrugging off my gut reaction to the call. They took me seriously and it paid off. Now, the only problem is how does a dispatcher explain this super power articulately in court, yet make it simple enough to be understood?

Dispatchers are Human

The person answering that 9-1-1 call or working the police channel is human. As such, he or she is susceptible to all the frailties that race may suffer.

Hour after hour, call after call, we hear overwhelming human emotion on the phone.. We listen to scared, hurting, confused, angry, and upset people. After all, why would people call 9-1-1, or even the non-emergency phone number, if they didn't have a problem they figure the police can or should handle?

We sit at the radio for hours on end assisting officers who want or need information quickly. Not just two or three officers, but at times as many as fifty plus officers who need to be dispatched to an event that is pending, to a disposition that needs to be taken, to run wants and warrants, to research, to premise history, to log-in traffic stops, etcetera, all at the same time. Officers get snippy when information isn't returned to them in what they consider an expeditious manner, not paying attention to the fact that several other officers also need assist/information/dispatch/etcetera from that same dispatcher.

It all means that the dispatcher must deal with their emotions in a manner that, hopefully, isn't affecting their level of service.

Dispatchers must consciously work at not snipping at the officer who wants to know why we haven't given him a complete wants and warrants and probation history requested for five different people, just after another officer asked for contact background on a suspect of a domestic violence in progress call he is en route to, while detectives are asking for a wagon to transport their prisoner since they are driving unmarked vehicles and thus don't have cages in their units.

We try not to get too exasperated at a caller who is calling for the fourth time that month about his/her out of control teenager who is mouthing off, again. Or the caller who calls 9-1-1 because they find their car has been broken into and doesn't understand why it isn't an emergency.

This job exposes us to other people at their most raw, emotional state of life. We hear women being beaten by their loved one while children cry in the background, or a neighbor calls in that the parents are disciplining their kids again. We listen to a father crying because he is trapped in his vehicle after an accident, and his baby isn't crying. We hear shots over the air while an officer requests back up as he comes under fire.

Because dispatchers are human, we have to deal with the feelings, the psychological and physiological reactions that result from a constant barrage of critical events, hour after hour, day after day, year after year.

So, dear reader, if you are a police officer, please be patient while waiting for your information, for a good dispatcher will be your best backup. The information is coming.

If, dear reader, you are a private citizen, please excuse my tone of voice if it is a little sharp. Possibly the call that came in before yours was upsetting, but because of my job, I can't get up and walk away for a while. I must answer the next phone call.

And, if, dear reader, you are another dispatcher, you are not alone.

Calling 9-1-1

Let's talk about calling 9-1-1. This number is for life and death emergencies and crimes in progress only! The number is not to be called to ask for a non-emergency phone number because you're too lazy to call 4-1-1 for the information or look it up in the telephone book. Nor is 9-1-1 to be utilized to report that you woke up to find your car stolen or broken into.

I regularly have the opportunity to speak to groups about proper 9-1-1 use. I tell them four things to remember:

1. In ten words or less tell the dispatcher what is happening.

For example: I think I need an ambulance.

I was in a car accident.

I see a house on fire.

2. Where is this happening?

Know your home address. Keep track of your location as you travel.

3. Shut Up.

There's no nice way to say this, but as a dispatcher I have a list of questions I need to ask you. You may have things you want to tell me, but they probably are not the items I need to know right away. There will be an opportunity to tell me later or tell the officer. But for right now Shut Up and let me ask the questions and get the information I need to know.

4. Breathe.

Your adrenaline is madly pumping. You're excited, anxious, and scared. That means your mind is not working as it should. So take a deep breath, and then take another. Focus on my voice and let me try to help you.

These four items may seem elementary to you, but they are daily issues for every public safety dispatcher. Our job is to get information quickly, assess your needs, and send help if necessary. We can't do that efficiently if you complicate our job by allowing your emotions to get the best of you.

Part Three:

Investigators

Shannon Leeper

is a Master Police Officer/Detective with the Lenexa Kansas Police Department, a suburb of Johnson County, Kansas. She began her law enforcement career 13 years ago. She has spent more than six years in the Investigations Division, working a caseload focused on crimes against children and on sexual assault and domestic violence. Shannon is a tireless advocate for women and children in her community and works closely with Sunflower House, a child abuse prevention center. In 2010, her efforts were recognized when she received the honor of Child Advocate of the Year for Johnson County, Kansas.

Shannon may be small in stature, but she has been described as a pit bull when dealing with suspects. That said, she makes sure to leave it all at the door at the end of each day. She is a firm believer in putting God and family first, cherishing time spent with her ever-so-understanding husband and two precious girls. Seldom is she seen without a camera in hand, hence her nickname The Paparazzi. She finds photography and writing therapeutic escapes from the daily grind. Those who know Shannon best will recognize the mantra she borrowed from Mark Twain: *"It's not the size of the dog in the fight. It's the size of the fight in the dog."*

30

Dakota's Story

by Shannon Leeper

"It's called posturing." That was the response from the nurse watching over the bruised and battered body of a diaper-clad little boy. And so began my first child abuse investigation and the case that set me on the path I was destined to follow.

It was March 15, 2005. The chill of a long winter in the Midwest was slowly fading. I was new to the Investigations Division of the Lenexa Police Department, with a mere ten weeks of experience under my belt. I was eager to learn, and Jake Boyer, a seasoned detective, called me after midnight, to tell me about a case that was just reported. He asked if I would assist with the investigation. I will be forever indebted for the confidence he placed in me at that moment and during the subsequent years working side by side.

My first assignment was to head directly to Children's Mercy Hospital in downtown Kansas City, Missouri. I had no idea what to expect. I knew an eighteen-month old child was being treated for suspicious injuries. I would be the first investigator to catch a glimpse of the tiny victim and meet the relatives standing by. A potential suspect had been identified. She was known to the family, which added to the tension during those first critical hours of the investigation. I rushed to my car with my keys, camera, and notebook in hand. I did my best to navigate through the night into the downtown area without the luxury of a navigational device, no easy feat for me.

Parking in the dimly-lit lot, I made my way through the winding halls, up to the wing where the victim was being treated. I was allowed immediate access to the child's bedside without any preparation regarding his condition.

It literally took several minutes for me to process the reality of what appeared before me. A sweet-faced toddler, named Dakota, appeared to be resting peacefully, but the noise of medical machinery replaced my anticipated silence in the room. So many tubes and devices attached to his small body, such an inherently incongruous sight, one I will never forget.

The nurse approached, and I explained my need to take photographs to document the child's injuries and condition. Fortunately, she was very patient and dedicated to her chosen profession. She helped re-position his chubby little arms and legs in order for me to hold my camera in one hand and a ruler in the other in order to accurately capture the size of the injuries. She pointed out things I wouldn't have immediately recognized without her gentle guidance. Speaking very deliberately, she explained each mark on the child's body. She answered my questions honestly and without hesitation.

As I watched, Dakota begin to make small movements, drawing his arms inward, toward his body; I assumed any activity was a positive thing. That is when the nurse educated me about abnormal posturing, and why it is a very ominous sign, suggestive of severe head injury. When all was said and done, I didn't have to ask what the child's prognosis was. Things were as bad as they could get, and the child's mother was waiting in the hall without a full understanding of the gravity of her baby's condition.

Later that morning, I learned just how severe Dakota's injuries were. I was present when Dakota's grandfather learned there had been no tragic accident. I can still picture the look of disbelief on his face as I delicately tried to explain that someone had intentionally caused the injuries that would later claim his grandson's life. I felt like an intruder during those hours I stood guard, watching the nurses and doctors thoroughly investigate and document a progressively worsening condition.

At 4:17 pm, on March 15, 2010, little Dakota Wayne Smith succumbed to his traumatic injuries. I was no longer investigating a case of child abuse—it had become a homicide investigation.

I worked diligently alongside the most persistent group of investigators I could ever hope to partner with. We knew almost immediately who inflicted the horrific injuries which were comparable to those of a head-first fall from a ten-story building. We had plenty of theories about what those last moments of consciousness were like for little Dakota, but the suspect refused to acknowledge what happened.

Despite her assertion that she didn't know what caused Dakota's injuries, the evidence was indisputable against Jessica Harber. She was arrested on March 21, 2005, and charged with 1st degree murder. Jessica was the girlfriend of Dakota's father at the time. When Dakota left the care of his mother and grandparents for a visit with his father and Jessica, they never imagined that someone they entrusted to care for Dakota would end up taking his life. It was devastating for the family, and I developed a bond with them almost immediately. I grieved for them and for the little boy, whom I would only know through family photos, video clips and stories.

Over the next eighteen months, the investigators, medical professionals, and prosecutors worked doggedly to address each potential defense to the murder of this innocent child. The team endured a heartbreaking funeral, long drives to and from a small town in Missouri to interview potential witnesses, the execution of search warrants, the unnatural autopsy of a toddler, deciphering medical records and the terminology that went with them, and countless hours of listening to jailhouse phone calls between Jessica, her family, and boyfriend.

We listened to her ridiculous rants about her situation and her obsessive insecurity regarding Dakota's father. Her poor mother constantly coddled her to prevent her from saying something that might potentially damage the airtight case against her. The only humor came from the choice words Jessica used to illustrate her family's displeasure with me and the others responsible for seeking justice for Dakota. If I were to add up how much those phone calls cost her family, I'm positive that it would amount to a small fortune. In addition to the tremendous financial strain Jessica caused her family, her verbal abuse was equally damaging. The one thing I hoped to hear Jessica say was that she was sorry Dakota was gone. I never heard those words.

More witnesses ultimately came forward. They had shared close quarters with Jessica in jail. They talked about her temper tantrums and provided chilling details of Dakota's murder, gleaned from conversations they had with Jessica over lunch or card games. We learned Dakota had been murdered because he was standing too close to the television. Because that little boy didn't scoot back, it cost him his life. Tragic. That Jessica chose to call her mother and boyfriend, rather than 9-1-1 after realizing Dakota was unresponsive, is unconscionable. Moreover, for Jessica to betray the trust of Dakota's family and be present during those final moments after life support was disconnected, turns my stomach to this day.

In the summer of 2006, a resolution to the case was in sight, and preparations were being made for an acceptable plea. I was on maternity leave at the time and held my firstborn daughter on my lap while watching Jessica refuse to admit her guilt after previously accepting a reduced charge of 2nd degree reckless murder. Her refusal to abide by the agreement opened the door for an upward departure in her sentence. The end result: a prison sentence of 20 years and 6 months. She was transferred to a prison in Topeka, Kansas, lost an appeal, and will not be eligible for parole until the year 2022. Justice served, if there truly is such a thing.

Five plus years have passed since Dakota's death. I think of him often and the imprint his short life left on my life and so many others. His death led to my passion for helping child victims. If fact, in 2008 I became the designated investigator within my agency for crimes against children, sexual abuse, and domestic violence. In September, I was honored with the 2010 Child Advocate of the Year award for my community. I attribute all of this to that first child abuse case and to little Dakota Smith.

I learned a great deal from the criminal investigation into Dakota's death, but I will be forever grateful for what his family taught me. They showed me the value of reaching out to the family of victims in order to help guide them through the confusing and often frustrating criminal justice system. I am certain I learned just as much from them as they did from me. My relationship with them has evolved over time, and they have been supportive and encouraging to me while coming to terms with the loss of their baby boy. They showed me the reward that forgiveness brings, and I am not only a better detective for knowing them, I am a better person.

Amy Sue Michalik

started her law enforcement career in 1998 as a police officer with the Atlanta Police Department (APD). She was the only woman on her watch, but it didn't take long for her to earn the respect of the men with whom she worked. In fact, it just took a punch in the nose. "Shorty White," as she became known on her beat, had a reputation for being a tough, hard-working cop.

In 2002, Amy moved from the APD to the Bureau of Alcohol, Tobacco, Firearms, and Explosives (ATF). As a special agent, Amy worked a variety of cases in the nine years since being hired. She has worked in Atlanta, Georgia; Miami, Florida; and San Bernardino and Glendale, California. She has taught new agents at the Federal Law Enforcement Training Center, been the Victim/Witness Coordinator and Senior Operations Officer in both Atlanta and Los Angeles, been specially chosen to work on two multi-agency Violent Crime Impact Teams (Miami & San Bernardino), and worked on the David Wilhelm Strike Force/Organized Crime & Drug Enforcement Task Force.

Amy developed health issues, causing uncertainty about her future in federal service. She began looking for other career choices and discovered the University of California, Los Angeles' Online Professional Screenwriting Program. With a renewed passion for life and a new found love of screenwriting, Amy took the opportunity to transfer to the LA Field Division with ATF to chase her Hollywood dream.

Amy attends the University of California, Los Angeles in pursuit of a Master of Fine Arts in Screenwriting while continuing to work for ATF. She is a finalist in the 2011 NexTV Writing and Pitching Competition, with an original TV pilot she wrote called "SHOOT". Shoot is about celebrity/fashion photographer, Dallas Cooper, who at the pinnacle of her career must reluctantly fulfill her promise to take up the family's legacy as an assassin when her father doesn't return from a mission.

31

Face to Face with the Devil

by Amy Sue Michalik

It started like just another day. As usual, I'm running late for work. I rushed into the kitchen to grab a jacket. I reached for my Georgia Bulldogs jacket but remember that my roommate, Turtle, liked to wear it so I left it. Instead I grabbed my Land's End Jacket, which fell on me about mid-thigh, in other words, it covered my gun.

I remembered that I needed to pick up my Reba McEntire/Terri Clark concert tickets. *May as well swing by on my way to work.* Phillips Arena is on my way, sort of.

As I drove towards Phillips Arena, several patrol cars whizzed by me, with lights and sirens activated. Then a few more and then a few more. *Hmmm, something's up.* It was not only the number of patrol cars, but they were from several different jurisdictions. I turned the car radio off and made sure my ATF radio was on. It was on, but silent.

Making my way to the arena, I parked my car in what I refer to as "police parking," because it's up front, and if there wasn't a spot, well, I'd make one. Actually there were a couple of police cruisers parked there as well because inside was a mini police precinct. So, literally, it was police parking.

The atmosphere was festive. People were dressed in the colors of their favorite teams. Orange and white (Tennessee)

212 John M. Wills

everywhere, blue and orange, too (Florida). It was SEC Championship time, baby. Atlanta was buzzing. Even this cold weather wasn't enough to keep the fans down. I shivered against the cold March wind as it blasted me in the face.

Sirens broke into my musing, for they could be heard coming from every direction. I got a really bad feeling about the sirens. All I need is to be in the wrong place at the wrong time and get caught. As I waited impatiently in line, the sirens incessantly cried and made me increasingly uneasy. I quickly grabbed my tickets from Will Call, looked at them, sixth row, nice. I smiled and put the tickets into the inside pocket of my jacket.

I began the trek back to my car. It was hard not to smile at fans' enthusiasm, especially when they are painted in their teams' colors and talking trash to opposing team fans. As I walked, a dark skinned black male charged towards me and stood out to me for a couple of reasons. The first, being that it was bitterly cold, at least by Atlanta standards, but this guy was only wearing a thin black blazer without a shirt. Secondly, I could only describe his body language as very angry. His fists were clenched at his sides; he stalked not walked, and his brow was furrowed. The man nearly ran into me. I stepped around him, and I believe that I even spoke to him, but only a word or two. I think I said something like, "Whoa, Dude." The sirens broke into my consciousness again. I looked back over my shoulder where I last saw the angry man and continued to my car. I called the office and was told to get there, ASAP.

I raced the couple of miles to the office and swiped my card, allowing for the barbed wire security gate to open. While it slowly created an opening for me to enter, I noticed the lack of vehicles in the lot. I hurried into the building, taking the stairs two at a time. The office, which usually bustled with agents from the DEA and ATF, in addition to the local cops, was a ghost town. Once I got to my cubicle, another ATF agent informed me that we both needed to suit up and go downtown—there's been a shooting at the courthouse. At that point, we hadn't been told too much.

In the parking lot, the two of us wordlessly suited up, not knowing what we were getting into. First the gun belt with the thigh rig, then the cuffs, baton, and last, the vest. What usually took five minutes to do was done in sixty seconds, and we both screeched out of the parking lot towards the courthouse.

As I neared the courthouse, I was completely unprepared for what I saw – chaos. No two uniforms looked alike. I drove by, looking for other ATF agents and/or a place to park. I saw crime scene tape, ambulances, and more police cars than I remembered ever seeing in one place at one time, except the city repair shop. Police officers, sheriffs, agents, and others were all in tears. I still didn't know what had happened, but it could not have been good. One of our supervisors came over the radio and told all ATF agents, except those at the courthouse, to stage at an apartment complex several miles away. No other info was provided. All at once, the caravan hit their lights and sirens and off we went.

With lights and sirens, it didn't take long to get to the staging location. Several other unmarked police type cars pulled up. A tall blonde got out of the car next to me and put on a plain blue bulletproof vest. She started asking me what we knew. I told her that I didn't know much, but I heard there was a shooting at the courthouse and that we were staging up here because this was one of the perp's girlfriend's apartments. When she didn't add anything to the story, I left her to join the rest of my agency that had made it to the staging location by now.

For a few minutes, we talked among ourselves, each one of us having a different version of a story, not knowing what was true. We all gathered around one agent who handed out copies of the mug shot of a dark skinned black male named Brian Nichols. The same agent launched into an incredible story of what has transpired over the last hour.

Brian Nichols had been on trial for the last week for the brutal rape of his ex-girlfriend. Nichols brought a cooler full of food and drinks to the rape so he could continue to rape his ex over and over for days while keeping her captive. The trial apparently wasn't going his way so he planned an escape. Nichols was being guarded by **one** Fulton County Sheriff's Deputy, a female. When she was taking him out of his cell to change or something, he overpowered her, took her gun, pistol-whipped, and beat her savagely. Using the back way, prisoners are brought into the courtroom by deputies. Nichols then proceeded to the courtroom he was being tried in. He encountered the Judge and court reporter that were on his case. He shot and killed both of them before running out of the courtroom and into the courthouse. Somewhere before he exited the courthouse, he came across two more deputies, whom he also shot and killed before fleeing the courthouse. Next, he carjacked a local newspaper reporter in the parking deck and made his escape. We were given his vehicle information, but Nichols' whereabouts were unknown. We were staged at the rape victim's apartment, thinking that he might try and take her out as well.

Our staging location suddenly seemed to be a hotbed for law enforcement and the media too. We didn't want the media to get a look at any of us so some stayed at the location while others were given various other locations to check. We scattered in all directions.

I was sent to a location forty-five minutes from the city to a house of someone he threatened in jail. It was funny, as I entered the neighborhood there are no less than six other police type cars around the neighborhood. I'm not sure who we thought we were fooling. I checked back in, no more information. Nichols was still at large. Every twenty to thirty feet, there was an unmarked car, all looking at this one house.

Some neighbors came out and asked what's going on and for the first time in my career, someone asked if we needed anything. Maybe public perception of the police is improving? Maybe. Someone thought he saw a curtain move inside the house and within an hour, the SWAT team arrived.

I'm the only ATF agent at the location, so this action was kind of exciting, if we could catch this killer. The SWAT team prepared to enter, while myself and several others from various agencies watched. First they shoot tear gas into the house and quickly follow with flash bangs. SWAT made their entry. Within about ten minutes, they were back out—the house was empty.

Okay, so much for that lead. I checked back in with my supervisor, who informed me that I am on the overnight shift so I should go home now and get a few hours of sleep. I looked at my watch, 3 p.m., and I was forty-five minutes, without traffic, from home.

Once home, I turned on the TV to hear about how we have been chasing our tails all day. Disgusted, I turned off the TV and tried to get some sleep.

Seven o'clock came way too quickly. I called in to see where to meet up. I was told we had information from the US Marshals that Nichols was holed up in a cheap hotel south of the city. I rushed down there to join my crew. I was there to relieve a couple of agents who have been working the case all day, but they didn't want to leave without the payoff. We got the key to the room, quickly set up on it, and rushed inside. Eight men, roughly, and me, make entry into a very small hotel room. Again, nothing. We spent the night, just like we did the day, chasing our tails. All Nichols sightings had to be checked out. At the end of my shift, I headed home, and still no one had any idea where this mad man was.

A couple hours later, my roommate hurried into my room and informed me they got him. I ran out to the living room to

216 John M. Wills

watch the news coverage. Nichols turned himself in, peacefully, but not before killing one more person, an ICE agent who was at his newly built house, laying tiles in his bathroom, when Nichols randomly happened across him. Nichols apparently shot and killed the agent and then stole his gun, badge and truck.

Within two minutes, my phone started ringing with friends calling me to tell me they saw me on the news. I tried to tell them that it wasn't me, for I was at home, I was asleep, but they didn't believe me. Nonetheless, I breathed a sigh of relief knowing that Nichols was in custody.

The coverage continued, and the news showed some footage of Brian Nichols from the parking deck across from CNN & Phillips Arena. He was wearing a black blazer that was too small for him and no shirt. I gasp! For a minute, I couldn't breathe and my head started to swim. I couldn't wrap my head around what I just saw. I ran into my room and grabbed my computer to look at that footage again. *No, it just can't be*!

There were so many thoughts running through my head. If only I had recognized him, that federal agent wouldn't be dead. If I had been wearing that other jacket, I'd probably be dead right now. I'm the only cop who ran across this guy and lived. I couldn't tell anyone though; I'd be fired. How do I justify the fact that I came face to face with a man that killed four people and I didn't know it? Better yet, that I chased his ghost for a whole day and night and didn't know either.

I guess they call it survivor's guilt, but I had no idea how much this incident affected me until five months later when one of my coworkers with the Atlanta Police Department was murdered by his own brother. I was inconsolable. My supervisor suggested I get some grief counseling, and I did. I was sitting on the shrink's couch just crying and crying. She simply stated, "Oh, you must have been really close to him."

I almost laughed when I answered, "No, not really." It was

then that I realized I wasn't dealing with the agent's death, but my own mortality. How close I came. Survivor's guilt all over again.

I stood alongside my vehicle and saluted the one containing the body of the slain agent as it was driven to North Carolina. I ended up assigned to the special task force named for him, Organized Crime and Drug Enforcement Task Force. I was also at the special dedication ceremony that included a fly-by of law enforcement and military aircraft, all the while feeling responsible, or at the very least negligent in his death.

Of course I know I'm not God and that I had no way of knowing who Nichols was, never mind what he had just done, but that knowledge doesn't make it any easier to live with.

Sandy Smetana

Dover, Delaware, became a police officer in 1982 with the Baytown Police Department in Baytown, Texas. She served as a patrol officer and field training officer (FTO) for 6 ½ years. She left Baytown and joined the City of Dover Police Department (DPD) in the fall of 1989, working patrol and serving as an FTO. Sandy worked various assignments, including: Patrol, Detective Division, Planning & Training Division, Community Policing Unit, Youth Unit and Hostage Negotiating Team. She was certified as an instructor and a master instructor. Promoted several times, she retired as a platoon sergeant in charge of a platoon of officers in the Patrol Division. She was the first female in the Dover Police Department to reach the rank of sergeant, and the first female officer to retire from the department. During her career she earned a Bachelor of Arts Degree in Behavioral Science, and a Master of Science Degree in Administration of Justice from Wilmington University.

While employed at the DPD, she was honored to become a Nationally Credentialed Law Enforcement Officer, and received her certificate from former US Attorney General Janet Reno. Sandy also received several awards, including two **Police Chief's Commendations**, **Officer of the Quarter in 2002** and **Class A and Class B Commendations**. She is a Lifetime member of Mid-Atlantic Association of Women in Law Enforcement (MAAWLE) and a Lifetime member of International Association of Women Police (IAWP). Sandra is also a member of the Fraternal Organization of Police (FOP) and has held several offices in her local FOP.

Sandy has two sons who are now following in her footsteps by giving back to the community. Her oldest son is a volunteer firefighter and her youngest is a Military Police Officer with United States Army Reserves.

32

Story Time at
the 7 Eleven

by Sandy Smetana

I was working with my partner in the juvenile unit one summer when we received a call from a concerned citizen. The caller advised that a sexual predator intended to pick up a child at the 7 Eleven, which was one block away from the police station. The caller added that the sexual predator was a male who had lured the male child to the store. We set up on the location, hoping to locate the child and the predator.

We were surprised when we located the concerned citizen who had called us, rather than the predator. No child showed up. We asked the caller to accompany us back to the police station to be interviewed; he agreed to do so. At first he was reluctant to talk to us, but after praising him for getting involved, lauding him for being a concerned member of the community, and explaining to him we needed to save the child from this predator and any others, he began to cooperate. We emphasized that we needed him, that he was key to our investigation.

We quickly realized our concerned citizen was in fact our suspect. The man stated he had found out about the alleged meet on his computer. My partner, using a ruse, told the suspect that he (my partner) knew nothing about the computer and needed the suspect's help to save the boy. The only way to do that was for us to utilize his computer in an effort to lure the criminal into the open. I emphasize that we only interviewed the suspect, rather than interrogated him, since we really had no crime to investigate. We asked him to bring his computer in so that we might examine it to find the boy in time to save him. The suspect agreed.

Surprisingly, when our caller returned with his computer we found it was well worn and held together with duct tape. Knowing how important it was to take someone like our suspect off the streets, we made sure we did everything properly. We obtained a search warrant for the computer and proceeded to examine the hard drive. Our search revealed child pornography, but we were stunned to discover something else—the man was in the process of adopting a child. The information was turned over to the state police, since the offense of possession of child pornography occurred within the jurisdiction of the state.

Kathryn Davison

 is a 15-year peace officer with the Casper Police Department in Casper, Wyoming. Her police areas of expertise are crimes against children, infant death investigation, forensic interviewing, and crime scene and hostage negotiating. She was a detective for several years and investigated many local high profile cases. She is a certified national trainer in Sudden Infant Death Investigation.

Although being a detective was the most rewarding position for Davison, she chose to go back to patrol in 2008 when she returned to the police department after a short absence. She works in patrol as a Field Training Officer, Evidence Technician, and Hostage Negotiator. Her hobbies include CrossFit training, all outdoor activities, reading, movies, and traveling. She and her daughter live in the country and enjoy spending quality time together.

The Locket

by Kathryn Davison

It was a crap shoot, but I knew something had to be in the files that no other detective had explored in the past. The Crawford decision had been an important milestone in my past child molestation cases. Why not a homicide? Crawford limited hearsay evidence in the child victim cases. However, why not look at the child's testimony in this case? What about looking at the medical records and viewing the doctor's notes? Could the doctor testify for the child? Especially with a child victim who had received psychiatric treatment at age three. It was worth a try. After all, I was working on what was to become a landmark case: the first bodiless homicide prosecuted in the state of Wyoming. Why not explore every avenue?

Beginning with the "soft" approach, I received a medical release from the patient for her files and sent them to the clinic. Now eighteen years old, she didn't remember a thing. The psychiatrist and psychologists who worked with her were long gone and had opened their own independent practices. They told me building a case would be difficult, and the clinic would fight me all the way. The clinic had already refused to release the records with the patient release after several follow-up calls. Even though it was all I needed by law, the clinic did not comply with the release form. I got the runaround for months. Finally, I had had enough. The clinic was holding up my case.

I spent days writing the search warrant, crossing my t's and dotting my i's. I knew if the warrant was approved by the judge, it would create a mess. No matter, the case had a gap. I needed to know what the child witnessed, felt, dreamed, said, and went through. And I wanted to know what went on in her mind over sixteen years ago.

The district judge thoroughly scrutinized my affidavit, but finally signed it with careful consideration. He warned me that I was opening a can of worms that had never been explored. He took a few days to research the warrant and its legality. Then he called me over to his office. He approved the warrant, stating I was in for a fight, and told me to let him know if there were any problems.

While driving the highway north to a beautiful mountain town hours away from my city, I was apprehensive. The Health Insurance Portability and Accountability Act of 1996 (P.L.104-191) [HIPAA] was a big deal now. I was pushing the limits, but armed with my patient release and search warrant, I drove to the local police department and contacted the detective division. They assigned me one of their investigators and a patrol officer to tag along.

Our mini contingent arrived and proceeded up the hill to the clinic. It was perhaps reminiscent of a battle in which the enemy held the high ground. As I walked into the front office, I could feel the place closing in on me. The staff was not friendly. I felt like a steak thrown into a lion's den. Composed, I introduced myself to the receptionist and informed her of my business. The two local officers were grinning, which didn't help. It seemed they liked trouble in their town; they liked stirring the pot.

Before too long, a woman who claimed she was in charge came out to greet me. She was cold and her handshake was clammy. I gave her a copy of the search warrant and stated my business. She backed up and told me to leave, that the files were not for release. That was the wrong move in this chess game.

Having tried the soft approach first, I shifted gears. "Perhaps you don't understand. I have a state search warrant. If you don't give me the files and tapes I am asking for, we will shut this place down and search the entire clinic. I imagine your patients would be very upset." I glanced over at the local cops—they were grinning ear to ear. They were ready to bring the whole police force to shut down this mental health clinic.

And so the chess game continued. Shortly, I was on the phone speaking with the clinic's attorney, telling him the same thing I had told the woman. I explained the patients would surely file a lawsuit and pull their files because the clinic was too stubborn to abide by a state search warrant. I further advised him that the head barricade bitch would likely be arrested for interference. Stammering, he asked me to hand the phone to the office manager.

"Helga" complied after speaking with the attorney. She took me to a storage room, cold and institutional, with white walls and a tile floor. It smelled like cleaners and disinfectant. The woman eventually gave me a banker's box full of files. No tapes. They had been destroyed, but were they destroyed a month ago when I had sent the patient release or years ago before the police got involved in a cold case homicide?

Raising Cain over the destruction of evidence, I shook the place with threats and possible jail terms. I could smell the fear. Nevertheless, they stood their ground regarding the lost tapes. Soon the phone rang, and the attorney asked to speak with me again. He assured me the destruction of the tapes was not done intentionally, but rather was a purge because of the years that had passed. I believed he was telling me the truth as he knew it, but I didn't have any faith or trust in the staff at the clinic.

After spending the day in the cold storage room, I took the box of evidence home. The local cops were disappointed that we didn't shut the place down. I smiled and told them we were only minutes away from doing that had the clinic not complied. The District Attorney was all for slapping them with interference; I can only speculate as to what the Judge would have done if his warrant wasn't complied with by the staff.

As I went through the contents of the box at home, minutes turned into hours as I read, non-stop, losing myself in the little girl's world. At times, tears streamed down my face as I realized the pain she had felt. Then, in the bottom of a folder, I found it—one cassette tape! *Could this be the evidence I needed?*

The tape was haunting. Much of the tape was inaudible. It was more than sixteen years old and had an eerie sound to it. Static. Voices. A child's voice. Wearing headphones, I listened to it over and over. It wasn't a tape ladened with evidentiary material, but it was the sound of the child's voice, and it took me back in time.

The documents held evidence of a tragedy no one would come to understand.

"Daddy cut mommy into two pieces." Chilling.

"Daddy put her where the Christmas trees don't have lights."

Those had been famous words in the case, which were heard over and over. What the other detectives from 1990 didn't know was there was much more. Pages more. Years. PTSD. Treatment. Recovery.

"Daddy hit Mommy. Mommy was running away, crawling in grass. Mommy was crying."

She cried. She begged her daddy not to hurt Mommy, but she was talking to her doctor, not her father. "Mommy dead."

The psychiatrist asked her why she thought mommy was dead.

"She had red on her face. She stopped running."

It would be years later before I would utter those same words in court, reading from the doctor's notes in the preliminary hearing. As I testified to her words, I read the transcripts belonging to her psychiatrist during the preliminary hearing. The courtroom was silent. It was the first time Misty's words were made public. The room was filled with reporters and citizens waiting to hear the evidence presented in a case that had gripped the city in a mystery for more than sixteen years; they all listened intently. My voice cracked, as my own motherly instincts kicked in while I testified.

She didn't have a mother to hug her, to tell her it was okay. Her mother had been taken from her when she was only three years old. Did she remember her mother's face? Did she remember what happened? The latter was a question that was posed to her when she took the stand and faced her father.

During the nights spent reading and researching, something happened to me. I don't know if I became too personally involved in the case, or if I felt tremendous sorrow for a small child who saw her mother murdered—perhaps both. Misty had never been hypnotized, which in the 1990s was a big thing. Had she been, the case would not be what it has become today, a historical case that resulted in the child's father's conviction, and her memories would have been challenged as having been planted, coached, altered . . . not her own.

Reading the hundreds of pages of therapy and treatment sessions was like reading a novel and getting wrapped up in the lives of the characters. The pages consumed me. I had a sterling silver carved prayer locket that was empty. I put Misty's mother's name in it and wore it every day, vowing not to take it off until the murderer was put in jail. Three years later, I was still wearing that locket to the first day of the homicide trial.

After Misty and the other family members took the stand, my partner Matt and I approached the waiting room where they were sequestered with Victim Services. I took the silver chain with the prayer box off my neck and told the family the story about the locket. I took the locket off and passed it to Misty. It seemed to be the right thing to do, to give it to her. Her grandparents and aunt sobbed. Matt and I had tears in our eyes as well, causing us to depart the room quickly to maintain our composure.

Walking down the hall and back into the history-making courtroom, I felt a hard "sock" on my right arm. Matt had punched me. "Don't ever do that to me again, dammit," he said, as he wiped a tear from his eye. We were both trying to fool ourselves into thinking that we hadn't personally invested ourselves in the case. How could we not after years of living it, breathing it, and working it every day? It had consumed the old detectives who had worked the case; now it was our turn.

Misty's testimony had been bittersweet. As she took the stand, she faced the jury and sat across from her own father. She was beautiful. Long red hair . . . she looked like him, but her mother's features were evident as well. The jury saw the resemblance too. Her testimony was short. She didn't remember. It was expected. We held our breath waiting for an attack on the girl who had already endured so much. The jurors all stared at the defendant; it was now his turn to question the witness—his own daughter. The District Attorney had planted the pawn in plain sight, anticipating an appeal, based on what might have happened between the two estranged family members once the father began his questioning. The defendant had the right to question his accuser, but he didn't get any answers because she didn't remember. Score one for the prosecution. Checkmate. However, we were relieved when no dramatic questions were asked by the defense.

Later, the psychiatrist and psychologist were allowed to testify, the defense claiming foul under the Crawford decision. The jury seemed strained after hearing the sorrowful saga the two professionals told on the stand. It was a landmark decision to allow the testimony that would later be challenged in the Wyoming Supreme Court appeal and upheld. The history-making case remains to this day Wyoming's first bodiless homicide conviction.

It was over, justice had finally been served, albeit after too many years and too much pain and suffering had passed. The case was closed, but for Misty it was far from over. The bits and pieces locked away in her memory would always haunt her. However, there is one memory that will forever be with her—that of a loving mother symbolized and safely preserved in a silver locket.

Sometime later, Misty enlisted in the Army and became a soldier. The silver locket she wore around her neck has been replaced by the dog tags she proudly wears every day she defends our country.

Bonnie Lowe

 is a retired, 30-year veteran of the Anne Arundel County, Maryland, Police Department. When she was 18 years old, she was the first female police cadet hired by her agency. She has worked in every aspect of policing except SWAT. Bonnie is a graduate of Anne Arundel County Community College and the University of Maryland's Law Enforcement Institute. She received additional training at the University of Louisville-Southern Police Institute, the FBI Behavioral Science Unit, and Johns Hopkins University. Bonnie was appointed as the first female police chief at a community college near Annapolis, MD. She is a court certified expert in sexual crimes and domestic violence and has investigated hundreds of crimes against persons and police misconduct complaints. She was an adjunct professor at Anne Arundel Community College in Annapolis upon her retirement from the police department.

Bonnie has received awards from the International Association of Women Police: The Police Chief's Award for Excellence in Law Enforcement, Police Officer of the Year on two occasions, The Baltimore Sun newspaper's Police Officer of the Year, and the State of Maryland Governor's Award for Crime Prevention. She worked as a consultant for the popular television show, "America's Most Wanted."

She served five tours as a contractor in international law enforcement missions. Bonnie has trained law enforcement commanders in Lithuania, Bulgaria, the Philippines, Kyrgyzstan, and Pakistan. She was one of the only Americans to receive a medal from the former Soviet republic of Kyrgyzstan and another from Bulgaria.

Bonnie is divorced with a 28-year old daughter and lives in Pasadena, Maryland, on the Chesapeake Bay.

After the Revolution

by Bonnie Lowe

After the revolution, the entire government changed. Members of the new interim government rose to power on an anti-corruption, transparency in government platform. Some of them had been incarcerated on trumped up charges by the former president, Bakiev, who is currently in exile in Belarus, and whose brother was the head of the secret police. Bakiev controlled everything in the country with the aid of organized crime and clan affiliations. The people had enough, and on April 7th the country exploded.

Dr. Jorey, my partner, said that he had never heard of a revolution happening so quickly and unexpectedly. He joked, "These Kyrgyz are something. They overthrow the government in one day, and then go back to their jobs the next morning, like nothing happened." A Central Asian newspaper described it this way, "300,000 Uzbeks are easy to control, but try to control only three Kyrgyz and it's impossible." They are foxy, nationalistic, and proud of their nomadic heritage. Hundreds of citizens of Russian decent have left the country in the last month. Most of the Kyrgyz, especially in the South, hate the Russians, and are encouraging them to return to their Slavic homeland. It's very comforting that they seem to like us, the Americans. They recognize a difference between the Russians and the Americans before we even speak. We smile at strangers. Former Soviets don't.

A couple of weeks after the uprising, I walked into the federal police headquarters, known as the MVD (Ministerstvo Vnutrennikh Del) and observed the police preparing for a ceremony. It was Victory Day, a huge holiday in the former Soviet Republic. It celebrated Russia's victory over the Nazis in World War II. The Chief of Human Resources greeted me in the lobby. One of the World War II veterans beckoned him. The old man, dripping in medals, asked in Russian, "She's an American, isn't she?" The chief said "Yes." The old veteran said, "Please give her a ribbon to wear. The Americans were on our side in The Great War." I told him that I'd be honored to wear the ribbon.

The ceremony in Red Square had included US and British troops. It was a big deal in this part of the world for everyone to witness the American and British military units marching in the heart of the former Soviet Union.

Later that day, I met one of the police colonels that had been systematically fired by the interim government because he was affiliated with the former regime. He took the ribbon off of my blouse and adjusted the folding. He said that he had been a member of the "Pioneers" when he was a kid, explaining that the Pioneers under communism were similar to our Boy Scouts. He explained that the wearing of uniforms and marching were stressed during Soviet times, so he was cognizant of the fold in the ribbon. Every military or police officer displayed a collection of medals on their uniforms. He told me that most of the medals were not earned; that it was not unusual to purchase an assortment of medals on the black market. Everything was for sale under communism....your medals, your rank and your position, and it still holds true today.

Most citizens buy their college degrees; their driver's licenses; and their titles. Most police and military officers buy their position or their rank. That's why criminals and idiots can become colonels or generals in the MVD if they're willing to pay. If they're connected by clan or political cronies, they're hired. They pay for the power or get appointed through nepotism. It's been that way forever in this part of the world. It'll take years to change the mentality and to put a dent in the corruption. The people don't know any other way to survive. For example, parents of five year olds have to give a gift to their child's kindergarten teacher in order for them to pass into the first grade. Most of the government is corrupt; the judiciary is corrupt; and many of the police officers are corrupt. Most of the time, the bribes are for need, not for greed. After all, how can a traffic cop raise four kids on $150 a month? The honest cops hate the practice of forced bribery by their commanders. Things have got to change.

Believe it or not, some of the citizens I've spoken with actually like this type of system. Why work hard to gain status or fight your way through the bureaucracy when it's easier to buy what you want and have instant gratification? Some of them admit that they're too lazy to go through the hassle. Bribery, money laundering, and drug trafficking sustain the underground economy. There's a lot of money to be made if you're a clerk in the passport office, a border guard or a traffic cop. They don't depend on their salary. Many of them make a fortune in bribes. For example, corrupt college professors accept bribes for passing students who don't attend classes. Medical doctors buy their degrees. That's why medical care is horrible in Central Asia. Jorey talked to a doctor last week who wanted to save sutures, so he partially closed up the patient's wound with scotch tape. The people are tired and frustrated. They realize that they'll never be able to compete in a global economy; make a decent salary; or experience real justice as long as the government promotes corruption and clan loyalty. The Kyrgyzstan economy has suffered considerably. There is no tax base. Legal and illegal financial transactions are in cash. There is no paper trail. Favors and bartering are the norm.

The Internet has opened a whole new world of knowledge for the people, and likely contributed to the protests. One of the MVD colonels referred to the video of the honest Russian cop on *YouTube* who boldly communicated the plight of honest Russian police who have to work in a sea of corrupt police. He firmly believes that the American anti-corruption program has raised awareness with the police on the impact of corruption on society and the economy. He said, "No more will the Kyrgyz have to rely on government propaganda for information. The government can no longer control freedom of the press or freedom of speech as long as the citizens can go to an Internet café, read news from all over the world and speak out against their own government. Listening to the Americans' teachings on the rule of law, transparency and democratic values has planted a seed in their mentality that the country's survival depends on fixing our broken system." Excellent observation.

Sandy Smetana

Dover, Delaware, became a police officer in 1982 with the Baytown Police Department in Baytown, Texas. She served as a patrol officer and field training officer (FTO) for 6 ½ years. She left Baytown and joined the City of Dover Police Department (DPD) in the fall of 1989, working patrol and serving as an FTO. Sandy worked various assignments, including: Patrol, Detective Division, Planning & Training Division, Community Policing Unit, Youth Unit and Hostage Negotiating Team. She was certified as an instructor and a master instructor. Promoted several times, she retired as a platoon sergeant in charge of a platoon of officers in the Patrol Division. She was the first female in the Dover Police Department to reach the rank of sergeant, and the first female officer to retire from the department. During her career she earned a Bachelor of Arts Degree in Behavioral Science, and a Master of Science Degree in Administration of Justice from Wilmington University.

While employed at the DPD, she was honored to become a Nationally Credentialed Law Enforcement Officer, and received her certificate from former US Attorney General Janet Reno. Sandy also received several awards, including two Police Chief's Commendations, Officer of the Quarter in 2002 and Class A and Class B Commendations. She is a Lifetime member of Mid-Atlantic Association of Women in Law Enforcement (MAAWLE) and a Lifetime member of International Association of Women Police (IAWP). Sandy is also a member of the Fraternal Organization of Police (FOP) and has held several offices in her local FOP.

Sandy has two sons who are now following in her footsteps by giving back to the community. Her oldest son is a volunteer firefighter and her youngest is a Military Police Officer with United States Army Reserves.

35

The Town Hooker

by Sandy Smetana

I was a DARE (Drug Abuse Resistance Education) officer for many years and hardly went anywhere without people recognizing me. I often went shopping, and when I had to write a check, I rarely had to show ID because the sales clerks knew who I was, referring to me as "Officer Sandy." I was assigned to the Juvenile Unit which was a part of the Drugs, Vice and Organized Crime Unit. At times, I was asked to go undercover to pose as a prostitute. I did this once in a northern county with another officer, and we were very successful. As I strolled the streets, the first "john" who stopped for me was a preacher. Of course, after he was arrested, he stated that he was going to preach to me about the errors of my ways. Another john even stopped, negotiated a price, and then went to an ATM to get the money.

One evening, I was supposed to meet for dinner with my husband and his boss, who was accompanied by his future in-laws. I had a colleague drop me off at the restaurant, rather than go all the way back to the police department to change and then twenty minutes more to the restaurant. For the undercover assignment that night I wore a pair of Daisy Dukes, which are essentially short shorts and a top that was much too small and tight. I did carry a bag with me with my other clothes intending to change into them in the restaurant bathroom.

This particular restaurant entrance is actually a bar, and as I walked through the front door all eyes immediately shifted toward me. Trying hard to be as nondescript as one could be wearing Daisy Dukes and low cut top, I spotted the group I was to meet, said a quick "hello," and walked as quickly as I could to the ladies room to change. I saw the shocked looks on my husband's boss and his future in-laws faces and knew I had some explaining to do.

After I had changed into more suitable clothing I joined my group of diners and explained my previous appearance. We all had a great laugh, but I noticed several males at the bar with their gazes fixed on the door to the ladies room waiting for the gal in the Daisy Dukes to emerge.

I even had some funny experiences working as a prostitute in my own town. Although almost everyone knew me, they stopped and tried to pick up Officer Sandy. One time I was working the street, and some of my DARE students kept riding their bikes up to me asking me what I was doing. I had to invent a cover story and politely tell them to go away. What was I supposed to do, tell them I was trying to arrest their fathers?

Another time a co-worker of my ex-husband stopped by and asked if I needed a ride. I told him, "No, I'm working." I had to tell him three times before what I was saying finally sank into his head. When it finally did, the look on his face was priceless. I felt so sorry for him that I wanted to grab his face and give him a big kiss, but I didn't because the undercover officers watching would have arrested him.

On another occasion, actually the same day, I had to have my cover officers chase away a male prostitute who confronted me and began yelling and accusing me of "horning in on his territory."

Jo Ann C. Kocher

Honolulu, Hawaii, is a native of New York City. She holds a B. S. Degree in Elementary Education from St. John's University and a M. S. Degree in Speech Education from Queens College. In June 1972, she was sworn in as the first woman special agent for the Bureau of Alcohol, Tobacco, and Firearms (ATF). She served in New York City until 1980 when she was promoted to ATF Headquarters. One of her collateral duties there was membership on the task force that later became the Interagency Committee on Women in Federal Law Enforcement. In 1984, the committee honored her by bestowing upon her its first Manager's Award for her contributions to women in law enforcement.

In 1982, Jo Ann became ATF's first woman Resident Agent in Charge (RAC) when she assumed responsibility for ATF's law enforcement mission in Hawaii and Guam. In this capacity, she supervised law enforcement operations, was the chief liaison representative for ATF with other federal, state, and local agencies, and handled administrative and personnel issues. She was active in several organizations, serving as the 1986 secretary of the Hawaii State Law Enforcement Officials Association and the FY 1990 Chair of the Honolulu-Pacific Federal Executive Board.

In 1996, Jo Ann was promoted to Assistant Special Agent in Charge (ASAC) in San Francisco. She had investigative and administrative oversight for several of ATF's field offices, as well as ATF's role in the UNABOM investigation. In 1997, she was selected by ATF's Deputy Director to serve on a focus group to restructure the bureau. Jo Ann retired from ATF in January 1999 and returned to Hawaii. She is currently writing a book about her experiences as ATF's first woman agent. She also works as a contractor for ATF doing background investigations, volunteers as a mediator for the Mediation Center of the Pacific and serves as her community's Neighborhood Security Watch (NSW) coordinator.

36

Whatever You Do, Don't Get Her Killed

by Jo Ann C. Kocher

Sitting in the unmarked, dark green, 1971 Ford sedan, we clearly saw Billy, a tall, NYPD detective with shaggy black hair, enter the tenement in New York's notorious South Bronx neighborhood. It was one of many in a row of identical, faded red brick high-rises lining the narrow street and cluttered with double parked cars. Soon Billy would make an undercover purchase of heroin. Knowing that someday, I too, would likely be in the same situation, I wondered what was going through his mind.

I sat in the back seat, trying to hide my edginess and dancing precariously with excitement. I was a new special agent of the Bureau of Alcohol, Tobacco, and Firearms (ATF), having been hired less than a year before. How would this, my first search warrant, wind up? The leader of the multi-agency group that targeted illegal narcotics dealers was driving. A bald, hardened police sergeant, his demeanor left no room for misinterpretation. He was in charge. Terry, ATF's representative on the task force, sat in the front passenger seat. Although he was about my age, he was a senior agent and had been in this situation many times.

As we waited for Billy to get to the apartment and make the buy, I thought back to events earlier in that January day of 1973. It did not begin well. Driving into work on the Brooklyn-

Queens Expressway (BQE), a dark brown, mixed breed dog tried to run across the three lanes of heavy but rapidly moving traffic. It darted almost in front of my government car, allowing me to see the terror in its eyes. As an animal lover, I was horrified. I barely missed hitting the stray dog. When I looked in my rear view mirror, I saw the car behind me strike it. I closed my eyes, hoping it died instantly and didn't suffer. I was nauseous by the time I got to the office, my psyche churning with the image of the petrified dog and its fate.

A few hours later, I sat at my gray metal desk in the squad room, still thinking about the poor dog. Out of the corner of my eye, I noticed Terry, an agent I had only met a few times, walk into my supervisor's office. I knew Terry was assigned to a special task force that concentrated on narcotics dealers and was made up of federal agencies and the NYPD. When Terry came out of my supervisor's office, he approached my desk. He was smiling.

"Would you like to go out on a search warrant tonight?" he asked me.

I wasted no time telling him I would love to go. As ATF's first woman agent, I had rarely been allowed to work "on the streets" since returning from training. It was frustrating and not what I had expected. I appreciated that Terry was willing to give me a chance. At last I was going to see what the real world of law enforcement was like.

"An undercover NYPD cop will be making a purchase of narcotics in an apartment in the

South Bronx," Terry explained. "We already have a search warrant for the place, and we'll hit it as soon as the buy is made."

"OK," I replied. I was familiar with the South Bronx, having done some substitute teaching there when I went to graduate school. I knew the area mainly from the kids I taught. It was impoverished and overcrowded.

"Your main job will be to search the guy's wife and older female kids, if they're in the apartment. We're pretty sure they'll be there." Terry was given explicit instructions when he asked ATF management if I could accompany the team on the operation.   The Special Agent in Charge, more commonly known to the agents as simply "the SAC," told him, "Whatever you do, don't get her killed." Terry laughed as he repeated the SAC's exact words, "If she ever gets killed, I'll never hear the end of it."

In the late afternoon, I joined Terry and several other federal and local enforcement officers for a briefing. I listened intently as they explained how Billy would enter the apartment and attempt to purchase heroin.   He had bought drugs there previously. For his safety, he would be wearing a hidden wire, which would allow all of us on the surveillance team to hear what was being said.   His partner would be stationed in a staircase immediately above the sixth floor apartment where the illegal activities were occurring.   After Billy was safely out of the apartment, we would make entry to arrest the suspect and execute the search warrant. I wasn't surprised that, as a rookie, I wasn't assigned to the entry team. I was just delighted to be there.

My assignment was made clear.   After other agents and police officers entered and secured the apartment, I was to come in and search the suspect's wife and kids for weapons and drugs. For the rest of the evening, I was to stay with her and the children while the apartment was being searched.

That evening, the three of us tried to appear invisible in the dwindling light of dusk, but we knew we stood out like an iceberg in the middle of the tropical Pacific. The two-year-old car, designed to blend into the neighborhoods where it would see most of its work, was one of the newest on the block. Other members of the task force sat in similar cars down and across the street.

Perhaps the car's white occupants in the predominately black neighborhood made passersby, who had seen too many police cars on their street, know we didn't belong. Or was it the running motor, needed to keep the police frequency active? Either way, we didn't expect to be there for long. Billy's partner had already taken up his assigned location on the stairwell. We were poised to execute the search warrant immediately after Billy made his undercover purchase.

We only had to wait about five minutes before he arrived in the apartment. His deep voice crackled through his hidden wire and through to the radios in our cars.

"What's up, man? You got the stuff?"

"Yeah, not as much as I expected."

"I'll take what you got."

"Where's the money?"

There was silence for a minute as Billy showed the cash. Then, his voice exploded. "Why are you pointing that gun at me?"

We bolted out of the car and into the crowded street. Other agents and police officers were already running into the building.

Bang...Bang. The unmistakable sound of gunfire erupted from the sixth floor dwelling.

"10-13 . . . 10-13," the NYPD sergeant shouted through his handheld radio, as he ran.

Dozens of federal agents and police officers raced up the dank stairways, suddenly void of tenants, but filled with the stench of stale urine. The universal cry for help would immediately bring more police screaming into the area. Our targeted location was unmistakable. Several other officers were there ahead of us.

They crowded the small, sparsely furnished apartment, carefully avoiding the dying black man sprawled on the kitchen floor. Was my heart pounding from the frantic run up the stairs or was it from fear? Would I do what was expected of me? What happened to Billy? I met him for the first time at that afternoon's briefing and liked him immediately. Although I was a newcomer to law enforcement, he welcomed me warmly to the team.

The relief on the other officers' faces told me that Billy was fine. One of their own faced imminent danger and was spared. I spotted him and his partner, who had fired the fatal shot into the drug dealer's neck, on the bottom of the stairwell landing, right outside the open apartment door.

"There's the wife," Terry yelled at me as I entered the narrow hallway. I couldn't help but see her slight husband, barely conscious with blood trickling from his neck onto the worn linoleum.

"Come with me," I motioned to her and her six kids. "I'm going to search you, and you'll stay with me in this room," I said, pointing to a bedroom.

I was astonished how calm she and her kids were. I couldn't say the same for myself. I struggled to remember everything I learned in training about searching people. I recalled the young secretary who volunteered to be "searched" during the practical exercise portion of that class. She had been cooperative. Would this heavyset black woman be the same?

Inside the sparsely lit bedroom with dingy gray, tattered curtains partially closed, I told the kids, aged three to twelve, to stay in one corner of the room. Terry stood between them and me, keeping an eye on all of us.

"Put your hands above your head," I told the woman, trying to sound authoritative, but fearing my voice quivered. She complied.

I started by running my hands through her unwashed hair. Carefully, I continued down her body, searching for drugs or anything that could be used as a weapon against us. I wondered if she was as embarrassed as I was. She showed no

246 John M. Wills

emotion. When I was finished, Terry told me to search the two oldest kids, both girls. I did, explaining what I was doing and why, almost apologetically. I wanted to tell them that I didn't enjoy this part of my job. I wished I could show compassion for them, knowing a loved one was dying. But I knew I couldn't. Doing so would be considered weak.

The eerie howl of an ambulance got closer and abruptly stopped as the vehicle arrived in front of the building. Police radios squealed as a continuing stream of officers, many of them with brass buttons on their shoulders, arrived. I remained in the bedroom with the woman and kids. We heard the paramedics wheel a squeaky gurney into the kitchen. Their tone was somber but urgent. The woman never asked what was happening or if she could see her husband. Soon, the ambulance, its siren starting up again, rushed to the hospital.

It was several hours before the other agents and officers completed the search of the apartment. When Terry told me we could leave, I sighed with relief and leaned against a wall near the front door. A sense of pride flooded through me. I had done the job expected of me well. A uniformed police officer shouted at me. "Don't do that."

"Don't do what?" I asked, recoiling to a straight position.

"Don't lean against the wall. You'll take cockroaches home in your clothes."

I still had a lot to learn.

It was late when I got home. I barely slept, tossing and turning with the events of the day continually replaying in my subconscious mind. I saw the man dying on the floor in front of his family, but the overwhelming nightmare was the panic in the stray dog's eyes before it was killed on the BQE that morning. I woke up, drenched in sweat, feeling worse about the defenseless dog than about the drug dealer who died. What type of person was I?

Terry told me to report to work early, for I would be

required to write a comprehensive account about the events I had witnessed. He explained that there would be a review of the shooting, and everyone present would have to recount the events as they remembered them. He also correctly anticipated ATF's response.

He arrived at the office before I did. As the senior ATF person at the scene, Terry was expected to brief ATF management on the shooting. By the time I got there, all the agents knew what happened. Many wanted to know how I had reacted. Terry gave me a glowing report, saying I remained calm and did my assigned job well. He even added a more than slight exaggeration, "She jumped over the suspect's body lying on the kitchen floor."

As I got off the elevator, several agents surrounded me. I was surprised to discover that most of them had never been involved in any shooting incidents, although many had been on the job a lot longer than I had. They were full of questions. Most revolved around the same theme.

"How much blood was there?"

"I've seen a lot more blood in the movies," I answered. As I was fielding their questions, my supervisor told me that the Assistant Special Agent in Charge (ASAC) wanted to see me immediately. I went to his office.

"I want to commend you on your professional performance last night," he said with a smile.

"I didn't do anything special," I replied, surprised he would even comment about it.

"At least you didn't faint." I think it was meant as a compliment.

The events of that evening changed things for me. Other agents realized I wasn't made of feathers and began to ask me to work with them. The members of the narcotics task force started to request my participation in search warrants, arrests, and surveillances on a routine basis. I stayed in the New York

Field Office for the next seven years, working on a variety of cases there and in other parts of the country.   However, I secretly suspect, even to this day, that the SAC always feared I would be killed and he would be blamed.

Alicia Hilton

is an attorney, a law professor, and a former FBI special agent. She received a B.A. in Sociology from the University of California at Berkeley and a J.D. and M.A. from the University of Chicago.

As an FBI agent, she was a member of a foreign counterintelligence squad in New York City and also worked undercover in two long-term criminal cases, posing as a drug dealer with ties to organized crime. She resigned from the FBI to attend law school.

Alicia practiced law in New York City as a litigation associate with Chadbourne & Parke and also with Shearman & Sterling. As a law professor, she taught Criminal Procedure, Criminal Law, Undercover Operations and Informant Management Law, and Cultural Property and Museum Law. She has served as a visiting professor of law at the DePaul University College of Law and the John Marshall Law School. In 2011, Alicia was a guest speaker at Baylor Law School, St. Mary's University School of Law, Texas Wesleyan School of Law, University of Hawaii William S. Richardson School of Law, University of St. Thomas School of Law, University of Tulsa College of Law, University of Arkansas School of Law at Fayetteville, University of Arkansas at Little Rock William H. Bowen School of Law, Hamline University Law School, Barry University Dwayne O. Andreas School of Law, University of Memphis Cecil C. Humphreys School of Law and Vanderbilt University Law School.

Alicia's legal scholarship has been published in the U.S. and in Australia. Her articles have been cited by a criminal justice casebook, by multiple treatises, and by law reviews, including the University of Chicago Law Review, the Georgetown Law Journal, the Texas Law Review, the Columbia Journal of Gender & Law, the Washington University Global Studies Law Review, and the Cornell International Law Journal. Alicia's law enforcement articles have been featured in Police Magazine, and she writes articles for Police Magazine's SWAT Blog, Women In Law Enforcement Blog, and Technology Blog.

37

Double Identity

by Alicia Hilton

I wondered what my Grandma would say if she knew I was wearing body armor and a gun under the hot pink sweater she gave me for my twenty-third birthday. She had always encouraged me to be what I wanted to be, but I don't think Grandma would be happy if she knew I had spent the past two years posing as a mob-connected cocaine dealer. Grandma died four months before I joined the FBI.

As I strode up Jerome Avenue in the Bronx, a number 4 train rumbled overhead. Though it was about 45 degrees outside, sweat rolled down my back. My mouth was so dry it felt like I'd been chewing sawdust, but I didn't stop at the bodega for a drink. I wanted to keep my hands free. Two teenage boys loitering on the corner were staring at me. They should have been in school, but they were probably working as lookouts for a local drug dealer. Were they staring at me because my jeans were so tight? Because they were wondering if I was a potential customer? Were they planning to rob me? Or had I been made? I knew the longer I played my undercover role, the more likely it was my cover would get blown. Working undercover made even the most level-headed agents paranoid, and that day all my senses were on high alert. I knew my black leather motorcycle jacket was bulky enough to conceal that I was wearing the Kevlar vest and the 9mm pistol, but I still worried that someone would be able to tell.

It was the first time I'd worn body armor to a meet. It was the first time I'd worn my gun in a hip holster while working UC, but this was no routine meet. Usually, I left my guns at home while I worked UC because most of the criminals I did business with would get suspicious if they saw I was carrying. They'd worry I was going to rip them off or that I was a cop if they saw I had a weapon. For suspects considered particularly dangerous, I brought a gun but carried it in a hidden holster, sacrificing ease of access for subterfuge. That day I needed to get to my gun fast. At locations spread across the Bronx, White Plains, Yonkers, Queens, and Upper Manhattan, FBI Special Agents on forty-five arrest teams were conducting a coordinated take-down. Somewhere on the side streets bordering Jerome Avenue, three of those arrest teams and search teams were waiting for my signal.

The busts would be the culmination of more than two years of work. Initially, the investigation had focused on public corruption, targeting corrupt employees at the DMV who sold fraudulent drivers licenses and vehicle registrations to drug dealers, terrorists, organized crime figures, and other scumbags who used aliases to enter and leave the U.S. or otherwise to facilitate their criminal activity. As evidence was gathered through undercover buys, surveillance and other investigative methods, the case expanded to include additional corrupt government employees who sold passports, green cards, social security cards, and birth certificates. Though none of the government employees were known to be armed and dangerous, some of the subjects at other locations carried weapons and had extensive criminal histories. They used their travel agencies, insurance agencies, and other businesses as fronts, laundering money and dealing in forged documents, drugs, guns, and counterfeit currency. Over the past two years, I had become quite close to some of these individuals. I knew that people like the brother and sister team I was about to do another transaction with would not hesitate to kill me if they thought violence would keep them out of jail.

Five minutes before the scheduled takedown time, I arrived at the location, where I was supposed to do the final deal, and discovered the business was closed, the glass front sealed off by a rolled-down graffiti-covered metal door. "Closed," I muttered for the benefit of agents monitoring the transmitter I was wearing.

Despite my concern about getting made, I didn't think that the subjects had been tipped off about their impending arrest. Criminals are notoriously flaky. They'd probably partied hard the night before and were sleeping off hangovers.

Even during the daytime, that section of Jerome Avenue is not the type of neighborhood you want to hang out in. I glanced around me, wondering if any of the arrest or search team cars was watching when I walked a couple doors down and paused in front of a pawn shop, pretending to admire a stereo and a pair of gaudy gold earrings in the window. Probably both were stolen. And I'd bet that most of the new merchandise sold in the pawn shop fell off a truck.

After waiting a few more minutes, I glanced at my watch and headed up the block. It would look suspicious if I waited on the street too long, and I couldn't risk meeting with agents surveilling the area. I stopped at a fast food joint up the street, used the bathroom, grabbed a drink, and then headed back. All the time surreptitiously looking for agents and the subjects I was supposed to meet. No sign of anyone.

Twenty minutes later, the business was still shuttered. I felt edgy and cold, but I didn't want to call off the bust. I knew if we didn't grab Tina, Joey, and their associates that morning, they would likely hear about the other subjects' arrests and flee the jurisdiction. And they were more likely to be armed and resist arrest if they were busted at their homes. Plus, doing one more deal right before the bust would be additional evidence against them that could be used at trial. I kept walking.

I circled the block again. The metal door was rolled up. The lights were on. I saw Tina at her desk. I felt my heart start pounding harder. Not from the brisk walk or the caffeine I'd been chugging all morning, but from the excitement that leads up to a good bust.

"Hey, Tina, how you doing?" I put the paperwork and photos for two passport applications on her desk. She didn't ask who the men in the photos were. She never did. She didn't care if they were drug dealers or terrorists or what their real names were. All she cared about was money.

"Good, real good." She shoved the paperwork into her top desk drawer and then looked back at me. "Where's Alex?"

"He had to take care of other business." I smiled. Tina didn't try to hide that she thought my undercover partner was sexy. She was like a dog in heat. Her husband was incarcerated in Greece. Her common-law husband in the U.S. also was behind bars for murder. If she knew that Alex was an FBI agent, she wouldn't be so eager to get in his pants. I smiled wider, knowing that my undercover partner was back at the command post, preparing to interrogate subjects after their arrests.

Tina's brother, Joey, came out of the back room and dumped a file on a clerk's desk. He always strutted around like he was a big man, but I knew his sister was the one in the family who ran the business. He was the type of man who only was good for bashing heads.

For once, I didn't have to fake that I was happy when he put his hand on my shoulder and tried to flirt with me. Everyone that we wanted to arrest at that location was on the premises.

I looked back at Tina. "The passports will be ready Monday?"

"No problem."

"Catch you later." I smiled at Tina, nodded at Joey, and

headed toward the door. I'd barely made it to the street when I heard sirens in the distance. Then saw flashing lights. The transmitter had worked.

Pretending to be just another bystander, I joined a group of gawkers on the corner and watched the cars skid to a stop. A procession of raid jacket-wearing FBI agents charged through the door. A couple of NYPD patrol cars arrived to assist with crowd control. No shots were fired. A few minutes later, Tina and Joey were led out, their hands cuffed behind their backs, and loaded into the back of separate Bureau cars.

I strolled up the street. An agent by the door waved me in. The members of the arrest and search teams who hadn't met me before had been shown my picture to eliminate the risk I'd be mistaken for a subject. Now that the bust had been made, I'd assist the search team in identifying evidence.

I opened Tina's desk drawer and pulled out the passport photos and applications. The middle drawer contained a stack of checks. Two were made out to Tina's other aliases. Welfare checks. One had been sent to an address in New Jersey, the other to an address in New York. The woman's annual income likely was several times higher than mine, and she had the nerve to scam the U.S. government for aid. Disgusted, I yanked open the bottom desk drawer and found an open box of colored condoms, one for each color of the rainbow.

In the back room, I found more surprises. A framed poster of Beavis and Butt-Head was hanging on the wall over a filing cabinet. The only other furniture in the room was a single chair that faced a battered wood table. At one end of the table, there was a dirty bird cage with a cockatiel inside it, pecking at a bowl of seed. The part of the table furthest from the door had been turned into a make-shift altar. Burning red and white candles of various sizes and shapes flanked a statue of the Virgin Mary. Her expression was serene as she bowed her head in prayer, quite a contrast to the snarl I'd seen on Tina's face when she was led out of her business in handcuffs. Imagining Tina and Joey riding in the back of the Bureau cars and cursing their fate, I laughed. Today, God was on the side of the FBI.

Mariann Baumbach

from Elizabeth, New Jersey, is a 23-year Port Authority NY/NJ police officer assigned to the K9 Unit. She also serves as a K9 instructor. She dedicates her story to her parents, Frank and Anna, who never imagined their daughter would become a police officer, much less be assigned to the K9 unit and bring home an 87 pound German Shepherd named Thor. They loved their "granddog," and Mariann is certain Thor is resting by their feet in heaven and keeping both of them safe.

Dope in the Garage

by Mariann Baumbach

Most people in the United States have never heard of The Port Authority (PA) Police Department. Even some who live in the New York / New Jersey area know that the PA polices the airports, tunnels, and bridges, but few know the size of the department—1,400 strong. We have police powers in two states, which make us unique. We patrol the above mentioned venues, as well as The Port Authority Bus Terminal on 8th and 42nd Streets in Manhattan, and the World Trade Center. Additionally, we also have our own accredited police academy. Yet there are those who look at us while we work in our dark blue uniforms and assume we are NYPD. However, take a look at the patch on our sleeves, and there you will see the difference. Some may say we are just security, a term all of us hate, but get a ticket or have yourself arrested by the PA and you will find out just how real we are—you now have a record.

Even though our department is large, it's nearly impossible to get assigned to a specialized unit because many of us are needed for traffic posts and airport duty. I should mention that we are the police and fire responders at three major airports, so getting an opportunity for an assignment to the K9 Unit doesn't come along very often. We now have forty-eight teams; when I entered the unit, we had eleven.

A posting for five openings in the Narcotic Detection K9

Unit came out in June of 1997. I was all over it. I submitted my paperwork, had oral interviews with the sergeant in charge of the unit, the lieutenant at the academy, and finally, one of the deputy chiefs. I was accepted and informed when and where to report for the class. The training was mostly uneventful, and upon graduation with my beautiful Shepherd, Thor, I was assigned to Kennedy Airport in Queens.

Although I'm a Jersey girl, I chose JFK Airport so I could help another officer in the class who lived much farther away and who would have had a terrible commute to the airport. Not that mine was a walk in the park either. I live about eight miles from Newark Airport, so crossing two bridges, driving on the Belt Parkway, and then going thirty-four miles out of my way was a burden, to say the least, but he was my classmate, and giving him a ride was the right thing to do.

Clearly everyone remembers the events of 9/11. On that horrific date, my department lost thirty-seven members; that day turned our world upside down. I knew every one of the souls who perished. After the attack we began working twelve hours shifts, six days a week. My shift was 7:00 a.m. to 7:00 p.m. Combined with my commute, twelve hour shifts began to turn into fifteen hours days. My day off was Sunday, and most of the time I slept. I had my dog to care for, but other than that I was thankful it was just me. I still don't know how some of my colleagues kept it together—seeing to family and meeting other obligations. I had enough trouble getting time to clean the house and write the bills.

By January of 2002, we were becoming accustomed to working the long days, and sometimes we'd go to "the pile" at 7 p.m. and work there for a few hours, sleep at one of the stations that was set up, and then go back to our regular assignment the next day. The pile was a heap of debris left over from the collapse of the Trade Center towers. Our job was to go there and stand in a line with buckets looking for anything of importance: body parts, IDs, etc.

One day, when I was looking forward to going home, a call came in to the K9 Sergeant at about 6:30 p.m. Listening to the conversation, I overheard him say, "Yeah we got one working. She'll be there in a little while to meet you." The sergeant hung up and came out of the office and explained the DEA in Queens was looking for a K9. I was to meet them at a specific location — a parking garage.

My jaw dropped. I wanted to kill him right there! I was already exhausted, and now he wanted me at the end of the day to go in the opposite direction of my home, do a job, come back to the airport to do the paperwork, and then head home?

"The next narcotic dog was due in at 7p.m., can't he go?"

"No, I want you to go. You have another half hour left on your shift and the call may turn out to be nothing. You'll probably be on your way home sooner than you think."

Really? Had he forgotten about the traffic around that area? *Well, he's the boss, gotta go and do what he says.* In my timid, quiet way, I slammed doors, banged open a kennel door, and then peeled out of the parking lot on my way to the call. I should also mention that we don't take the work vehicle home. We drive our own personal cars back and forth to work, so when I returned from the call, I still have to clean out the vehicle so the next K9 officer can pull his tour with his dog.

Thankfully, traffic was moderate, and I quickly arrived at the garage where I was immediately directed to a far corner. The DEA agents were standing by and requested we search three vehicles. They advised that they had the owners of the vehicles detained, and if my dog indicated the presence of narcotics on any car, they would have the owner open the vehicle. This practice of having a dog check for the presence of narcotics is a good tactic because the dog's indication gives the right to search the vehicle's interior. Thor is an aggressive indicating K9. He will scratch, bark, bite, and do whatever he needs to do to get to the source of the odor. He can find marijuana, cocaine, crack, heroin, meth, ecstasy, and drug tainted money.

I began my search on a small Toyota, but Thor immediately pulled me away to a red van parked next to it. The dog went to the driver side and then across the front of the van to the passenger side door. Next, he went underneath the double side doors and began barking. He slid back out and began scratching madly at the double side doors. I didn't wait for the DEA to get the owner; I tried and succeeded in opening the door. Thor jumped in and began again to scratch madly, this time at a black tarp lying on the floor of the van. He got underneath the tarp and began nosing suitcases around as best he could. Thor is an eighty-seven pound shepherd so moving the suitcases around was rather easy for him.

At that point the agents quickly converged on the vehicle, and I took Thor out of the van. The agents pulled a suitcase out, opened it, and found "bricks" of cocaine neatly packaged in saran wrap and duct tape inside the case. There were a total of 537 kilos of cocaine in the cases under the tarp! No money was found, which is what the agents were originally looking for, but this discovery was even better. That seizure still holds the record for our department as the largest single seizure by a K9. I was never so proud of my "son," and the DEA sang the dog's praises as well. I thought for all the bitchin' and moanin' I did about going to conduct the search, it turned out to be one of the highlights of my career.

Years later, my beautiful partner, Thor, passed away from hemangiocarcoma on 3/28/06 at almost eleven years old. It was a shock because he was so strong and powerful. I had hoped he would live to around age fifteen. I vividly recall the beginning of the end. We had just finished working a 3 p.m. to 11 p.m. shift, went home, watched a little late-night TV and then headed out for a walk. As we came to the corner of the block, Thor began walking sideways, like a crab. He walked into a sign post and then sat on the ground. I tried to get him to come into the house, but he just stared at me with a blank look. I left him there for a second, ran to my house, got my car keys, and off to the hospital we went.

I knew something was terribly wrong. The thirty minute ride to the 24-hour pet hospital was the longest trip of my life. I called ahead, and when I arrived the vet on duty immediately took us in. Thor just lay there on the table. He didn't move during the exam, didn't stir when they x-rayed him. Anyone who owns a dog knows this behavior is not normal. Within fifteen minutes the vet told me Thor had a mass in the belly area, and it was bleeding.

"What do you want to do?" The vet asked me.

"Are you kidding?" I cried out, "Do anything you can, and do it now!"

The vet operated immediately and afterward had my dog stay overnight; I also stayed and slept in my car in the parking lot. Thor weathered the operation fairly well. The doctor told me Thor should probably stay for a few days to get stronger. They removed his spleen, which any dog can live without, and sent a piece of his liver to be biopsied.

Long story short—Thor had cancer. He began chemotherapy, but by treatment number two it was too late, he was gone. When the vet called to tell me, I completely lost it and cried so hard that when I phoned my K9 sergeant to notify him of the death, he was unable to understand what I was saying. The day Thor died I went to work, still hysterical. My colleagues had no clue how to handle me. Let's just say the day did not go well.

My dog was my world, and there will never be another like him. Pictures of Thor adorn the walls of my home and his ashes rest in a beautiful box in a quiet room. I think of him every day, even though I have a new K9, also named Thor, but it's just not the same. When I retired, the department actually allowed me to keep the second dog, so now I have a six year old pet who thinks he has to save my house and car from everyone and everything that even comes near me. Truth is, I wouldn't have it any other way.

Phyllis Sciacca

of Alexandria, Virginia, was born and raised in Mineola, New York. She graduated from Stetson University, a small university in Florida, and went on to become one of the earliest female agents in the Federal Bureau of Investigation, serving in that capacity for 29 years. Women were not allowed to become special agents until after the death of J. Edgar Hoover. Phyllis worked bank robberies and fugitives, but her main focus over the years was white collar crime. She married an FBI agent she met in Buffalo, New York, and has been happily married for thirty-one years. Phyllis has a stepson and a granddaughter. She loves traveling and has visited all seven continents.

39

They're Looking
for Accountants

by Phyllis Sciacca

My story starts in 1972. I was one week away from graduating from a small college in Florida. Another gal and I were the only two women graduating in the accounting program in the Business School. We had finished our exams and were at Kay's house in Tallahassee. I was lamenting to Kay that I really didn't want to be stuck in an office all day looking at numbers. Kay was also in a quandary and wasn't too hot on being an accountant either.

Her stepfather was reading the newspaper. Having overheard our lament, he said there was an article in the newspaper about the first female FBI agent who was hired since J. Edgar Hoover's death. "You girls could do that," he said. "They're looking for accountants and lawyers." I thought, Wow, now that's something that could be fun! I contacted the FBI and was told that applicants had to be twenty-three years old and have one-year experience in the accounting field. So, off I went to Atlanta to live with some girlfriends and find a job until I reached that age. When I turned twenty-three, I re-applied. Surprisingly, not that many women had gone into the FBI during that year. I always thought I was the fifteenth female agent in the Bureau, but documents show I was the thirtieth. Oh well, so much for being good with numbers!

I was called into the Atlanta office for an interview. Back then interviews were done by the Special Agent in Charge (SAC) or the Assistant Special Agent in Charge (ASAC). Just my luck, the SAC was out and I was ushered in to see the ASAC. He was clearly uninterested and asked me one question, "Little lady," he said, "Could you shoot and kill someone if you had to?" I was so annoyed and wanted to say, "Call me little lady again, and I'll shoot you." But I didn't and instead said loud and strong, "Absolutely!" About four months later, after fingerprinting, a physical, and a background investigation, I received a letter of appointment. I was to be a Special Agent, reporting to Quantico May 6, 1974, and was being paid the princely sum of $13,379 a year.

I reported to Quantico and made it through the sixteen week training course to find out that my first assignment was Buffalo. I had asked to go to New York City (which no first office agent ever requests). The Bureau, in its infinite wisdom, chose to send me to Buffalo. I arrived there to find another female agent already assigned there. It was strange that with so few female agents, two were in a small office like Buffalo. One of the first things that happened was the office held an open house because they had recently moved to a new space.

I was assigned to greet the guests, which consisted of judges and high city officials. When the guests had gathered, the office coordinator, Dave Sanchez, introduced me to the group as the "office's Dickless Tracy." Needless to say I was mortified. Later, the Buffalo Police Department decided, for some unknown reason, to honor women in law enforcement. They did not have women in their ranks, other than traffic cops, so they contacted the SAC and asked if Shelly Hughes (the other female agent) and I would be their honored guests. Shelly and I sat at the head table and were talked about and honored. All this adulation and I hadn't been an agent for a year yet.

There was a need for female agents in other parts of the

country, and the Bureau called upon the few of us to do some interesting things. A problem came up in Boston. Two top ten fugitives were going to meet up with their girlfriends and flee the country. The two fugitives were wanted for blowing up a water tank and the courthouse and were violent, bad guys. Before there were female agents, male agents would take the squad secretary with them, or occasionally their wives, when they need some "cover" on surveillance. These bad guys were armed and extremely dangerous, so taking an unarmed civilian was not an option.

The FBI decided to fly in ten female agents to go with the guys and follow the girlfriends in order to catch the fugitives when they met up to flee the country. The girlfriends had been schooled by their boyfriends on how to ditch surveillance, so they were very hard to follow. Naturally, while I was the point (the one actually following them), they went into a small newsstand. The place was very small, so I opted not to follow them in but to wait outside until they came out. They didn't come out. They bolted out the back door never to be seen again.

Fortunately, a Boston agent had an informant who was in touch with the girlfriends and made arrangements to meet the fugitives in a bar outside of Boston. They put the ten gals with ten of the biggest male agents in the office in the bar, posing as a group of guys with their dates. I was sitting at the bar, the only blonde in the group. They told the informant to take a seat next to the blonde and wait for the fugitives. My job was to get the hell out of the way when the fugitives came in so the guys could grab them. As so often happens, the fugitive came to the door, didn't like the looks of the crowd (maybe so many big clean cut looking guys?), and turned around and left. The informant turned to me and said, "That was him; he just left the bar."

My purse was wired with the SAC on the other end listening in to hear what was going on. I started yelling into my purse, "He turned around and left the bar." The rest of the agents were around the perimeter of the bar. They started to close in, when a lone agent saw one of the fugitives. When he tried to grab him, a struggle ensued. The fugitive and the agent were fighting over the agent's gun. Back then we all carried revolvers. The agent hit the cylinder release and kicked the bullets out of the gun, for he felt he was losing the battle. The fugitive got the gun, put it to the agent's head, and pulled the trigger. There was no loud explosion, just the sound of an empty cylinder. At that point, numerous agents converged on the scene and the fugitive was apprehended (no thanks to any of the women I might add).

While in Buffalo, I was assigned to the fugitive and bank robbery squad. This was the first time the Bureau ever had a woman on the squad. For the most part all the guys were helpful and courteous. There was one exception, Dick Wilson. Dick was true to his name—a dick! He would not lower himself to work with a female agent and was vocally dismissive of the Bureau for hiring us.

One day I had dropped my car off at the garage for servicing and had just come back to the office. When the elevator reached the Bureau's floor, the doors opened and there was Dick. He said, "We just had a bank robbery, turn around." I told him I didn't have a car and was so bold as to ask him for a ride. Dick gave me an, "Oh crap," smirk and said, "I'll drop you at the bank." The unspoken part of that sentence was "I'll drop you off and then go catch the bad guys like only us men can do."

We got in the car and started out. The Bureau radio broadcasted the license plate of the getaway vehicle, and lo and behold, it crossed in front of us on a side street. Now, I must pause and tell you that it was a typical Buffalo winter day, snowing like a son of a bitch and about ten degrees below zero. We put the red light up, the siren on, and I called in on the radio to say we were in pursuit. The car pulled over, and we both jumped out. I had my gun out, trained on the driver. I looked over and there was Dick trying to get his gun out. His coat was all buttoned up, he had gloves on, and he couldn't get to his gun. He was literally trying to rip the buttons off his coat to get it open, but his wife must have sewed the buttons on with extra durable thread because they would not yield. I yelled to the driver to keep his hands on the wheel where I could see them and then stole another look at Dick. He was still struggling to get his gun out.

The bank robber was compliant, so Dick, in a fit of frustration, gave up, walked over to the car, yanked the door open, grabbed the guy out by the collar, and threw him up against the hood of the car. He reached for his handcuffs and couldn't get those out either, for his coat had imprisoned his whole body. I nonchalantly handed him my cuffs. Dick patted the guy down, cuffed him, and threw him in the back seat of the Bureau car. He then went over to search the car for the bank robbery loot. He still had not said one word to me.

I stayed with the prisoner, called in to the station, told them we had the guy in custody, and gave them our location. After advising the bank robber of his rights, I started to talk to him. The lookout broadcast over the radio was for two black males. I asked where his partner was. He told me he dropped him off at an address about six blocks away. I yelled to Dick. He came back to the car with a rifle the guy had in the back seat. We got some other agents to follow us while the bank robber pointed out where he left the other guy off. Agents grabbed the second guy.

From then on, Dick and I had an unspoken agreement. He would stop making disparaging remarks about female agents, and I would not tell the guys what an ass he made of himself on the arrest. That lasted for a few years, and then Dick started bad mouthing female agents again. It was amazing, but that story about his problems during our arrest somehow just leaked out.

After Buffalo, I went to Alexandria, Virginia. I arrived in Alexandria and was the first and only female agent in that office. While in Alexandria, I had some good cases. One case involved ammunition paid for by the US government, which was sent to El Salvador to help their government battle the rebels. When Congress appropriated the money, they stipulated the goods had to be of US manufacture. That way, while we helped the government of El Salvador, we spent (and kept) the money in the US. One company that supplied ammunition said they were sending US goods but were in fact sending Yugoslavian ammunition of poor quality that caused the soldiers' guns to jam. This practice was allowed to go on, as the military commanders were getting kickbacks.

So off I went to El Salvador during a civil war, a very unsettling time. The Bureau told me to take my gun, a revolver. So there I was with a snub nose revolver when everyone else had an M16 or other large military weapon. I was with a DCIS agent, Doug Smith, who was also armed with a similar small caliber weapon. The Department of Justice (DOJ) sent an Assistant Attorney General, Vicki Toensing, and some other high officials to meet with high El Salvador government officials. They arranged a meeting with President Duarte of El Salvador. FBI Headquarters told me I could not go to the meeting with Duarte, as "street agents do not meet with heads of state." They finally agreed that it would look bad if I was the only one who didn't go, so they relented and told me I could go, but I was not allowed to talk.

Well, when the President summoned us, we were in the middle of an interview with a Death Squad Colonel. We were yelling at him, telling him we knew he was taking bribes and that his men were being killed because of him. The high DOJ officials told us to keep after him and left us to go off to meet the President. We continued the interview, but the Colonel would make no admissions. The man we were interviewing was rumored to be responsible for the killing of three Agency for International Development (AID) workers a few months previous. The AID workers were staying at the same hotel we were staying at.

Our situation was very uncomfortable after that interview. After meeting the President, the DOJ officials immediately flew back to Washington and left us to finish up. While we were there, someone shot at the embassy and one of the bulletproof cars (we were in the second car which wasn't shot at). Our rooms were also searched while we were at dinner. We got back to Washington safely and prosecuted the US people involved in the sale of the ammunition. The government of El Salvador did not do anything about their military leaders who took the bribes to accept the ammunition.

Prior to the Iran Contra affair, I was assigned a case that involved using US funds to pay for weapons for the Nicaraguan contras. The US government had authorized only humanitarian aid for the contras, and any money provided could not be used for "lethal" aid. Off again I went, this time to Miami, where I interviewed the three leaders of the Nicaraguan contras. That was fascinating! These men agreed to be interviewed in Miami because they wanted the US to continue funding their effort and did not want to appear to be uncooperative. I had to sympathize with them though. They used the money for food to support their troops, but they felt they had their hands tied. If their men did not have the weapons to fight, they would be killed, and food and medical supplies would not help them. It was also hard to track where the money went. They had to buy food from local farmers to feed their men while on the battlefield. They obtained "receipts" for the food, but the farmers did not want the Nicaraguan government to know they were selling food to the contras or they would be shot as traitors. It was a lose-lose situation.

The commanders did as well as expected and used the

money for medical supplies and food. There was one commander who admitted using the money for weapons, for the men were being overrun, and all the food in the world wouldn't save them from being wiped out. Aside from the three leaders, I interviewed one of the battlefield commanders known as "El Negro" Chammoro. He was kicked out of Honduras but was being smuggled back in to the country that evening. I met him before he was whisked off to be air lifted back into battle. When the Iran contra scandal broke, the Bureau absorbed my case into it, for they wanted control of everything involving the contras.

My story would not be complete without discussing the events of 9/11. On that day, I was sitting in the office at the Resident Agency (RA) in Tysons Corner, VA, when word came out about the first plane hitting the World Trade Center. We all went into the conference room and watched CNN. Suddenly, we heard the Pentagon had been hit and looked out the window to see the smoke. We were called into the conference room while management decided what should be done.

We all hopped into our cars and raced toward the Pentagon. Amazingly enough there was no traffic heading in that direction, but there was gridlock with people trying to get out of DC. We reported in to the Command Post, and it was immediately evident that there was mass confusion. The fire was still burning, and there was nothing to do until it was under control. Meanwhile they sent us to interview survivors and witnesses. I interviewed one man who had just entered the Pentagon situation room to bring the news that the second tower had been hit when the plane hit the Pentagon. Two people in the room with him were killed. He saw a hole in the wall and climbed out, literally climbing over the windshield of the plane to get out. He thought it was the windshield of the plane, but it may have just been the windshield of a truck that had been parked in one of the inner rings. It was amazing to talk to him, for he was just realizing the enormity of what had happened while we were talking.

From there, I was told to find four generals who had an office overlooking the parking lot to see if they had seen the plane coming in. The command post had no names of the generals and no location for them. I felt a little stupid walking around asking if anyone had seen four generals in the Pentagon. I did find an admiral and wound up settling for him. He had an office down from where the plane hit and was calling to people through the smoke to direct them out. He gave me the name of a fixed wing flight instructor who was in the parking lot who saw the plane hit. He had been sent home, so off I went to his house in Woodbridge, VA.

It was about 9:00 p.m. by the time I got there, but nobody was sleeping that night. He told me how he had seen the plane coming in, wheels up, and that the pilot had "spooled up" or gunned it as he drew a bead on the Pentagon. The witness was pretty shook up. We returned to the Pentagon and followed minor leads until the staff sent us home, about 2:00 a.m. with instructions to report back to Tysons Corner at 6:00 a.m. When I got home, I was washing my hands in the bathroom sink and noticed black specs in the sink. I asked my husband (also an agent) what that dirt was. He said, "Look in the mirror, you've got soot all over you." I hadn't had time to look and had no idea I was full of soot.

The next day we went to Tysons Corner and were told the ASAC who was in charge of the hijacking investigation at Dulles airport did not need help. He had ten agents out there, and he thought that was enough. The supervisors knew he was in trouble and sent sixty of us to the airport to assist. The supervisors went along also, as the ASAC obviously was not thinking straight. I was assigned with four other agents to interview all American Airlines employees who had access to the plane. There were about 120 people who had badges that would get them into the area where the plane was parked.

We started doing the logical interviews first, the ones who cleaned the plane and inspected the plane before it went out. At that point we were still not sure if the box cutters were put on the plane by someone else, or if the hijackers brought them aboard. These employees were beside themselves. They had lost crew members they knew, plus a secretary from their unit had been a pass rider on the plane. They were so upset thinking that maybe they missed something.

One female inspected the plane before it was allowed to be boarded. She normally would have gone back while it was being loaded to watch, especially since there were two passengers on the "pull list," for the ticket agent was not satisfied with their answers to the security questions. Back then, if an employee was suspicious of a passenger, he put them on the "pull list," which meant their luggage was not loaded until the passenger physically boarded the plane. Two of the hijackers were put on the "pull list." However, on that day of all days, an employee had a minor accident out on the tarmac, and the female inspector went out to deal with it, missing the plane's departure. She was visibly upset thinking that maybe if she had been there to look at the passengers or searched the plane better this tragedy wouldn't have happened.

We continued with our interviews, and on the second day the ASAC came to me and asked where we were. I told him that we still had twenty people to interview, and he told me that couldn't be true because he already told FBIHQ the interviews were finished. I told him they were not done. Not being the sharpest knife in the drawer, he then said "Why do we need to talk to people who weren't on duty that night?" I told him these people still had access to the plane with their badges and needed to be questioned to rule them out.

The ASAC then said, "Why do we care? The hijackers were killed." I looked at him and found it hard to hide the fact I thought he was a complete moron and explained, like you would to a child, that if we caught someone else who assisted the hijackers they could be charged with the hijacking. Plus, I threw in that I did not think this was an investigation in which we should take any short cuts but should be completely thorough. He told me he wanted the interviews done by 7 p.m. that evening because he didn't want to go back to FBIHQ and tell them he was wrong when he told them they were done. Not long after that, they needed a team to set up a command post at National Airport. He immediately put me on the team to get rid of me. Fortunately, he had competent supervisors with him at Dulles Airport who went around him to get things done they knew should be done.

It wasn't until the third night, after working long days and nights that the full impact hit me of what had happened. I found myself driving home with tears rolling down my cheeks. It was the first time I allowed myself to feel any emotion. Until then I was just doing what needed to be done and focused all my energies on the task at hand. But you can only do that for so long and then the emotions catch up with you. It was one of the most important investigations I have ever worked on.

My philosophy is that you don't have to be physically strong and/or masculine to be an FBI agent or a police officer. Most of what we do does not involve physical contact, but you do need to have an aggressive attitude; I do. (Note to the reader: People's names in the story are not their actual names, and the opinions expressed herein are mine, and not those of the FBI.)

Peggy Tobin-Trice

attended the University of Nebraska on an athletic scholarship and received her B.S Degree in Criminal Justice. In 1990, Peggy began her career with the Bureau of Alcohol, Tobacco, Firearms, and Explosives (ATF), and was stationed in Tulsa, Oklahoma. She continued her education while residing in Tulsa and received a Master's Degree in Criminal Justice from Northeastern State University.

Peggy has been assigned to the Tulsa Field Office during her tenure with ATF, and has assisted in the training/instruction of the field of gang culture and identification through her board position with the Oklahoma Gang Investigator's Association and ATF. She also assisted in preparing the 2007 Oklahoma Gang Assessment Summary, per the Oklahoma District Attorney's Council and the U.S. Department of Justice. Subsequently, Peggy has been acknowledged as one of many editors for the "Quick Reference Guide to Gang Symbols," per the Oklahoma District Attorney's Council and Northeastern State University.

Peggy has received the following accommodations: Certificate of Commendation from the United States Attorney's Office (3 times); ATF Certificate of Award-Special Act or Service Award (3 times); Oklahoma Gang Investigator of the Year Award from the Oklahoma Gang Investigator's Association, and the U.S. Department of Justice, Project Safe Neighborhoods, Outstanding Gang Investigation Award.

Laurel Ledbetter

has been employed by the Tulsa Police Department for over 13 years. She is currently a sergeant assigned to the Internal Affairs office. Prior to joining the Tulsa Police Department, she received a Bachelor's Degree in Criminal Justice from Northeastern State University. Subsequently, she has also earned a Master's degree in Criminal Justice from NSU.

Laurel worked as a patrol officer for a total of five years in the Uniform Division North. She was assigned to the Organized Gang Unit for a total of three years, and the evening shift of the Narcotics Unit for another three years. Sergeant Ledbetter was promoted in 2007 and was a field supervisor at the Uniform Division North before being assigned as an investigator in Internal Affairs.

She has received gang training all over the nation from a variety of sources, among them, the Los Angeles County Sheriff's Department, the Bureau of Alcohol, Tobacco, Firearms and Explosives, the National Institute of Law Enforcement, the Texas Gang Investigator's Association and the International Outlaw Motorcycle Gang Investigators Association. She completed the Drug Enforcement Administration's basic narcotic investigator's school and was certified as a clandestine lab expert by Network Environmental Services. Laurel has taught gang classes at the Tulsa Police training academy, focusing on African American street gangs and outlaw motorcycle gangs.

She received the Tulsa Police Department's Medal of Valor and the Chief's Award twice. She was honored by the National Association of Insurance Woman with their annual Officer of the Year award, and has been the recipient of the Amicus Curaie, presented by the City Of Tulsa Courts for excellent warrant service.

Laurel has been assigned to the U.S. Attorney's Office in the Northern District of Oklahoma where she and ATF Special Agent Peggy Tobin were responsible for the completion of the Ceasefire case. For their efforts, Agent Tobin and Sergeant Ledbetter's case was named as the United States Department of Justice, Project Safe Neighborhood Case of the Year in 2007.

Tulsa Oklahoma Operation Ceasefire

By Peggy Tobin-Trice and Laurel Ledbetter

In June of 2003, I had been a special agent with the Bureau of Alcohol, Tobacco and Firearms, and Explosives, (ATF) for thirteen years. During those years I had worked a variety of investigations involving different types of defendants. My passion had always been working gang conspiracy cases involving narcotics, firearms, and violent crimes and I was about to embark on one that would be a journey for me and my other fellow law enforcement partners in Tulsa, Oklahoma.

In March 2003, Michael Summers, also known as (AKA) "Mikey D," AKA "Green Eyes," was released from prison. He claimed to be an original gangster (O.G.) of the Hoover Crips. Because Summers resided in the streets of Tulsa, he dubbed himself the "Five Star General" of the Hoover Crips to the police and others. Summers even had five stars tattooed on his shoulder in order to reinforce that perception. After his release from prison, Summers stated during a traffic stop, "It is time to kill or be killed." He continued his narcotics trafficking and violence through the 107 Hoover Crip Organization, and had his soldiers distribute narcotics and take care of anyone who disrupted, disrespected or retaliated against the "set." One of the special characteristics of this group was that four of our main targets were brothers and one was their sister. A common practice among Hoover Crips in Tulsa was to pass around firearms for the purpose of homicides, shootings and drive-by shootings. Law enforcement in Tulsa knew that the Hoover Crips in Tulsa used witness intimidation as a means to avoid prosecution. The Hoover Crips were known by law enforcement to commit drive-by shootings and homicides as a means to control witness testimony or the lack thereof.

In April, May, and June of 2003, Tulsa had eight gang related homicides, with three being committed in four days. In January, February, and March of 2004, Tulsa had eight gang related homicides. Three of these had occurred in four days. All of these shootings had been between the Hoover Crips and the Neighborhood Crips. The homicides had been initiated by the Hoover Crips and directed by Michael Summers. Law enforcement in Tulsa knew that something had to be done. Thus, a task force was formed to deal with the rising homicide/shooting incidents in Tulsa.

During June of 2003, law enforcement officers from Tulsa Police Department, ATF, DEA and FBI formed a task force entitled "Operation Ceasefire." ATF and Tulsa Police Department took the lead in this investigative effort. Investigators identified a list of 50 names of documented Hoover Crips who were involved in criminal activity. Soon, a two-pronged approach was implemented. The first one was a proactive approach, which included search warrants, developing and continuing to work with confidential informants, and confidential sources. An intelligence gathering approach was also engaged by getting reports from police records, gang files, photo books of all targets, violent criminal involvement and Department of Corrections information. Lead investigators were myself, Special Agent Peggy Trice, Tulsa Police officer Laurel Ledbetter, two former Tulsa Police Officers, one FBI Special Agent and one DEA Special Agent. This task force was the start of what would eventually evolve into the first RICO case in the Northern Judicial District of Oklahoma, namely, Tulsa, Oklahoma.

On April 19, 2003, Justin Price was murdered in the street in North Tulsa. Witnesses stated that Curtis Deon Jones, AKA "Straightface," AKA "Deon," a Hoover Crips gang member, was involved in that murder. According to witnesses, Jones had stated that Stewart was "slipping." Witnesses also testified that Jones stated that he had killed a nappy head on 55th Street with a Tech 9 firearm. It should be noted that "nappy head" is derogatory term for Neighborhood Crips. Witnesses stated to Ceasefire investigators that Jones stated that he killed a Neighborhood Crip because his cousin got killed by one a few years ago. Ceasefire investigators also learned that he (Jones) was waiting in the bushes for Price and ambushed him.

On May 11, 2003, James Stewart, AKA "Yohn", was killed at a convenience store in Tulsa. Witnesses placed Paul Summers as the shooter of Stewart. Witnesses further stated to Ceasefire investigators that there was an ongoing dispute between Stewart and the Summers brothers. Witnesses further stated to investigators that the Summers brothers believed Stewart to be a snitch, who supplied information about the Hoover Crips' illegal activities to law enforcement. Ironically, James Stewart had not been working for the police in any capacity.

On October 16, 2003, one of our lead investigators and former Tulsa Police Officer, while assisting on surveillance team during a controlled undercover narcotics purchase with an undercover police officer in a known narcotics area controlled by Hoovers in Tulsa, witnessed a homicide/robbery occur across the street from his location. The suspect, later identified as "TT," ran across the street and pointed her weapon at the officer. Subsequently, the officer shot and killed "TT" in self-defense. Once "TT" was identified, it was learned that she was Michael Summers' sister.

After the shooting, a crowd developed, chanting and attempting to incite a riot. That night following the shooting, S/A Trice as well as other investigators learned that Michael Summers was walking around with a SKS firearm and was going to kill the officer responsible for his sister's death. Pursuant to this information, one of the officers in the gang unit developed information to obtain a search warrant in a residence near where TT's death had occurred. The initial residence where the search warrant was executed revealed no firearms, but the abandoned residence next door revealed several firearms, one of which was an SKS firearm. We soon learned shortly after the shooting that Paul Summers, Michael Summers, and Roy Summers (AKA "Long John") were discussing locating and plotting the murder of the officer that had killed his sister. We were being told that this information was coming from someone inside the Tulsa Police Department Records Division who was providing sensitive law enforcement information to the Summers brothers. This odd coincidence of the unrelated shooting being Michael Summers' sister had stepped up the investigation to a higher level with these gang members plotting to kill an officer.

On February 18, 2004, S/A Trice was contacted by a former Homicide sergeant of the Tulsa Police Department, reference a Confidential Source (CS), walking into the Tulsa Police Department Homicide Unit requesting to give information about the Summers brothers. Subsequently, S/A Trice worked with this individual to provide intelligence information relative to criminal activities by the Summers brothers as well as others that were hanging around.

The intelligence being provided came in at the right time. From December of 2004 to March of 2004, a known source to law enforcement, dated Roy Summers and was around this crowd on a regular basis. The source of information described an incident involving the funeral service for Charlie Summers,

AKA "Charlie Woo," brother to the other Summers brother, who had been killed on January 16, 2004 in a gang related shooting which was unsolved at the time. CS described attending the graveside service for Charlie Summers and hearing Michael Summers yell out "I'm gonna kill the rest of them motherfuckers." CS also described hearing Paul Summers bragging about how they got Cornelius Finch AKA "Half Dead," who was killed on January 20, 2004. Finch had been killed in retaliation for Charlie Summers' death. Several CS's also helped to identify firearms these gang members had in their possession. One of the firearms was a semi-automatic with no grips, which would later be used in a homicide. Through our CS, we were able to corroborate that someone at Tulsa Police Department's Records Division was providing information to the Summers brothers. As we would later learn, not only was a civilian employee providing information, but also a Tulsa police officer was as well.

On the evening of February 26, 2004, our CS contacted me and told me that he/she had just pulled up next to Robert Fellows, Greg McKinney, Roy Summers and Phillip Summers at a stoplight. CS said that all four were dressed in dark blue hoodies, and that Roy Summers stated "they were about to ride up on some motherfuckers." With that information I immediately telephoned a former sergeant with the Tulsa Police Department Homicide Unit, who assisted in getting the Tulsa Police Department Helicopter Unit to locate the vehicle. Subsequently, the Helicopter Unit located the vehicle with the use of the FLIR, an infrared camera device. When they did, all occupants of the vehicle fled on foot. Eventually, Roy Summers and Robert Fellows were apprehended, yet a visual with the FLIR indicated two of the occupants had placed something in the bushes. The next morning Ceasefire investigators searched the area and recovered a Bersa .380 caliber revolver with no grips.

On February 23, 2004, Shelly and Ples Vann were killed in their home in Tulsa. The Vanns were the parents of an Original Gangster (O.G.) of the Neighborhood Crips in Tulsa, Lawrence Tennyson, AKA "Bud." Bud had been hated by the Hoovers for a long time, and Phillip Summers had made it known on the street that he wanted to "get" Bud. The investigation revealed that Gregory McKinney, AKA "Act Bad" or "A Cat," Phillip Summers AKA "Stey High," AKA "Phil Phil," and Robert Fellows AKA "Raboe," went to the Vanns' residence. Fellows stayed in the vehicle parked in front of the Vann's residence. Summers and McKinney went inside the residence and killed the Vanns. This homicide was pivotal in that the Bersa .380 had been identified through ATF's National Integrated Ballistic Information Network (NIBIN), as a match to the firearm utilized to kill the Vanns. NIBIN was established by ATF in 1999 in order to compare automated ballistic images made on fired cartridge cases and bullets recovered from a crime scene or a crime gun test fire. They then compared those images against earlier entries via electronic image comparison. Subsequently, a short time after the .380 was recovered, a .45 auto pistol, which was thrown from a vehicle by Phillip Summers, was later recovered by citizens clearing out brush on their land and turned into the police department. This .45 also matched up though ATF's NIBIN as the second firearm which had been used in the Vann Homicide.

Phillip Summers implicated himself as participating in the murder of the Vanns in a letter to the wife of Charlie Summers AKA "Charlie Woo," which was recovered by police officers. Interestingly, the .380 that was recovered and verified to be used in the Vann homicide, per NIBIN, was the same firearm used to shoot Brian Armstrong, a Neighborhood Crip Associate, on January 10, 2004, which was a successive count in our indictment.

Another noteworthy event had occurred that we were

unaware of at the time of the homicide. A CS's vehicle had been borrowed by Robert Fellows the day of the homicide and subsequently used in the homicide of the Vanns. Also, the morning after the killing, a CS had been over at a residence with Roleithia Summers, when Robert Fellows, Greg McKinney and Phillip Summers showed up. According to CS, McKinney and Summers each had firearms, and all three were making comments about Bud being surprised when he got home.

On March 3, 2004, one of our CS's was threatened by Roleithia Summers and two other black females at a hotel room. They were threatening him/her her because they believed him/her to be a snitch. This incident was at the direction of Michael Summers. A firearm was placed next to the CS's head and the trigger was pulled, but the firearm either malfunctioned or was not loaded. As Roleithia was leading the CS out of the hotel, the CS was able to get away. Notably, the same day this threat occurred, Ceasefire investigators were placing a GPS on the CS's vehicle and hardwiring an apartment to be utilized by one of our CS's. Needless to say, with the threat, none of those things occurred, and one of our CS's was no longer a source that we could utilize.

On March 5, 2004, a tape-recorded conversation ensued between Michael Summers and one of our CS's. During that conversation, Summers stated he believed the CS to be working for the police, and that the police bought the CS a phone. I and the other Ceasefire investigators felt this statement was odd and believed this was another example of someone on the inside that was helping the Summers brothers. Summers made the statement to our CS, that he would go "Straightface." Summers stated "I don't even give a fuck, and I don't play them games. The coldest thing is I don't even have nothing against you." To all of us, the term "straightface" meant committing a murder without any worry or concern, as well, as no disguise. Moreover, the term also meant killing a person without any remorse or care.

After countless attempts at undercover operations, trash pulls, search warrants, and the lack of witness cooperation, Ceasefire investigators decided we had exhausted our investigative efforts, so the next step was a Title-III (wiretap) on Michael Summers' phone. Summers was on electronic monitoring by the state on a narcotics charge and he had a probation officer. With that, we had information if his phone number was to change and his whereabouts through the GPS. I volunteered as the affiant on the Title-III. I had been previously involved in a few as a monitor/response team. I knew that a Title-III meant long hours and lots of tedious work. Thankfully, I had plenty of assistance and support.

On April 23, 2004, the Title-III was obtained for narcotics and homicide. Due to the potential of the interception of homicide crimes as being part of the Title-III, it was going to be monitored 24 hours a day. Logistically, we had to monitor the Title-III in Oklahoma City, which was a couple of hours away. Thus, we had to deal with five-day rotations and bringing officers/agents to Oklahoma City to assist. The first day of the interception we learned that Summers' narcotics supplier was no longer a black male named, Chris Gibson, a known source of crack cocaine and marijuana. The shift had gone to Inez Valdez and Jesus Trejo, two unknown Mexican males residing in the Tulsa area.

The Title-III ended on May 23, 2004. During the Title-III, we had approximately 2,000 completed phone calls. Michael Summers never got off the phone. His calls were constant. Ceasefire Investigators executed five search warrants during the wire which produced several firearms, approximately two pounds of marijuana, and approximately two pounds of cocaine base. We also coordinated with US Marshals in Bakersfield, California in order to arrest Paul Summers AKA "Tom Tom," now a fugitive, for an outstanding murder warrant in the James

Stewart case. Paul Summers had called Michael Summers during the Title-III, which had revealed Paul Summers location. After about two weeks into the Title-III, my partner Officer Ledbetter, discovered she was pregnant. This would be the first of two pregnancies during this case, illustrating how slowly the wheels of justice turn.

After the Title-III was over, we knew we had our "Enterprise" and had enough evidence to produce the first RICO case in the Northern Judicial District. Subsequently, we began to gather evidence and call in witnesses to the Federal Grand Jury, a total of 96. During this time, I became pregnant and gave birth in the latter part of 2005.

On May 31, 2005, we indicted 13 defendants on 147 counts to include RICO; VICAR; Possession of Marijuana and Cocaine Base with Intent to Distribute, Maintain Drug Involved Premises, Intimidation of Witnesses, Use of Communication Facility to Facilitate a Felony; Felon in Possession of a Firearm AFCF, Money Laundering, Possession of a Firearm during the commission of a Drug Trafficking Crime, and Aiding and Abetting. We superseded this indictment on December 19, 2005. We added some additional counts and listed our cooperating defendants as unindicted co-conspirators.

On August 9, 2005, Gregory McKinney was killed by an unknown assailant in Tulsa. This murder is still under investigation by Ceasefire investigators, as well as the Tulsa Police Department homicide detective who worked the case. McKinney's homicide is believed to be related to McKinney's cooperation in the Shelly and Ples Vann homicide.

On March 1, 2006, a former Tulsa police officer who had worked in the Gang Unit during our investigation, and a records clerk at the Tulsa Police Department, were indicted on obstruction charges unrelated to our investigation. However, during their trial our case was mentioned numerous times as to his involvement. We now understood why some things that had not made sense during the investigation, such as dry holes on search warrants, informants being threatened, undercover operations being compromised and informants and witnesses telling us that the Summers brothers had "someone" on the inside. Finally, it all made perfect sense.

The investigation was groundbreaking for Tulsa because of its specific focus on one street gang and its leadership, its high level members, its enforcers and several of its significant drug suppliers. An alarming spike in gang-related murders, a gang war orchestrated by the leader of Tulsa's most active criminal street gang, led to this targeted initiative. Tulsa's skyrocketing murder rate spurred the Deputy Attorney General to designate Tulsa as one of the original 20 cities to receive a Violent Crime Impact Team (VCIT). The RICO investigation and prosecution was the first of its kind in this district. It enabled law enforcement and prosecutors to draw upon a variety of gang-related criminal activities, including six murders, drug trafficking, shootings, witness tampering and weapons offenses to wipe out the leadership of the Hoover Crips and expose them to substantial prison sentences. The investigation produced a 147-count federal RICO indictment which has resulted in 13 guilty pleas, including seven charges to RICO, 176 cumulative years of imprisonment and a remaining defendant who is facing capital murder charges in state court. One of the convicted co-defendants in the RICO case has testified in the Vann's state murder trial. Additionally, 57 targeted gang members were charged and convicted in state court through the cooperation of the Tulsa County District Attorney's Office. The total drug amounts were: marijuana, 128 pounds; cocaine base, crack cocaine, 24 pounds.

The effect of the investigation and prosecution was immediate and dramatic. It virtually wiped out the known leadership of the 107 Hoover Crips. In the eighteen months preceding the investigation, Tulsa averaged nearly four firearm-related gang homicides per month.   In the three months immediately following the arrest of the RICO defendants, there was only one gang firearm-related homicide per month, and during the six month period following the arrests there was an average of less than two gang firearm-related homicides per month.   The partnership of federal, state and local law enforcement produced by this investigation has spilled over and continued in subsequent investigations and operations.

Part Four:

Chaplains

Reverend Jan Heglund

of Fairfax, California, is a chaplain with the San Rafael California Police Department and the San Francisco Division of the Federal Bureau of Investigation. She has been a chaplain for 16 years. Jan is married with four children and four grandchildren. She loves running to stay fit and also reading. She finds one of the biggest blessings in life is waking up in the morning.

Law enforcement chaplaincy is her passion, and she considers it a privilege to help people during some of the most important and difficult times of their lives. Serving as chaplain at the FBI Academy at Quantico, Virginia, at Ground Zero and as a chaplain at National Police Week in Washington, D.C., were powerful experiences for her.

Reverend Jan is on the Board of Project Grace, a non-profit organization for women who have lost a child. The organization takes women on working trips to Europe. She is a founding member and Chaplain Coordinator of First Responders Support Network, only the second place in the world that does what we do: host a week long healing workshop for those suffering from PTSD. Jan is also on the Advisory Committee for the Arts, Humanities, and Social Sciences Department at her local Dominican College.

Chaplain Heglund received the Outstanding Clergy of the Year Award from NAMI, California, and the Woman Making a Difference for Women Award from Soroptimists International. Jan considers it an honor and blessing to be included in this publication.

Do I Have To Talk About God In This Small Space?

by Reverend Jan Heglund

GOD HAD A PLAN.

Did I ever imagine, while attending Grant High School in Portland, Oregon, riding my favorite bike and playing hide and seek in the summer, that I would be totally changing my planned career later in life? Could I have foreseen at nineteen that my mom would die and I would quit college where I was majored in Business, or that I would be praying over someone in a hospital in California?

After I moved to San Francisco, and became the administrative assistant I always wanted to be, I could not have imagined in a million years that I would be voted Clergy of the Year by NAMI (National Alliance on Mental Illness). How could I ever have known, that, after marrying and converting to Catholicism, divorcing, experiencing living as a single mom, and surviving the death of a grandchild, that I would, as an ordained Episcopal Deacon, be standing at a podium giving the key note speech at San Rafael High School graduation in the Marin County Veteran's Memorial Auditorium, and that the local paper would carry the entire speech?

Life has a way of happening. As a law enforcement chaplain, I recently stood at that very same podium delivering the Eulogy for a much loved and treasured law enforcement individual's celebration of life. Shared below are stories and experiences that have happened in my many years as a law enforcement chaplain with the San Rafael Police Department and the San Francisco Division of the FBI. I have been instrumental in starting chaplaincy programs in other agencies, and my career has opened many doors, such as working at 9/11, being the chaplain at the FBI Academy and one of the chaplains at National Police Week in Washington, D.C. My experiences have taken me to Nicaragua and Greece and changed my life in a way that is hard to explain. I guess my message is that, later in life it is possible to pursue a dream you didn't even know you had until it came knocking at your door. You can ignore it, but your life will be forever changed and enriched if you walk over and turn that four hundred pound knob.

THE BEGINNING

I had just started as a police chaplain and was riding along in a police car for the first time. Aware that no one wants someone in their car chatting constantly for an eight hour shift, I continued to ride along and enjoy the quiet. At a certain point, after having glanced at the face of the young officer sitting alongside me, I said, "I bet I know what you are thinking."

Startled, the officer replied, "You do?"

I said, "Yes, I bet you are thinking, 'What in the world is this person doing sitting in my car, and OMG, it's a woman, and, worst of all, am I going to have to talk about God in this small space?' All I am going to say is everything said in this car stays in this car."

The officer didn't stop talking the entire shift.

BEADY EYES ARE DECEIVING

We were the responding car to a domestic violence call. The building was narrow with steps going up to a front door. When we entered, we realized we needed to go up another flight of stairs. At the top, the hall divided the rooms, with the living room on one side and the bedroom on the other. The officers in the first car had separated the very angry woman and her husband on each side of the hall. Sitting on the floor of the living room was a tiny woman who had the meanest eyes I had ever seen. She was helping a young child with her homework. In the next moment, the ugly words came rushing in a scream out of her mouth as she yelled to her husband. Her husband, who I never saw, screamed back obscenities. With this, one of the first responders, a young officer, put his arms up as if to hold back the waterfall of words, and said, "Now, now, remember we were going to take a time out." The combatants, completely ignoring his words, caused the officer finally to notice me standing in the framework of the door, in uniform and with a clergy collar on. He said, "And here is Rev. Jan, our chaplain," as if I could, with my crown and white halo and wings, solve the weight of the world.

Hearing that, the woman said in a voice mean enough to make her beady eyes look compassionate, "I HATE chaplains!"

I replied, in a very soft, kind voice, "That is ok. You can hate chaplains."

She looked at me for a moment and said, "Did you hear me?! I said I REALLY hate chaplains."

Again, I replied, "That is completely okay. You can hate chaplains."

Her retort, "Can I talk to you out in the hall a moment? I need to talk to someone about my mother-in-law." She took my arm, guided me to the hall, and continued to tell me about her life with her mother-in-law. All four officers watched in amazement that turned to disbelief when, upon our departure she put her arm around me (no small job, for I was as tall as she was short) and said, "Honey, do you have any place for Thanksgiving?" When I replied I did, she said, "Well, anytime you are in this neighborhood, you just come right up these stairs, and we'll have ourselves a cup of tea."

When the officers descended the stairs, bewildered, they asked, "How did what just happened, happen?"

INVOLVING THE COMMUNITY

A homeless woman rolled her wheelchair up to the front counter of the police department and reported a local business man's wife had given birth to a stillborn child. The police clerk relayed that information to me and I brought up the situation that morning in the briefing meeting and asked whose beat that store was in.

When one of the officers replied it was his beat, I asked him if he could drop in and offer his condolences to the husband and his wife. I was then able to drop by the shop, giving them information about counseling and a support group for grieving parents. They are still grateful.

*****

We have a police volunteer who, upon request, calls homes once a week on behalf of a relative or friend who is worried or concerned about the health of their loved one who lives alone. One day while talking with a frightened woman who lived alone and facing dialysis, the office person remarked, "I feel so badly for this woman. She is going to have dialysis, and she is alone and frightened." The employee said, "We'd better let Rev. Jan know."

They called me in my car, and I immediately contacted my church and asked about a St. Stephen minister. A St. Stephen minister is someone who goes through fifteen weeks of training in preparation for being a "partner" for someone who is housebound. That person is interviewed and screened in order to be admitted to the program. I told the woman at church about the woman on the phone, and she said, "I will call you right back." She did, with a name of a woman who had a similar background. Before I even arrived at home, I called the frightened woman and told her that a St. Stephen minister would be calling her on Monday to set up a day of the week she could come and simply be a friend and to help her with whatever she needed.

The St. Stephen minister did call, and she continued to visit the lonely woman every Wednesday for eight years until the woman died. This particular case involved the police department office staff, the clergy, the church and the neighborhood. It was a perfect example of all of us working together to help each other.

UNLIKELY INVITATIONS TO THE OTHER CLUB

Shortly after I started at the police department, I was asked to preside and preach over the law enforcement funeral of a beloved, young officer who had died of cancer. I had never even seen a law enforcement funeral, but with the help of others, I did facilitate the funeral. The ceremony was held at a large nearby church. Six months later, the priest of that church called and asked if I would come over to the attached school and talk to the students about Martin Luther King, Jr. Day. I said, "Of course." Gathering my white vestment that day, I arrived at the church office. When the secretary opened the door, the first thing I said was, "Do you have anything that will get coffee out of a vestment?" True to form, even though my family keeps encouraging me to stop drinking coffee in the car, I had spilled coffee all the way down my robe.

The night before, this wonderful priest called and said, "Now that I think about it, why don't you preach at all four services on Sunday?" I asked, "Have you forgotten, my friend, that I am a woman and Episcopal clergy?" He replied, "No, I heard you preach at the policeman's funeral, and I want you to come and preach here. My office staff fell in love with you the moment they opened the door."   About an hour later, the assistant priest called and said, "I've got another good idea. Why don't you come and preach at the 5:00 Family Service on Saturday, the night before, and we are also having a baptism?" I agreed.

I processed in with the Gospel book, read the lesson, and preached. After I preached at the biggest service on Sunday, the priest stopped everything just before distributing communion and said to his very large congregation, "You have just seen Rev. Jan process in, read from the Gospel and preach. It is with a heavy heart that I have to say that I cannot, by church rules, give her communion so I am going to give her a blessing. "At this point, he walked across the altar and crossed my forehead and said a blessing. He then walked back to the center of the altar area and said to his congregation, "Now let us all pray that sometime in the future we will all be at the same table." I told him it was his finest hour. He did not put down his faith tradition but explained why I was not receiving communion and what he was going to do instead. In closing, I told the congregation they had two very loving priests and I hoped they appreciated them.

That event was life changing for all of us. A woman with tears in her eyes came up to me after the baptism and said, "You will never know what it meant to have a woman on the altar when my daughter was baptized." A year later, someone came up to me in the local drugstore, asked if I was Rev. Jan and when I said, "Yes, I was," she took my hand and said, "We have been praying for that for so long."

About a year after my appearance at the large church, another smaller local church in a nearby city called. The priest said he had heard about me preaching and wondered if I could come and preach at his church. I experienced irony. The last time I was at that church, I was Catholic, married to a different man, and my children were attending the parish school. Here I was now: an Episcopal woman, divorced and remarried, resulting in a different name, and ordained clergy.

That priest did not acknowledge or explain my presence and that was fine with me. I was standing, in my vestment, my arms down at my sides, watching the parishioners receive communion and return to their seats by walking behind me. All of a sudden, I felt someone press a communion wafer in my hand. I turned around to look and saw a very elderly lady walking back to her seat. She never turned around. That small gesture has remained one of my treasured memories of my ministry.

A NOVELTY IN POLICE CIRCLES (to put it mildly)

The female priest I worked with at the time said to me, "You know that retirement home you take communion to on Sundays? Well, I want you to think of something they can do to live out their ministry. Just because they are elderly does not mean they cannot be contributing to the world." So I tried to think of something. Then I remembered the cloistered nuns! They can't do anything but pray. I had a great idea. I ran it by our police chief, and he said, "Go for it, Rev. Jan."

Remembering that when dealing with law enforcement remaining Ecumenical is vitally important, I put out a short general email explaining I was going to enlist members of a retirement community to pray for those in the police department who desired prayers for themselves and their families. I asked that the police employees put their name in a plain envelope and put the envelope in my box, marked "Confidential." I would then pair up the person who requested prayers with a retirement individual who was willing to pray for that individual every morning for the entire year. I had so many requests from the police department that I ran out of people at the retirement home. I had to stand up at the church where I was serving and ask for more volunteers. That program operated the entire year, and many times when I was at the department someone would come up and ask, "Rev. Jan, you know that person who is praying for me (match ups were confidential), could you ask them to include my sister? She has just been diagnosed with breast cancer."

A NEW VIEW OF WATER

One of the officers in our department seemed to always be called to the scene of tragic accidents. As he said, "How is it that I always seem to be the first responding car?" He was, and the incidents involved four horrific accidents.

Early in the morning, I was called by a sergeant who described a terrible accident where my friend had been the first to respond. The sergeant asked if I could go to the accident scene and told me where to drive to avoid the yellow tape. I arrived to find the sergeant talking to my officer friend. Meeting my eyes, the sergeant said, "Rev. Jan, have you had breakfast?" Although I had just finished, I said, "No, and I am starving." He handed me some money, and said, "Would you take this officer to breakfast? He is starving."

That was all that was said, and the officer and I left to have breakfast. We talked and talked and talked some more. Afterward, we got into his truck and we talked some more. I could see his shoulders were beginning to droop, he was breathing easier, and his voice had become calmer. The morning passed, and I thought that perhaps he wanted to go home. I didn't want him to miss the opportunity, so I asked if he would like to go home. I told him I was fine with just going back to the police department. He hesitated a moment and then said, "No, let's go by water."

I had explained that years ago when my son was going through a rough time, in desperation I had called a counselor who told me, "Walk him by water." My friend and I did just that and I learned a valuable lesson. The presence of water in a person's vision has a calming effect. I think it helps one's perspective. The world is much bigger than we or our problems are.

NO, IT ISN'T FAIR

Many police departments operate a program named, "Are You OK?" The premise is that if someone is worried about a loved one living alone miles away, a volunteer at the police department in that city will call every day to make sure the person is okay. If the individual does not answer on the third ring, the police department sends an officer out on a "Well Check."

We were assigned to conduct a Well Check at a home where the shut-in woman had not answered her phone. Unfortunately, before we got there her grandson happened to come by, entered her home and discovered she had died. It was a day when the rain was coming down in buckets. We arrived to see the teenage grandson on his knees on the sidewalk screaming and crying sorrowfully over the shock of finding his grandmother. He was drenched from the cold rain. I simply got down on my knees on the sidewalk while a stream of rain became a river around us and held the young man while he wailed. He kept saying, "It isn't fair! It isn't fair!"

I answered as I continued to hold him, "You are right, it isn't fair." To express any other opinion would have been the most unfair.

I WONDER WHAT A DEAD BODY LOOKS LIKE

On one of my first ride-a-longs, we were called to a hotel downtown. A woman had died of natural causes in one of the rooms. The detectives arrived and checked everything. The officer and I waited out in the hall. The detective came out of the room and the officer said, "Do you want to go in the room and see her?" Although all of my relatives, except for my very-much-alive brother, have died, I had never seen a dead body, so I thought to myself, "There is no time like the present to find out if I can do this." I went in and looked at the woman who had died in her sleep, lying on top of the covers. I was intrigued and discovered I could do this. I just might be in the right business.

I also was on a ride with a young officer when we got a call to perform a Well Check on a residence. The drapes were drawn, the car was in the carport, and the car hood was cold. I have learned that a cold hood is a bad sign. The minute the officer in front of me put her hand on the doorknob and started to turn it, I knew I was getting a whiff of a smell I had only heard about. The apartment was very small, and the woman had taken her life many days before. That odor is a smell like no other and seeps into your clothing. I was asked if I had any perfume, which I did. Usually in these cases, Vicks salve is used in a nose mask carried in the trunk of the police car. There was no Vicks in the car. We used my perfume to protect our senses against the smell. The sergeant and others came by, and I was moved by how caring and sensitive they were to this new young officer and her reactions. I ended up giving her a small bouquet of flowers with a small jar of Vicks tucked inside with a note that read, "Just to remind you there is still beauty in the world."

WOULD YOU LOOK AT THAT GRANDMA IN A VEST!

My grandson spent Wednesday nights with us when he was small. It gave his parents a break, and he loved to be served breakfast in bed before we went down the hill to the end of the block where his school was located. On this particular morning, he announced he needed to take something for show and tell to his fourth grade classroom. I told him he could take whatever he wanted. He said, "I think I'll take your bulletproof vest."

I responded, "Go for it."

At the end of the school day, he trudged up the hill and came in the door with eyes that sparkled. I asked him how it went. He said, "Nia (his name for me), it was so cool, and you will never guess what! I am the only kid in my classroom whose grandma wears a bulletproof vest!"

"What a shock," I thought to myself. "Score one for grandma." (What a cute story!)

EVERY PARENT'S WORST NIGHTMARE

If someone had asked me how I would handle a suicide call with the young teenage suicide victim still in the next room while we attended to the parents, I would have answered, "I really don't know. I have never had that experience."

We arrived at the house and were greeted by the victim's parents who were screaming everything I probably would have been screaming if I were in their places. I pray on my way to every call, asking for God's guidance that I may see what may not be obvious, hear what may not be said, and be a source of comfort and care.

As odd as it sounds, I seemed to operate outside myself somehow, observing how I was handling this difficult and tragic situation. I thought to myself, "How do I seem to know to ask if I can make these parents tea, or ask if there is a close friend they would like me to call, or if I can make a run to the airport if someone needs to be picked up, or when just to be quiet? How is it that what I am doing and saying seems to be helping?" No one was more surprised than I was.

Much appreciated by officers who have the rest of their shift to work after all the matters are taken care of, I am able to stay as long as the family wants me to. That night they asked if I could stay, and it was very late when I finally got into my car. I was still amazed at how I was feeling, how I could minister to these parents and still be able to handle this heartbreaking situation.

I got in the car and the first thing I said was, "Thank you, God, thank you, thank you, thank you. Please use me again and again!" Then an epiphany happened! I had to smile as I thought to myself, Well, Jan, this is a no brainer. If you believe God called you to ordained ministry, but more importantly, this specific ministry, why are you surprised that He enabled you to do it?

That God, He/She is certainly amazing!

I'VE NEVER WALKED AMONG SO MANY ANGELS

The area inside St. Paul's at Ground Zero was semi-dark. The lights were dimmed, and the only sound was soft snoring by the rescue workers sleeping in the pews, some holding stuffed animals that had been sent by children, some sleeping up in the choir stalls. Lilting above the stillness was the sound of violin music being quietly played. Some nights it was the sound of the piano played every so softly. Lit candles created dancing shapes on the walls.

When the tragedy occurred, I told my husband I was going to New York because I wanted to be a participant, not just an observer. At the police department, the chief stopped in the hall and said, "I hear you are going to 9/11, Rev. Jan." I told him I was and I was leaving in two days. He said, "Turn in all your charges. The police department will pay your way."

Like many other volunteers on my shift, 12 p.m. to 7 a.m., I helped dish up food from the endless buffet line and was available as a pastoral presence when a police, fire, or other worker came through the door.

"Watch for him," we were told. I can close my ears today and hear the sound of slow, exhausted, heavy boots making their way up the aisle, entering this respite for whatever was offered, for a chance to look at goodness. I noticed the fireman enter the door and stand in the aisle, as if he didn't know who he was or had forgotten where he was going. I walked up to him and asked if he was okay.

Without looking at me, he said, "This is the very worst day."

I said, "What makes this the worst day out of all these worst days?"

"I have never uncovered so many body parts."

I sat behind a policeman sitting in a pew. He had his head in his hands, his elbows on his knees. I leaned forward and asked, gently, "What can I do for you?"

Without turning around, he said kindly, "You can get me a plane ticket out of here."

I said, "Let me guess, a one-way ticket?"

"You've got it."

A police captain who had become my friend asked that a car be brought around, and he escorted me to the family platform overlooking the hole at ground zero. Families were escorted there by a volunteer and allowed to be there for twenty minutes. The temporary wooden wall was covered by notes. One I still remember said, "Mom, you must have been so afraid. We are so proud of you."

When I returned to SF, an article I wrote was printed in the paper. In the middle of the night, I had awakened as the words formed nonstop in my head, spilling out onto the pages in front of me instead of every cell of my body.

I was a witness to the terrible things some people can do to others, and at the same time, I was a witness to the good that is inherent in others. There is no way to describe the courage, the strength, the dedication, and determination of those who came through the doors at St. Paul's. They were selfless, often to the detriment of their own mental and physical health. Not one person came through that door who didn't thank us over and over for what we were doing. It was hard to listen to their stories because we were aware of how they were giving of themselves without being asked. Their gratitude gave new meaning to the saying, "If you want to bug a police officer, tell him 'thank you' because he feels he is just doing his job."

So we ask, "Why did this happen that so many innocent people should be killed, so many families rocked with a vibration that endures today in their most private thoughts?" It reminds me of the story of the teenager who has just got his driver's license. He asked to use the family car and was told, "No." Frustrated, the boy asks, "But why? I am a good driver and now I have my license. Just give me a reason why I can't have it." The point is that the reason does not really matter, nor would it change anything. He just wanted the car. We just want 9/11 not to have happened, but it did.

And where is God in all this suffering? There are illnesses and accidents in life, and no one knows this better than the first responder community. There are people who are capable of doing terrible things to others. In my experience, God helps us through the tragedies we encounter.

God also appears through us. My days at St. Paul's were evidence of this, every hour. Hundreds and hundreds of people were unselfish in giving and caring. Officers remarked, "It's a little like home here inside St. Paul's. It is peaceful and quiet. I came in and I don't want to leave." There was certainly the presence of evil in the event, but there was also the presence of goodness and love in those who gave their time to minister and heal.

Dr. Mary Glenn

of Pasadena, California, has served with the Alhambra Police Department for over ten years as the co-founding/lead chaplain. She is also a certified police chaplain trainer. Mary works as the Director of Collaborative Partnerships and Education with City Net, a non-profit organization that engages, educates, and empowers Christians, catalytic leaders, and collaborative movements in cities and neighborhoods for holistic transformation. She educates and writes curriculum to help people engage their lives and faith with the cities they live in.

Mary is an adjunct professor with Fuller Seminary and Bakke Graduate University, where she received her D.Min. in Transformational Leadership. She is an ordained pastor, having served over 15 years in youth and community outreach ministries, and is a graduate of both Regent College and Fuller Seminary. She loves the television programs, Southland and 24, naming her dog after one of the characters, Jack Bauer.

Two Babies

by Dr. Mary Glenn

Grief is a necessary part of the process of responding to death. "Let grief run its course, as it must." It is healthy, especially when done in the context of community. How we embrace grief is just as important as grieving itself. Many of life's situations faced in the day to day job of an officer demand that one grieve. In the past ten years that I have served as a police chaplain, I have seen law enforcement officers face painful situations that would push any human heart to the tipping point. In late 2005 and early 2006, two deaths had a huge impact on the Investigations Bureau at Alhambra Police Department and on the community at large: the deaths of Baby Sarah Chavez and Baby Therese Rose. I remember that period of time as if it was yesterday.

Baby Sarah Chavez was born on December 2, 2002, and died on October 11, 2005. She was born with Vicodin in her system. When she was just two days old, a case file was opened on her. The social workers placed her with her godparents. Eventually she was placed in the home of a lesbian couple who loved Sarah. The couple said they saw signs of abuse from the moment Sarah arrived at their door, and they begged child welfare officials to investigate more fully. However, Sarah's biological family fought to get her back because they didn't like her being in the home of a gay couple even though this was a safe and loving haven for this precious child. Her biological family won in court and took her back. She moved in with her great-aunt and husband and their five year-old son. On October 10, 2005, Sarah was taken to the hospital because her arm was severely fractured. Sarah also had internal injuries from being hit in the stomach. She died from blunt force trauma to the abdomen, which completely severed her small intestine. Baby Sarah's great-uncle was found guilty of Assaulting a Child Under 8 resulting in death and Child Abuse resulting in death. He is facing twenty-five years to life. Baby Sarah's great aunt spent fourteen months in jail before she was freed.

Baby Sarah should never have been placed in the care of her great-aunt and uncle, but somehow she slipped through the system. It was hard to watch how this tragedy involving the death of children impacted the detectives. They had to see Sarah's beaten body, collect evidence, learn details and put together a case. People sometimes forget that law enforcement officers are professionals who are human. They feel just like everyone else does. It can be especially difficult for those who are parents. Absorbing this kind of pain can be overwhelming, yet they are just trying to do their job.

Just a few months after this tragedy, another heartbreaking event occurred in Alhambra. On March 12, 2006, a newborn baby, Therese Rose, was thrown onto the train tracks by her mother, although a Safe Haven Surrender Sight (located at Alhambra Fire Department) was just a few blocks away from the train tracks.

The newborn was found March 12, 2006 with the umbilical cord still attached. She landed on the train tracks, fifty feet below street level. The child's body was found near train tracks, wrapped in plastic bags, just south of Missions Road near Fremont Avenue. Parishioners of Saint Therese Church, near where the body was found, named the child Therese Rose and held a candlelight vigil and funeral service for her, attracting hundreds of mourners and huge media attention.

This case impacted all of the community. A commonly asked question was, "How could a mother do this to her own child?" But I heard no one ask, "How did this impact the detectives who worked this case, especially those with children? How would they be impacted by seeing this innocent newborn so blatantly discarded?" The same detectives who handled the Baby Sarah Chavez case worked on the Baby Therese Rose case because their work focused on investigating homicides.

It is interesting to note that the babies were unknowingly buried close to one another in the same graveyard. At the police department, there was always a sense that these two innocent lives were intertwined. They forever changed and impacted the lives of those involved in working on their cases.

In both cases, chaplains responded to the need by helping the department and the community heal from both losses. In the case of Baby Sarah, I was able to spend time with the accused couple's son. In fact, I spent hours upon hours with this boy, providing a safe place for this youngster who had witnessed so much tragedy in his short life. I just tried to stay focused on giving him a safe environment to be a kid.

I spent time with this young boy at the children's room at the Alhambra Police Department. The children's room has been a place where children in crisis spent minutes or hours. It was a room that had no decorations, old and limited supplies and did nothing to give hope or peace to a child in need. After this tragedy, I resolved to do something to create a safe place for children and their families in times of crisis just like this. Who knows what kind of difference this could make?

We, the chaplains, recruited members of the community (service clubs, churches, individuals, police associations and more) to pitch in for this great cause. A local pastor offered his services by designing and painting the room with a beautiful mural. Diapers, crayons, blankets, and stuffed animals were donated. The room was dedicated on July 10, 2008. Those in attendance included many members from the community at large, local media, city employees, church representatives, the Alhambra PD Chaplains, and the two detectives who worked these two tragic cases. The children's room was officially named the Baby Therese Rose / Sara Chavez Kids Corner. This room now serves as a reminder of God's peace and hope in the midst of pain and injustice. The Alhambra PD Chaplains led the endeavor to remodel the children's room at the police department. It was an opportunity for us to share a real need with the community, knowing that we couldn't do this project on our own. We can make a difference through collaboration and partnership.

These two cases bring light to the kind of darkness law enforcement officers must not only observe and investigate, but also process on a personal level. How does it impact the officers who must see the pain and injury inflicted upon these innocent lives? These officers, in the course of doing their jobs, see human tragedy that no one should witness. They can be impacted and broken by what they experience. For the detectives involved in this case, we ask what kind of hope and peace are they given in the midst of the demands of their jobs? We pray that the remodeling of the Children's room, prayers of remembrance and messages of hope bring them God's peace in a very real and tangible way so that these children's deaths will not have been in vain. Moreover, we hope that our ministry of presence (as police chaplains) during these times of incredible tragedy and crisis will bring comfort and support to our local police. This is part of the work and call of the police chaplain.

Part Five:

Corrections

Marianne T. Jervis

was born and raised in Haddon Heights, New Jersey. As a youngster, her artistic abilities in classical piano earned her first place in a Catholic Youth Organization U.S. National talent competition. She cut a record with Capital Records and was given a music scholarship for Julliard School of Music in NYC. Marianne also began intense training in martial arts and after many years earned a 2nd Degree Black Belt.

She became a State of New Jersey Corrections Officer and enjoyed the job of securing and supervising inmates. She became aware of violence in the workplace and became an International/National certified C.I.S.M. (Critical Incident Stress Management) team member. On September 11, 2001, she was dispatched to the critical incident in New York. She worked as team leader at Ground Zero, directing other C.I.S.M. members from New Jersey and Pennsylvania to the site.

In 2003, she retired from corrections. Marianne has received several awards in Washington, DC, for "Speaking Out," "Winning on Policy," and "Positively Impacting Policies in the Workplace, State and Nation for Working Women". She returned to college and was chosen by the Phi Theta Kappa Honors International Scholar Laureate Program to interact with government officials and heads of state in Austria, Prague and Budapest.

Marianne works at Kennedy Memorial Hospital in Stratford, New Jersey, accompanied by her two small therapy dogs, Angel and Sandy. Whether in hospice, emergency, x-ray, or physical therapy, the trio help patients relax and become more receptive to treatment and testing. Her life experiences, training and education have afforded her the opportunity to become a beacon of light, paving the way of hope for those trying to work out of abusive or crisis situations.

I'm Your Mom Now

by Marianne T. Jervis

It was a cool, clear, and brilliantly sunny August morning. Bernie, the mailman, handed me a postcard which read, "Start Date 9/18/93" at the top left corner just above the State of New Jersey Department of Corrections address. My heart jumped at the words **start date** and **Officer Recruit with the State of New Jersey Department of Corrections.**

I was beyond overjoyed. *I made it! I made it!* I sang to myself. All the testing, waiting, and praying had finally paid off. After many hours of rigorous testing, interviewing, and a complete physical and psychological exam, I had finally been accepted as an officer recruit. Running toward the kitchen phone, I could hardly wait to tell my family and friends the good news.

It was everything I had dreamed of, and I was finally making my mom proud of me. I was amounting to something more than a singer/songwriter/musician, and I was making my family, neighbors and friends proud. The person who I thought would really have been most proud of my accomplishment was my loving father. I just knew he was smiling a big smile for me in heaven. At that moment I sure missed my dad. He died in a car accident on his way to work on June 7, 1989.

I did my homework, endured rigorous training and passed my tests with flying colors at Skillman Boot Camp (The

Corrections Officers' Training Academy or COTA) located in North Jersey. For the next couple of years, I saw a lot of action while stationed at Jamesburg State Prison, one of the oldest and most dangerous correctional facilities in the state of New Jersey. It was a juvenile facility, and more often than not, it was over inhabited and understaffed. The juvenile testosterone and egomania soared as the young adult inmates exhibited coping mechanisms, such as exaggerated false bravado and fearlessness.

Gang wars were not uncommon. The slightest disagreements or simple verbal disputes involving egos and inmates' territories, neighborhoods, or where an inmate was born, served as a flashpoint for battle. For example, Newark would fight Paterson, Camden would fight Trenton, and so on just for the sake of fighting, showing off, or killing time in prison. I guess it was supposed to be a macho thing for them. Yet no matter how injured or scarred an inmate got, they never seemed to comprehend the reality of their violent acts.

In any event, I continued to perform my duties to the best of my ability and set a good example by teaching the positive reinforcement as I was taught by my teachers and peers. I endeavored to set the precedent, especially for the sake of the inmates who were trying to get their lives together and who had no parents or authority figures. These individuals were visibly trying to learn how not to resort to violence, repeat history, or abuse drugs, all of which are the primary causes of juvenile incarcerations.

I recall one inmate in particular. He was one of the most assault prone, defiant and incorrigible inmates I had ever come across. I will call him Mr. Parren. This inmate set fires on the unit by sticking toilet tissue into the electrical outlets. He used these fires as a distraction to mask his drug dealing and violent beat downs of inmates he had forced to be subservient to him. However, following many incidents of rage with Mr. Parren, I cornered this violent ring leader and informed him that I was no longer going to tolerate any more of his outbursts or abusive acts. Well, you could have heard a pin drop on my unit. I had had enough and was finished with beginning my shift in this manner each day.

Mr. Parren looked me straight in the eyes and let out a very sinister laugh saying, "You can't make me do nothin'." At that point, I flipped over almost every table and chair in the inmate day space. Mr. Parren looked shocked and scared as he yelped, "Please, Miss J, you 'bout lost your mind."

"Oh well, Parren, you don't care anyway, right?" After a few more "Please, Miss J's," I decided I had scared him enough and thought it was time we talked. I could see the relief in his face as he pleaded with me to talk to him and calm him down. I began, "Parren, I don't care how many bodies you got or how many you put down. I read your rap sheet, and I have a good mind to call center command and have them send your mom over so she can put a foot in your backside."

Parren softly replied, "My mom is in Clinton State Prison."

Not wanting to show vulnerability to his response, I answered, "Well, I will just talk with your dad."

"I don't know who my dad is. I heard he was dead."

I shifted in my seat and digested the information from his point of view. My only thought was, *Wow*. However, being on a mission to regain control of my unit, I firmly responded. "Then Parren, I will be your mom, and as long as you are here you will do what I tell you or I will put my foot in your backside." He looked fiercely into my eyes with an, "I dare you to make me" glare while I gave him a look that I hoped would pierce his soul. Fortunately, he was smart enough not to go there. I cut through the ice by ending with "Parren, when I was young, I never wanted to listen to my mom, and by the way, my dad is dead, too."

He searched my eyes as I continued, "But as long as you are

alive, you should do things that will make your mom and dad happy and proud when you finally meet each other again." His eyes were wide and glassy as I said, "You should find better things to do with this time to bring life or add laughter to people's lives, instead of death. Being cool isn't so cool when you end up in jail like this." I jokingly ended the conversation with a question. "Parren, how many cool dudes do you see in this jail? Not one, right?" We both began to laugh, and he swiftly quipped back, "Miss J, they get real cool when the heaters break down inside this jail." We both laughed again.

Next, I had to focus my attention on the unit I was supervising. For now, it was temporarily quiet as the inmates absorbed my every movement during this exchange. Some inmates attempted to win me over or bring my guard down by asking if I needed anything done. Some even volunteered to sweep and mop the corridor. I shook my head a stern "No," and ordered them out of the area. As the inmates swiftly ran from the doorway, I moved toward the door of the day space area and assured Parren it was going to be okay. I laughingly called back to him in a language he could easily understand. "Parren, if anybody is going to be a pimp around here, it will be me because I am the number one pimp and everyone else will always be number two."

I stopped for a moment, barely believing what I had just said. What a culture shift that was for me. But Parren broke into a wide grin and said, "You are crazy Miss J, but I like you because you tell it like it is, and you have a lot of heart." Needless to say, inmate Parren became less prone to assaults and more disciplined and respectful.

I was later transferred to Riverfront State Prison in Camden, New Jersey, where I faced many challenges. I worked as a State Senior Corrections Officer and supervised approximately 150 inmates. During the course of my duties, I was assaulted by an inmate who tried to drag me into his cell. I survived that attack and several others, finally deciding that I had had enough. Although worn down from the stress and constant survival mode I found myself in, I picked myself up by my bootstraps and mustered every ounce of positive energy and courage that was left in me.

My experiences as a corrections officer left a positive impact on me, enabling me to become a better person. Specifically, the challenges I faced and overcame led me to create a thoroughly comprehensive workplace violence prevention program, which is presently being made available to major corporations, medical and educational facilities, and victims of violence or abuse.

Today, I am fortunate. I have a good life, and I'm healthy. I've continued my education and am currently pursuing a law degree to better assist victims of abuse. As I live with PTSD, I continue to counsel victims of abuse, violence, critical incidents, and trauma. My goal is to educate victims, as well as the public, about the symptoms, causes, conditions, behaviors, and safety risks prevalent in our ever-increasing world of violence and abuse. My heart goes out to all victims who are struggling through their present crisis situations.

In my spare time, I spend many hours at hospitals and nursing homes visiting the sick and comforting dying patients, accompanied by my two tiny therapy dogs, Angel and Sandy. We get to see miracles happen almost every day, and for that I am thankful.

Mickey Koerner

grew up in central Iowa and as a student she was very active in sports. She learned to fly airplanes as a teenager, and continued flying during her college years at the University of North Dakota, where she graduated with a B.S. in Aeronautical Studies and an M.S. in Educational Research Methodologies. She has maintained her flight instructor certificate since 1991.

Mickey trained several people during the early 1990s, and one of them encouraged her to apply to become a deputy sheriff. She did so, and worked for the Polk County Sheriff's Office for three years. During that time she was assigned as a transportation deputy for the jail division. After she left the PCSO she continued to assist in flight training deputies and transported inmates, via airplane, back to Polk County for bed and breakfast.

Currently, Mickey works for an airline and flies in the southern United States. She continues to support her friends who are police officers and has contributed short stories and devotionals to several books. She believes that if a person knows Jesus Christ as Lord and Savior, He will use that person, regardless of their field, to find the lost and encourage the fellow believer.

Jail Time

by Mickey Koerner

I was a deputy sheriff assigned to the jail division for three years. It was not the job I intended to do, nor what I aspired to be. Nevertheless, a carrot was dangled in front of me so I accepted the job in hopes that I would someday catch the carrot. However, much like the donkey that walked behind the carrot, I never did catch it. This story, however, isn't about the carrot, but about what I learned while I worked inside the jail.

Much of my time was spent assigned to floors housing 40-70 inmates who were awaiting trial, transport or release. I spent the bulk of my time assigned to the first floor, where those charged with murder were kept, the second floor, where Immigration and Naturalization Services held prisoners, and the third floor, which held sexual offenders. I absolutely hated it. Much like the Biblical story of Jonah in the belly of the whale, I felt that I was in the belly of the jail, with the acidic juices of humans at their worst eating away at my emotional health and mental stability.

Then one day a thought struck me in a way not unlike the way any of the inmates would have decked any deputy jailors if they had the opportunity. *These guys aren't much different than me. The only difference is that they have committed felonies against another person. I've committed huge offenses against others and God, but society hasn't seen my transgressions as being punishable by jail or prison.* While I'm not saying these men shouldn't be locked up for some period of time, or perhaps, for life, I am saying that none of us are innocent in the manner of how we relate to each other and to God.

That notion took a while to recover from.

I started to look at the inmates for who they were, each one made in the image of God and each with human weaknesses and foibles. I began to look at myself in the same way. Then I realized that only the blood of Christ could make us right with God and with each other.

Needless to say, I was not very popular with my colleagues and some inmates, but I started treating my co-workers and the inmates differently. The majority of my captive audience knew there was something different about me, and would sometimes question me about it. When they did, I told them about the love God had for the world and how He gave us Jesus Christ, His only Son, who died for us so that we would never have to spend an eternity in prison. Most listened, some repented, and a few became Christ followers.

My colleagues gave me much the same reaction. Some of them are believers today, and they are out on the road being good cops, a reflection of our Lord. Others are still trapped in their own personal hells and headed down a long, destructive road. However, my confidence is not in the arm of the law, but in the arm of our Lord.

I left the jail and began to work with the missions for several years. God used that time to prepare me for service in the aviation industry where I've discovered that many people are also trapped serving self, false gods, and the flesh. It doesn't matter where people choose to serve, but I am most thankful when a person chooses to serve and follow Christ as a police officer. Many prayers for your protection, my friends.

Rachel Kowalski

is a 38-year-old divorced mother of a beautiful 16-year-old daughter. She began her career with the Rhode Island Department of Corrections in 2004. Over the years she has found her job to be difficult at times, yet a good learning experience. She is fortunate to have great coworkers and a strong union that ensures her work environment is safe. Yearly training allows her to maintain her qualifications, regardless of budget cuts.

Through her trials and tribulations as a correctional officer, Rachel has learned many things, not only about criminals, but about people in general. She feels that we are all one bad day away from making the same mistakes many of the inmates have made. Growing up in the military, she was unaware of the struggles people endure, whether it be buying drugs and robbing people to support their habits, or just plain selfishness and deviance toward others.

While working with RIDOC, Rachel earned her Bachelor's Degree in Criminal Justice by attending night school. She did this while raising her daughter and working full-time. Working in corrections is unique in many ways; you meet a variety of people and learn the harsh lessons about making the wrong choices and hanging out with the wrong crowd. Her career has made her more aware of how biology, socioeconomic status and environment impact criminal behavior. Working in corrections does change a person in many ways, particularly in relationships with friends and family. The key is to recognize that it does and to learn *to leave work at work*. Who we work with in corrections on a daily basis is reflective of society.

45

Just Another Day

by Rachel Kowalski

I am a female correctional officer, and for the past seven years I've worked with female offenders at the Rhode Island Adult Correctional Institution. I've been involved in a variety of situations, some of which were funny, and others that were not. The story I am about to share is somewhat odd to be sure, but one that mothers might possibly understand at some level.

About five years ago, I was the committing officer assigned to process female inmates into our facility. I also ensured they were seen by Records and ID for inmate photos. One particular female who arrived from court earlier in the day was there, not for any serious charge, but because she had mental problems. In situations like hers we house those inmates in the isolation unit where they can be monitored around the clock by an officer and a surveillance system.

My partner and I proceeded to isolation to get this woman from her cell and take her to Records and ID. Arriving at her location, we discovered the inmate was very reluctant to accompany us. The first thing that caught our attention was that she was standing at the back wall—naked. It was evident to us from the woman's physical appearance that she had borne children, how many and how recently, we weren't able to discern, but our best guess was that she had recently given birth.

Sensing our presence, she turned and suddenly began screaming at my partner and me.

"You all want a piece of me? You ladies are just jealous of this gorgeous body." She fondled her breasts while she yelled at us.

Trying to ignore her strange behavior, we first ordered her to get dressed and then turn around. Our policy mandates that inmates must be handcuffed while escorted.   She seemed oblivious to our commands; her only response was to continue her aberrant behavior and shout nonsensically at us.

Not wanting to upset her any more than she obviously already was, my partner and I stood in the cell doorway about seven feet away from her. We waited patiently, hoping her outburst and outrageous behavior would subside.   Then, without warning, the woman began to squeeze both of her breasts simultaneously, causing milk to squirt in dual streams in our direction.   To our astonishment, the lactating woman managed to hit my boots from that distance. Trying to maintain some professional decorum despite what had just occurred, my partner and I, nonetheless, turned and looked at each other, remarking on what a strange but impressive feat we had just witnessed.   As odd as her behavior was, we were both saddened to see a woman acting in this manner.

Unbeknownst to us, while this incident was unfolding, a male building lieutenant happened to approach our area and observe the nude female inmate, as well as my boot, which was now covered with breast milk. Apparently this scene was too much for him to comprehend; he turned pale and passed out. We later learned that as a result of witnessing this inmate's behavior, he made a decision: that day was to be his last day working with female offenders.   He was subsequently transferred to an all-male facility.

As for me and my partner, this was just another day in the life of a female corrections officer working with female offenders.

Shelley A. Wykoff

 came to the Federal Bureau of Prisons, Department of Justice, in March of 1997, after serving almost six years with the local government at the Erie County Prison in Erie, Pennsylvania, where she worked as Senior Correctional Officer. She furthered her education by obtaining a Master of Science degree in Administration of Justice from Mercyhurst College, Pennsylvania, while working fulltime. She was awarded the James V. Kinnane Professional Scholarship. She earned a Bachelor of Arts in Criminal Justice with a minor in Sociology from Edinboro University. Professional certifications have included Advanced Basic Prisoner, Arson Investigation, EEO Counseling and Lead Self-defense Instructor.

Shelley is a contributor to several professional memberships: Women in Federal Law Enforcement, American Correctional Association and the National Rifle Association. She supports the troops with contributions to the anysoldier.com campaign for the Afghanistan and Iraq wars. She also began a scholarship for any soldier in need at Mercyhurst College in memory of her maternal grandfather, Frederick William Morong, and mother, Janina Morong-Wykoff, a philanthropic endeavor that has been very rewarding. Shelley has also funded and donated a family quilt to the Friends of the Little River Light House in Cutler, Maine, delineating the ancestry of the Morong family to the U.S Lighthouse Service, later to become the United States Coast Guard. She also is active in a variety of civic organizations, including the National Wildlife Federation.

Shelley's family, consisting of many nieces and nephews, is an important aspect of her life. Outside of professional interests, she likes to travel and read and enjoys living on her farm with her chocolate Labrador retrievers.

Hootch Attack

by Shelley A. Wykoff

L ike most days back then, and most today, although at a different duty station, I rose early, taking in the beautiful mountain sunrise with my Keurig coffee cup flavor of the day at my side. After having been once again energized by this ritual, I stepped out to the nearby dirt road path with my loyal chocolate Labrador, Kelly, to get in my daily two mile run.

As it turned out, I was going to need every ounce of that caffeine later in the day, as well as the practiced mindset not unlike that of a soldier. I pictured myself as a "guerilla in a constant state of warfare," surrounded by the swirling mists of sabotage.

As I drove to work that particular fall afternoon, I enjoyed the intense colors of the surrounding foliage covering the mountains. A random thought crossed my mind that the beauty of the area seems to disappear once I get out of my SUV and get inside the prison. The trees morph into metal, steel and concrete with a myriad of different hues of grey. Rose colored glasses certainly are of no use here. My mind harkens back to the second quarter of that year when I was the E/W Compound OIC (officer in charge), charged with support to all of the eight units on "The Hill."

I began supervising a movement for the rec yard. Soon, my eyes came to rest on the face of a young inmate whose forehead was creased with worry and whose face had panic written all over it. He was trying to do his best not to violate the rule of no running toward me on the compound. Immediately, with my many years of experience in the business, I recognized something was seriously wrong by his body language alone. He finally reached me and blurted out "Miss Y," (Wykoff) you need to come, and come quick, my cellie is bleeding out, and there is blood everywhere!"

I immediately got some quick details and radioed on the alternate channel for the assigned unit officer to meet me at the door of the affected unit. Luck was on our side. It was a cloudless blue sky and most inmates were on the yard which made for a nearly empty unit. After clearing the remaining inmates from the area, myself and the assigned officer, cautiously holding our breath, approached the cell. I peered into the small grey cell, and immediately my eyes focused on a blood trail on the tiled white floor that led to the bunk bed. There was a deep red stain, seemingly spreading at an uncontrollable rate on the bedding. My eyes then rested on what was underneath that bundle of covers, a large man was quaking and shaking, crying out in a feeble voice for help. At that point, relief washed over me, I knew he was still alive, albeit in very bad shape. Blood was everywhere. It seemed all of my senses were being assaulted simultaneously. I smelled a noxious odor, and a wave of nausea peeked and crashed in my stomach like waves in the ocean. Then, and only then, was I able to absorb the adrenaline creeping into my system.

I stepped out and radioed for medical assistance, closed the compound, and ordered the unit be locked down. It seemed an eternity before we could begin the short journey across the secured compound. Then a nagging thought kept re-playing in my mind. *I hope he isn't dying, I hope he isn't dead. Is he gonna die on my watch?*

The paramedic on duty finally arrived with more support.

We lifted and transported the victim by medical cart to the internal hospital in the health services area across the compound. Once transferred to the gurney, the other support officers left me there to provide security and assist the doctor in stabilizing the inmate.

A few minutes into the assessment, it was apparent the victim was still very intoxicated. The assumption was he was lit on homemade jail house hooch, a variety of soured and mixed fruits combined with sugar, yeast, and a form of heat to cook the liquid into the "nectar of the gods," as the inmates called it. I sent up a silent prayer to the patron saint of correctional officers, St. Michael. I uttered, "St. Michael, please be on duty with me," and I prayed the inmate did not turn violent in any manner against my person.

My adrenaline was still pumping, almost as if Niagara Falls was crashing and cascading over the bluffs right next to me. I could hear the falls so clearly, as if the wondrous body of water had actually moved from Canada! The sound was intense. The inmate kept repeating to me, "I done had worse in the state, I was just gonna lie there for a while, then get my sewing kit and dental floss and sews myself up, I can still do it too."

The doctor overheard this and responded, "Sir, if you would have done that, an infection would have settled in, and you very likely would have died by your own hand." Swirling around the room was the noxious odor that still seeped from the inmate's pores. As he lay there, the hooch seemed to abate his pain, but the level was declining enough for some degree of lucidity to return, and I was able to probe him with some very pointed questions regarding how he came to be in this state. I assisted holding gauze, astringent, and Lidocaine, while the doctor cleansed what appeared to be several straight razor type cuts across the length of his throat, down his chest and left cheek areas. The mountain of gauze on the drop cloth kept growing over the next hour from the slice across the man's throat. The cut was from carotid to jugular. Each part of the anatomy of the throat—arteries, ligaments, muscle, and fatty tissue—was exposed and pulsing from the stress of the wound.

The inmate re-counted his story as I held a cool cloth to his forehead. He explained he bought some "good shit" from the "wine maker" on the compound and then mixed it with his Kool-Aid. After consuming a large quantity, he knew he should stop but the chains of addiction wrapped him tightly in the haze of intoxication, stealing his self-control and any will to stop. An urgent message for vengeance began to nag his intoxicated brain. He remembered that two doors down was an inmate he needed to settle a little score with. He had been disrespected by him earlier that week. He slipped his hand quickly under his mattress to reassure himself his homemade razor weapon was at the ready, and he knew once the blade was at his victim's throat the inmate would obey his order not to scream or alert the "PO-lice."

He'd teach him a lesson by violently shoving his pulsing manhood deep into his anal cavity, sodomizing him for hours, until he knew never to disrespect him ever again. He was intent on showing his victim who dominated and ran things . . . to show him not only was he in control, but that he controlled everything, EVERYTHING in the man's world now. His thoughts began to materialize, forming a plan. He was ready to pay him a visit and display his prowess and power.

At least now I knew why the struggle ensued between the two men. Inevitably, the inebriated state and large size of the attacker, allowed the smaller, sober, intended victim to turn the tables on his attacker. The much smaller inmate was able to steal the weapon. I also knew why the intended victim inflicted the wounds where he did. The victim was in survival mode, fighting for his life, and fearful of the ravages of prisoner rape.

After the inmate was sewn up, about four hundred stitches later, I learned that if there had been slightly more pressure applied by the razor on the throat cords, the throat arteries would have completely severed, and the man would have died. We later learned the straight razor was embedded and melted into a toothbrush handle to be used as a weapon. The inmate stayed for a course of IV antibiotics and was placed in a medical observation cell overnight for monitoring. The inmate's attacker was found at a later date and internally sanctioned for his brutal attack.

As for me, that night I was sure happy to hear that resounding "clang" and "click" from the kong gate closing behind me, setting me free into the night. I stopped in the cool midnight mountain air, under the glow of the moon, and shouted, "It's a Michelob Ultra night," and made a beeline for the parking lot and the comfort of my Ford Escape.

As I entered my sanctuary, home sweet home, I was greeted by all three of my Labradors. Their sweet kisses made me feel welcome. Tonight I relished this daily ritual even more due to the watch I had just worked. Then, a funny thing happened—it almost seemed like Kelly's tail had become a magic wand and she promptly sat, as if I had given her the command, and in between her chocolate paws I saw an ice cold beer! Well, at least that's what I thought I saw. Life was good!

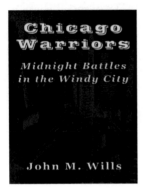

Title: *Chicago Warriors™ Midnight Battles in the windy city*

- Author: John M. Wills
- Price: $27.95
- Publisher: TotalRecall Publications, Inc.
- Format: HARDCOVER, ISBN: 978-1-59095-843-8
- PAPERBACK, ISBN: 978-1-59095-841-4
- EBOOK, Nook, Kindle, ISBN: 978-1-59095-842-1
- Number of pages: 352
- 13-digit ISBN: 978-1-59095-843-8
- Publication Date: 2009

A Chicago Warriors™ Thriller

Chicago Police Officer Pete Shannon's life is about to take a dramatic turn. His wife has a dark secret that she's about to reveal to him; his partner's life is about to be in jeopardy, and worst of all one of his own colleagues will present him with one of the biggest challenges of his life. Pete's strength, both physical and spiritual, will be put to the test as he and his partner work the "graveyard shift" on the mean streets of the "Windy City."

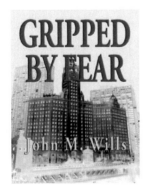

Title: *Gripped By Fear*

- Author: John M. Wills
- Price: $27.95
- Publisher: TotalRecall Publications, Inc.
- Format: HARDCOVER, ISBN: 978-1-59095-772-1
- PAPERBACK. ISBN: 978-1-59095-773-8
- EBOOK, Nook, Kindle, ISBN: 978-1-59095-774-5
- Number of pages: 288
- Publication Date: 2010

A Chicago Warriors™ Thriller

Pete Shannon and Marilyn Benson find themselves working their biggest case yet in their new role as Chicago Police Detectives. In this second book of the Chicago Warrior Thriller Series, a madman has inexplicably targeted women who labor as office cleaners in downtown Chicago, sexually assaulting them as they travel to and from their job.

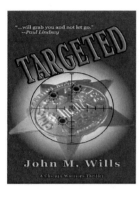

Title: *Targeted*

- Author: John M. Wills
- Price: $27.95
- Publisher: TotalRecall Publications, Inc.
- Format: HARDCOVER, 978-1-59095-794-3
- PAPERBACK, ISBN: 978-1-59095-795-0
- EBOOK, Nook, Kindle, ISBN: 978-1-59095-796-7
- Number of pages: 352
- 13-digit ISBN: 978-1-59095-794-3
- Publication Date: 2012

A Chicago Warriors™ Thriller

Chicago Police Detectives Pete Shannon and Marilyn Benson are thrust into a homicide investigation, taking them away from the Violent Crimes Unit where they are normally assigned. A crazed gunman has been randomly targeting cops for his own deranged satisfaction. The duo finds themselves teamed with a pair of old-timers who do their best to interfere with the detectives' leads and make their lives miserable. The hunt for the serial killer becomes a life-altering experience for the partners as they face individual challenges that threaten to destroy them.

At the same time, Father Ed Matthews, a Catholic priest, has been accused of for child molestation at the southwest side parish where he's assigned. Pete and Marilyn arrest him, but as the priest begins his journey through the Chicago judicial system, he flees the city and becomes a fugitive. He begins a journey away from the priesthood, from which he may never return.

About The Author

John M. Wills is an award-winning novelist, former Chicago police officer and retired FBI agent. His thirty-three years in law enforcement have included working violent crime, drugs, undercover assignments and teaching street survival internationally. He was awarded two of the Chicago Police Department's highest commendations for Valor, and ended his career teaching at the FBI Academy in Quantico, Virginia. His short stories and poetry have also won awards and are published in several anthologies. John has published more than 125 articles on police training, firearms and street survival.

For more information on John M. Wills please visit John at:

http://www.johnmwills.com

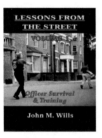

Title: *Lessons From The Street:*
Officer Survival & Training Volume 1
- Price: $14.95
- Publisher: TotalRecall Publications, Inc.
- Format: Format: Paper Back   ISBN: 978-1-59095-658-8
- EBOOK, Nook, Kindle, ISBN: 978-1-59095-870-4
- Publication Date: 2011

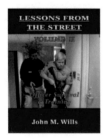

Title: *Lessons From The Street:*
Officer Survival & Training Volume 2
- Price: $14.95
- Publisher: TotalRecall Publications, Inc.
- Format: Format: Paper Back   ISBN: 978-1-59095-659-5
- EBOOK, Nook, Kindle, ISBN: 978-1-59095-673-1
- Publication Date: 2011

Stay safe, brothers and sisters!